José Serebrier

Portraits of the Maestro

José Serebrier

Portraits of the Maestro

Michel Faure

AMADEUS
PRESS

Lanham · Boulder · New York · London

Published by Amadeus Press
An imprint of The Rowman & Littlefield Publishing Group, Inc.
4501 Forbes Boulevard, Suite 200, Lanham, Maryland 20706
www.rowman.com

6 Tinworth Street, London SE11 5AL, United Kingdom

First published in French as *Un chef d'orchestre et compositeur à l'aube du XXIème siècle* (L'Harmattan, 2001).

British Library Cataloguing in Publication Information Available

Library of Congress Cataloging-in-Publication Data

Names: Faure, Michel, 1942– author. | Corigliano, John, 1901–1975, writer of foreword.
Title: José Serebrier : portraits of the maestro / Michel Faure ; foreword by John Corigliano.
Description: Lanham : Amadeus Press, 2021. | Includes index.
Identifiers: LCCN 2021010636 (print) | LCCN 2021010637 (ebook) | ISBN 9781538155004 (cloth) | ISBN 9781538155011 (epub)
Subjects: LCSH: Serebrier, José, 1938– | Conductors (Music)—Biography. | Compoers—Biography.
Classification: LCC ML422.S47 F37 2021 (print) | LCC ML422.S47 (ebook) | DDC 784.2092—dc23
LC record available at https://lccn.loc.gov/2021010636
LC ebook record available at https://lccn.loc.gov/2021010637

Contents

Photo gallery follows page 140

Foreword

I first worked with my dear friend José Serebrier at the very beginning of my compositional life. I was just thirty, and it was the late 1960s, when José programmed my newly written piano concerto with an orchestra in Madrid. The soloist was the pianist who had premiered the work in San Antonio, Texas, and we both flew to Madrid for rehearsals and concert at the famous Teatro Real.

At the first rehearsal, it became obvious that the ensemble was not the first orchestra of Madrid. Upon looking at the xylophone part, the percussionist exclaimed that he had never before been asked to play two notes at once. It was then that I began to appreciate Maestro Serebrier's conductorial skill. He took that orchestra and built an amazing performance with it. Much of the concerto is extremely fast and has constantly changing meter. It is extremely difficult to perform—even with a first-class orchestra—but thanks to brilliant conducting, the audience never knew it was a problem at all. I should add that José asked me to sit in the audience for the concert—a practice that I had studiously avoided for years due to nerves. So I went backstage, then outside the theater, and then tried to come in from the audience entrance. But I did not have a ticket and was not allowed to enter the hall; I had to stand in the traffic in front of the concert hall, waiting for the end of the performance. I was admitted only after the concerto was over. But I already knew that it would be a great performance thanks to my new friend, José Serebrier.

Through the following years, José and I enjoyed many happy collaborations and spent wonderful evenings together with his wife, the extraordinarily gifted soprano Carole Farley. I also got the chance to hear José's music, which is so fantastic. The recent release of his piano concerto based on *B A C H* is an amazing work, and it should become extremely popular both with pianists and audiences. He is as both conductor and composer extremely communicative and urgent. And of course his compositional craft, like his conducting craft, is perfect in every way.

The last time we worked together was in the summer of 2016, at the Beijing Modern Music Festival. José conducted the opening night with the Beijing Symphony Orchestra and programmed my clarinet concerto with the excellent British clarinetist Michael Collins as soloist. Like so many of my works, this is an extremely difficult piece, utilizing new techniques and notations. When Leonard Bernstein had conducted the world premiere in New York in 1977, he told me it was a "test for conductors." Many members of the Beijing Symphony Orchestra were confused by my instructions, but José, ever the teacher, explained all the difficulties to the players. And then, as conductor, he molded the work to perfection. This piece has orchestral players surrounding the audience: five French horns are around the audience, two trumpets are together in the back center, and two clarinets are placed in the back left and right of the hall. The conductor must communicate with these players as well as handle the soloist and orchestra. Bernstein was probably right about the piece, but if it was a "test," then José knocked the ball out of the park.

José is a great artist and a truly great friend. He has shared his gifts with the world, and I am so happy to have him in my life.

John Corigliano, 2020

Introduction

My acquaintance with José Serebrier began after a concert given by his spouse, the American soprano Carole Farley, at the Corum, Palais des Congrès, in Montpellier, on the first of January 1994. Accompanied by l'Orchestre National Philjarmonique de Montpelier, Languedoc-Roussillon, under the baton of Hubert Soudant, she had sung, beautifully, arias by Grieg, Lehár, Cole Porter, and Emmerich Kálmán—the usual musical melting pot of New Year's Day festivities, extremely popular with survivors of New Year's Eve banquets. Same as the one in Vienna, a televised Strauss mix, this concert took place from noon to 2 p.m., in time to renew one's appetite. It was in the hubbub of the postconcert reception that José and I were introduced to each other by René Koering, head of music at Radio France. A mutual fondness immediately arose between us, and over time this fondness became friendship. We met again at the Opéra Comédie de Montpellier when José came to support Carole in her premiere of Koering's operatic satire *Marie de Montpellier*, in which she performed the role of the composer.

José and I did not see each other again for more than a year. I kept writing to him, appealing to him to tell me more about his life and career, peppering him with questions, putting forth my proposal that I was sure we had more than enough material to write a book about him. After much insistence over more than a year, I eventually received from the United Kingdom and the United States an impressive quantity of letters, photographs, and programs, which in their kindness and flavor touched me deeply. Being a professional journalist, I was not accustomed to such spontaneity, such enormous generosity, such complete trust. A transcontinental dialogue was born. From this fruitful exchange and from the quality of the text I received, this book was born.

I saw José again several times—in concert with violinist Pierre Amoyal in a program combining Tartini, Schumann, and Schoenberg; in concert with pianist Fazıl Say (George Gershwin, Tchaikovsky); conducting without soloist a most exciting program (Copland, Glière, Ginastera, Bizet, Falla, Wolf-Ferrari, Dvořák); and privately for unforgettable moments of great friendship. José is one of those men who irrepressibly inspire friendship. You cannot resist him. His personality, while intellectually complex and subtle, immediately charms, because he is without emphasis or ostentation, steeped in sincerity and naturalness. Some might see naivete, but for myself I discern the strength of innocence. Violinist, composer, orchestrator, and conductor, a complex figure, colorful and enticing, whose artistic culture, intensely felt, is oriented toward others, with great passion—a passion as Slavic as the repertoire he loves. The ivory tower is decidedly not his residence, and he has no love for fashionable societies, for affectations that are, sadly, so profitable.

Completely immersed in his own era, José Serebrier expresses in his music great intensity (*Poema Elegíaco*; *Partita*; Violin Concerto, *Winter*)—the fears, the alienations, the mortal contradictions, but also the exaltations and tumultuous intoxications. In this little book, I wanted to bear witness to an artist, a musician, a man whom I love and admire, whose unshakable friendship and infinite patience are so precious to me. Worried that I may betray his message by either exegesis or approximation, I have let him speak for himself, an essential corpus of the book. Let's listen to him.

Michel Faure, 2000

Itinerary of a Child Prodigy

What sort of childhood did you have,
and what was your first encounter with music?

Contrary to the experience of most of my colleagues, music had no part in my early childhood. We did not even have a record player at home, 78s at the time. Until I was nine years old, the only entertainment I had were games and sports activities for children of my age. My central ambition at that stage was to become a writer. My father was a frustrated novelist, and my early literary aspirations only aroused my father's temper. Any spare time he enjoyed was spent working out new novels or short stories. He amassed mountains of manuscripts, none of which was ever published. He assuredly wanted to protect me from writer's anxiety. Even so, my imagination ran wild. My mind was on constant alert, and my natural tendency toward the arts stood waiting to be challenged.

Two occurrences triggered my taste for music. I had just turned nine, and I was listening to the small radio in our kitchen when I felt literally carried away. It was for me an incredible discovery, an almost divine revelation. As far as I can remember, it was the first time that I was paying any attention to or interest in a piece of music. Admittedly, I had been attending school concerts, but none had really caught my attention. The piece of music I had just heard had completely overwhelmed me. I feel absolutely no shame admitting that what was to shape my life forever was the *1812 Overture* by Tchaikovsky. That day was the start of my profound affinity with Slavic music. I had fallen in love with it. The other concomitant occurrence was due to Cupid's arrow. I fell in love with a girl of my own age, who was a school friend. To my regret, she only had eyes for this dandy violinist, and she swooned over him every time he performed at school concerts. I took the immediate decision to learn to play that instrument. I asked my young rival for his teacher's details and walked to the teacher's home straightaway. He sold me a violin, for which I had to pay using my own savings. The day I was due to take my first lesson the bus drivers decided to go on strike. At that time Montevideo was crippled by countless strikes. Undaunted and galvanized by my ambition, I walked eight miles there and back to receive my first introduction to the violin. I arrived home at nightfall, my new violin tucked under my arm. I had to face my angry father, who had been extremely worried. I received the worst conceivable punishment from him: no access to my violin for a full month. Apart from this incident, which was difficult to swallow, my parents never discouraged me from learning to play the violin. Their encouragement limited itself to paying for the lessons. Contrary to my literary ambitions, my musical ones did not seem to worry or trouble my father in any way. This was probably because he was neither aware of what was involved nor guessed where it could lead. He seemed impervious to the inherent difficulties in the profession.

For my first lesson, I composed a small piece for solo violin. I still wonder today how this was even possible, bearing in mind that I had absolutely no knowledge of music. My teacher was neither pleased nor impressed. He was a popular tango musician. He often gave his young pupils the opportunity to play in his orchestra at dinner dances. A few weeks later came my turn to find myself playing in his ensemble, alongside students and adult professional musicians. This was my first ever public performance, and I got paid for it. At first, I could not fathom why. Why should one be paid for having such fun? From time to time, with my violin case well in view, I walked past the home of the little girl who had involuntarily inspired my new direction. I remember her, running to the porch entrance, looking tirelessly puzzled; I was going back and forth, too shy to approach her. Much later, for a while, we shared an intense passion.

Hardly six months after I had started the lessons, without any other type of musical education, I started to compose a sonata for solo violin. Not only was my knowledge of theory and harmony rather basic, but I had no idea about any existing musical form. I dropped out of the tango teacher's lessons and took a decisive step forward by contacting the most prestigious violin teacher available—Jascha Fidlon. He was a legendary character. He ostentatiously showed off a photograph, taken in Russia, of himself with Leopold Auer and Jascha Heifetz, who was five years his junior. He proudly kept reminding us that Auer had regularly requested that he teach the young Heifetz when he was not available.. He had, nevertheless, ended up playing in an orchestra. And when that orchestra toured South America in the 1940s, he claimed political asylum in Uruguay, which was at the time of the Second

World War a haven of peace for refugees, especially of Jewish descent. Fidlon got a job in the SODRE Symphony Orchestra, the only one in the country, and he asked to be integrated into the back row with the second violins, to be free from having to play whenever a Mozart work was performed, requiring less than the full strings. I remember him as an angry and brooding man. Yet he was an amazing teacher who started a remarkable school for violinists, some becoming world-famous soloists. I was in no way ready to study with him, and retrospectively I think that he required nerves of steel to teach a beginner practicing on a tiny instrument. It was one of his pupils, Israel Chorberg, one of my sister Raquel's friends, who had suggested to my family that they let me study with Fidlon. Later Chorberg became one of the most famous freelance musicians in New York and performed my early solo violin sonata many times in concerts all over the United States.

A solid technician, an exceptionally qualified teacher, Fidlon never encouraged me when I brought my new compositions to the lessons. He did not find it reasonable for a nine-year-old boy to compose before knowing the basic principles of music. The ease with which I was progressing must have puzzled him. My family was staying out of all that and was not applying any pressure on me. My only fear was that Fidlon would throw one of his formidable fits. Furthermore, as he had absolutely no interest in my compositions, I kept them to myself as time passed. I soon attempted to write some modest orchestral works. Having received absolutely no classes in orchestration, I purchased a Spanish edition of Rimsky-Korsakov's two-volume orchestration manual, which I passionately devoured. I inquired at the Municipal School of Music if I could study harmony with Vicente Ascone, Italian-born and head of the school. He, like Fidlon, had found paradise in Uruguay. He had left his native Italy to become one of the most beloved figures in the Uruguayan musical life. As head of the only official state school of music, he was a very charming man, and his teaching—more than adequate—guided me through the mysteries of *Harmony* by Dubois, the book used at the Paris Conservatory at the time. He kept reminding me that, within a period of six months, Wagner had absorbed all that there was to be learned about harmony. Clearly stung by his remarks, I set myself up to break that record. At the same school, I kept my violin lessons under the tutelage of Juan Fabbri, concertmaster of the national SODRE Symphony Orchestra. The Municipal School of Music, like all the other schools in the country, from primary school to university level, was tuition-free. I therefore bid farewell to dear Mr. Fidlon. When Fabbri retired, he was replaced by SODRE's new first violin—in my opinion, one of the best instrumentalists working in Latin America—Miguel Pritsch, a true gentleman, humble, and blessed with a terrific sense of humor. He is the one who encouraged me to finish my sonata so it could be performed.

That he did, successfully, recording it for the National Radio and performing it on a regular basis. I dedicated it to him, thanking him for putting his trust in me and for his help. I was twelve at the time.

Who were your parents? Where did they come from? What did they do?

My parents met on the boat that brought them from Europe to South America. They got married six days later when they arrived in Montevideo. My mother, Frida Wasser, was born in Poland in 1902 in a shtetl called Beltz (She died in Miami, Florida, in 1985). Beltz no longer exists or has changed its name. When she was eighteen she moved to Hungary, where she spent a few years before immigrating to Uruguay with her mother, her brother, and two sisters. She was a deeply religious person and was respectful of all the kosher traditions to the letter. She regularly attended the synagogue and took every opportunity to pray. My father kept saying to whoever would listen that he was an atheist. Nevertheless, he always respected my mother's convictions. He was born in a Jewish family in Kiev (Ukraine) in 1900 (he died in Montevideo in 1966), the eighth-generation direct descendant from the Ba'al Shem Tov, founder of Hasidism. Most of his relations were religious people, quite high hierarchically. But my father had always been a rebel against anything dogmatic, which he found dangerous. Most of his family had settled in Philadelphia, but he had opted for Uruguay, which was then very welcoming to European emigrants fleeing communism and the growing anti-Semitism that led up to the Shoah. That was in 1929. My older sister, Raquel, was born in 1932, and I was born in 1938, on December 3. Our family name has always been Serebrier. It is a Russian word derived from *serebro*, meaning "silver." Serebriakov—or Serebriakoff—is probably the surname of distantly related families—for example, pianist Pavel Serebryakov, famous pianist and dean of the Saint Petersburg Conservatory after Glazunov's departure for Paris.

David, my father, had first followed his older sister to Philadelphia. She got married and had a large family. The Philadelphia family circle was quite large and still is. Men are mostly attorneys, and the majority have their own law firms. My father, who was an engineer, preferred to settle in Uruguay, where he founded his own industrial company, specializing in commercialization of sunflower oil and its by-products. His cousin, who bore the same surname and first name, immigrated to Israel and became David Caspi—which means *silver* in Hebrew, therefore the equivalent to the Russian *Serebrier*. I had the pleasure of meeting him on my first conducting tour of Israel in 1963. He was a tall man, a renowned and admired architect, who took an important part in the reconstruction of the old city of Jaffa.

My father's business prospered for a while. But eventually the market crashed. He lost a lot of money and had to change careers. He opened a shop selling clothes and luxury goods. Not once did he ever contemplate leaving Uruguay. He loved the country. My sister, Raquel, became a dentist and worked for a long time at the National Institutes of Health in Maryland, mainly doing research. She married Alfredo Halegua, a successful Uruguayan sculptor. They live in Washington, DC.

You mentioned a particularly funny anecdote about a strange diet . . .

In fact, when I was a little boy, I was so thin that my worried parents took me to a doctor, who prescribed for me the most radical and unimaginable cure. Arguing that I was too young—I was three at the time—to attend primary school, where children were usually aged five or six, and that missing school for six months would have no impact on my future, he prescribed the following: I was to remain in bed and only get up when it seemed essential. I was to consume only high-calorie food, and I was to drink, three times a day, a large bottle of Guinness—stout—which at the time seemed to me to be just a thick black medicine. I can still picture my parents buying case after case of that beer that I was to drink with some effort and deep disgust. I think that the "doctor" was trying, with this primitive method, to transform my metabolism.

How was Montevideo and how was the political and social climate in Uruguay at that time?

At the time I was born, Montevideo was a true paradise, a privileged place with magnificent landscapes and a solid economy. It felt good to live there, and many immigrants had made Uruguay their home—Spaniards, Italians, Russians. Jews represented about 10 percent of the population. We had a democratic government, social life was stress-free, education was compulsory and free, musical life was thriving, artistic activity was very dynamic. And there were countless girls who were . . . *so* pretty. I have very fond memories of my early childhood there: lengthy hot days spent on the beaches with close access to the town center, or in Piriápolis, a popular seaside resort. Punta del Este was the most exclusive resort in Uruguay and above our means. But my family led a comfortable lifestyle without deprivations.

Until 1956, the year I left for the United States, musical life in Uruguay was exuberant. The SODRE orchestra was at top level, and conductors like Erich Kleiber and Fritz Busch used to spend a lot of their time there (Kleiber's yearly cycle, dedicated to Beethoven's nine symphonies, became legendary). Highly qualified teachers had arrived from Europe. Stage shows were extremely successful. Composers, performers, poets, novelists, painters, and sculptors were competing alongside. Unfortunately, the market proved to not be large enough for so many professionals in a country of less than four million. Uruguay counted more dentists, doctors, and lawyers than craftsmen. The situation started to seriously deteriorate economically and socially just before my departure. The same thing, indeed, occurred in various parts of South America. The best intellectuals and professionals started to leave, impoverishing the country that, ten years later, became the victim of a monstrous and galloping inflation, considerably reducing the living standards of an embittered population soon on the brink of revolt. That catastrophic situation mainly resulted because of the nationalization of all the main public-utility companies. You could retire at age forty-five on full pay. There was no income tax, and much of the population was working for the state. A utopian situation, with no link to actual economic reality. In short, a country in shambles. Periodically, an old dream would be revived among the political parties' brain trust—replacing the presidential regime with a government largely representative of all the parties, from the majority to the most marginal, a completely proportional executive, steered in the same way by an oversight committee of presidents. This was devised to prevent any possibility of a dictatorship, the power not being controlled by just one person but by a group of people representing the majority party, with some minority participation.

Uruguay had never had a dictatorship—contrary to Argentina, our neighboring country separated by the Río de la Plata, and whose example was worrying the Uruguayan officials. The plan to replace a single president with a "group" of nine, five from the majority and four minority, was voted on and became, in fact, a constitutional act. That was, of course, a disaster. Too much plurality killing the plurality. In addition, each member of the comity had under his orders a stream of assistants and advisers, and the state budget became colossal, all-consuming. All the projects proposed by the majority kept being blocked by the minority at each stage, and the executive found themselves in a situation where they could not do anything. We had to resign to repeal that constitutional clause. But the economy had suffered considerable damage, and the elite kept emigrating. During that crisis period, the *Tupamaros* started to appear, a new—and weird—political terrorist movement that was astonishing the Uruguayans. Their members were not, as one might have thought, poor and exploited farm and factory workers but young bourgeois, some from influential and very wealthy families—a typical urban movement that wanted to "fix" and "clean up" the system, to eradicate all previous influence, to expose and break up long-established political games. The result was quite the opposite of what the *Tupamaros* had been hoping for: the army, which until then had been disorganized, lazy, and inefficient, started to become structured, disciplined. It gained strength, won the battle against the *Tupamaros* and, intoxicated by its own power and by pretending to restore the public order, usurped the power and started to rule with an iron fist, without any power sharing or resemblance to the previous democracy. For the first time, the country fell under a totalitarian regime. As a result, all civil servants and diplomats were replaced by military personnel.

It took a long time to get rid of that pernicious military dictatorship. Fortunately, as always in Uruguay, not a drop of blood was shed. The military power had been aware for a while of the peoples' aversion and contempt toward them, so they decided, as a way of appeasing them, to make a gesture in favor of democracy. They ran elections, knowing that they would be unfavorable to them. And this proved to be the case: Democracy was reinstated. The financial consequences proved beneficial, and a bloodbath was avoided.

Is your Jewish background important in your choice of music?

I cannot say that I am particularly aware today of Jewish education's impact, but surely there must remain some traces in me. The Jewish community in Montevideo was an important one, but it remained, all the same, a minority, and I must have sometimes felt "different." Hasidic music and the religious ritual surely permeated my subconscious with very subtle, but permanent, traces. Nevertheless, the climate and color of my music have always been Slavic. Any musical note I write sounds Slavic, even if I try to make it sound Latin, as in my youthful Second Symphony, *Partita*, for example. It was on my first trip to visit my paternal family in Philadelphia that I was really made aware of my ethnic and cultural heritage. I made the acquaintance of my aunt, a marvelous *mamele*, a Yiddish mama, who would gather the whole family together once a month. She adopted me as one of her sons. My father had never mentioned her or the rest of the family to me. On the contrary, my aunt never ceased talking about him with devotion and a touch of nostalgia. All members of the family felt proud of their Ba'al Shem Tov heritage. And I was accepted as their young South American cousin and as the ninth direct descendant of the founder of Hasidism. The only words of Hebrew that I ever learned were those uttered at my Bar Mitzvah. I had learned them by heart without quite understanding what they meant.

When I was about seven or eight years old, I belonged to a Jewish youth organization, and I spent part of my summer holidays in a young pioneers' camp founded by that organization. I had terrific fun, the best of times. The aim of that organization was, however, to prepare young South American Jews to immigrate to Israel, to help build the first kibbutz. I had absolutely no idea at the time about that plan. I went to the summer camp for fun.

During my first tours in Israel, it appeared to me that these kibbutzim had played a crucial role in the building of the new country, but the prevailing ideas there appeared strange, incomprehensible to me. It was a sort of utopian, futuristic society in which money had no place, where children were brought up in a community group rather than in a family environment, where work was the main preoccupation. When somebody received an outside guest, there was a great deal of excitement. I immediately realized that most of the members felt frustrated, would have loved to leave, to be set free and have a personal life. At the end of the sixties, some kibbutzim suffered many defections, including some of the founders. For some, it was a traumatic experience, as they had now been deprived of the group protection. Nevertheless, the kibbutz remains a great institution to those who have a sense of sacrifice and a mission. There is no doubt that the South American Jews possessed it, and they played a pivotal part in the creation of the new country.

I inherited from my father a more secular approach to life. Having to deal with a religious family, including many rabbis, he had become a rebel. He did not believe in God. The strict religious education that he had received had produced the complete opposite effect on him. He never talked about it and never tried to influence my sister and me. My mother was usually the only one going to the synagogue. My sister and I would sometimes accompany her during the holidays.

In Philadelphia, I was also invited to Sabbath every Friday, a sweet and friendly family reunion around the central and charismatic chief of the clan, my aunt. This turned out to be a new experience for me—the first on the family side. In Montevideo, we hardly had any contact with my mother's sisters, our closest relatives. In Philadelphia, I took great pleasure in these meetings. On the cultural side, I then learned how to appreciate Jewish traditions, and I started reading Yiddish writers: the Singer brothers—Joshua and Isaac Bashevis—Sholem Aleichem, Isaac Leib Peretz.

How old were you when you first started conducting?

My music ambitions never ceased to grow. Having come across posters praising a couple of young Italian conductors as they were successfully touring South America and the huge impact they had on the public—never seen before—I was persuaded that if an eleven-year-old could conduct an orchestra, so could I.

I was rather more attracted to the vast symphonic repertoire than the still-limited violin concerto repertoire. I then decided, on the spot, to become a conductor. With that aim in mind, I found myself at the Minister of Culture's office and requested to meet with the head of the music department, the famous Lauro Ayestarán. He welcomed me warmly and immediately put his trust in me. He was one of the most significant figures in music of his time. A musicologist and a historian, his encyclopedias still carry authority. I wanted him to allow and help me to create a youth orchestra—a tradition that had already been established in the United States but not yet in South America. With his help, I obtained assistance from the public authorities. His gave me his blessings and a letter of recommendation that opened all doors for me—and furthermore allowed me to skip school without needing to provide any explanation. I immediately went in search of children able to play any instrument well, and to do so I visited all the schools in Montevideo. In less than a week, the orchestra was fully organized, and we soon started our rehearsals. I started conducting, unashamedly, as naturally as you breathe, assuredly with some apprehension but overall confident and certain that everything would work out fine. We did not have printed scores; rather, each player had his or her own handwritten version. The first readings were easy to perform for beginners, the *Tales of Hoffmann*'s Barcarolle by Offenbach. It progressed to the four suites by Bach—a huge jump.

We were soon visited by Ayestarán and he was so impressed with our work that he scheduled our first public concert in the national university's auditorium—the Paraninfo. I was far too young and inexperienced to realize all the implications and unaware of the public due to attend, including the president of Uruguay with his entire cabinet of ministers. Suddenly I was put in charge of a large official ceremony. I must have had some notion of the importance of the event, as I had planned to perform Bach's four suites.

What followed has become legend, kept alive by those present in the audience that day. Having absolutely no experience in conducting an orchestra, I naively thought it impossible to perform while reading the score. I did my best to convince all these youngsters, aged between twelve and seventeen, that they had to learn all of Bach's scores by heart. A few of them didn't feel equal to the challenge and pinned the scores onto the back of the chair of the player in front of them. The evidence can still be seen in photographs taken at the concert. The president, Luis Batlle Berres, and members of his cabinet were seated right behind the orchestra, facing me. At the end of the concert, the president got up and walked across the stage so he could shake my hand and express his admiration for "such a remarkable orchestra, especially taking into account the fact that the musicians were playing by heart, without music." Having not seen any music scores and unable to conceive that it could all have been memorized, he was convinced that we had performed by ear. I was too shy at age eleven to reply to the president and so I didn't answer him.

For four years, we performed in the capital as well as in other towns around the country. I must have been considered a dictator, as one day the orchestra left the stage in protest after I had imposed too many rehearsals of a piece. Nevertheless, the musicians were all friends, and today some of them occupy enviable positions in American orchestras. Some changed careers. As for myself, I was set on pursuing that field and was considering starting a professional orchestra that I brazenly called The Telemann Chamber Orchestra. My music sophistication was on the rise, and I dropped Tchaikovsky in favor of Baroque.

What were your first attempts at composing?

In parallel with my studies at the Municipal School, I started attending courses on a regular basis with another Italian immigrant, Guido Santórsola—lessons crucial for my training. He taught me basic music theory and composition techniques. His wife, Sarah Bourdillon, gave me my first piano lessons. Responding positively to my interest in the keyboard, my parents bought me a piano—a significant financial investment for them, a gift from Heaven. I started composing seriously, using the piano to control the harmonies. My first score was an *Elegy for Strings*. I was fourteen years old.

To my utter astonishment, *Elegy for Strings* was soon performed all over. An Uruguayan conductor, Juan Protasi, conducted it on Radio France, in 1954 or 1955—I cannot quite remember exactly when. There must surely be a recording of it somewhere. During the same week, Santórsola conducted it in Belo Horizonte, in Brazil. He also premiered it in Montevideo. To this day, I perfectly remember the review: Apart from the usual conventional comments, it said, "It was obviously an impersonal, elegiac work, as no fourteen-year-old boy, living in Uruguay, could ever feel so sad to write something so dark and moody." The elegiac force attributed to my music remains to this day, and many of my later compositions confirm it; the Slavic soul, I guess.

Three years later, when Leopold Stokowski gave the world premiere of my First Symphony in Houston, a reporter wrote on that occasion, "Here we have a seventeen-year-old who composes his music with his heart on his sleeve." A comment not miles away from the previous one.

Although it was a wonderful experience to conduct my own youth orchestra, I quickly aspired to conduct a real, large, professional orchestra.

The inaccessible SODRE, the national orchestra, was a very respectable and admired institution at the time. For years Erich Kleiber had inspired a solid Beethoven tradition there. Fritz Busch had later taken over, and many of the major conductors performed there as well: Hermann Scherchen, Nikolai Malko, Artur Rodziński, Antal Doráti, not to mention great composers like Paul Hindemith. It was a time and a place, as I mentioned previously, ever so favorable to the development of music, theater, poetry, painting. Unfortunately, that utopian paradise was mainly an illusion, and black clouds soon began gathering in the sky, as soon as the incredible conflict at SODRE between Paul Paray and Argentinean composer and conductor Juan José Castro destroyed all illusions.

Castro had been, for some time, the inspiring leader of the orchestra and was enjoying huge acclaim among the public, musicians, and critics. The orchestra's board of directors, appointed by the political authorities, had, nevertheless, decided not to renew his contract. Furious, Castro's reaction was rather unusual: He published a letter of protest, addressed to the public, in all the newspapers. The public reacted immediately. At the close of his final concerts, he received endless applause, sometimes lasting over an hour. This pacific attitude in support of Castro had no influence on the board, which went ahead with the decision to get rid of that truly charismatic figure. The more the public protested in showing their support for Castro, the more stubborn the board grew. There was a real risk that the situation would grow violent. But in time, the supporters' enthusiasm waned, and soon only a few spectators were left to support him. In the end, Castro left. It was the best outcome for him, as he was immediately appointed conductor of the Melbourne Symphony Orchestra. Uruguay's loss and Australia's gain. Much later, while on my first tour in Australia, I immediately made friends when I told the Melbourne Symphony how Castro had treated me like an equal when I had been a mere child: confirmation that he was still very much loved in Australia, as he has remained very popular in Montevideo.

The board of directors then appointed Paul Paray as the SODRE Symphony Orchestra's music director. The public immediately scapegoated him. As he appeared to conduct the first concert of the new season, the room became unmanageable. Fifteen minutes later, amid continuous noise and screams, Paray had to leave the stage. I believe the concert still took place, despite the clamor of a public that wanted Castro back at the podium. At the start of the following concert, Paray addressed the public, expressing his admiration and respect for Castro, expressing his regrets that he had left. He wasted his time; his kind and courageous speech was exuberantly booed. But great professional that he was, he nevertheless conducted brilliantly. Then, somebody leaked to the media the salary he was receiving—which up 'til then had been kept secret. That was the final blow: the uninitiated, the average person who had no idea about salaries paid around the world, found his salary of thirty-six thousand dollars scandalous. For the public of the fifties in Montevideo, this sum was an absolute fortune, the equivalent of what some cinema stars get paid to do one film nowadays. Dissatisfaction turned into real hatred, and Paray had to resign and leave. It was a turning point for him, as he was offered the leadership of the Detroit Symphony Orchestra, where he achieved an exemplary tenure with concerts and a great discography.

It was around that time that the National Conservatory of Music was formed and conductor Carlos Estrada assigned its leadership, following a competition. The first thing he did was to get rid of the perceived threat caused by Guido Santórsola, who'd had his eye on the position of professor of composition. Following an unbelievable plot, a true Machiavellian conspiracy, Santórsola was expelled, humiliated, and his Uruguayan career destroyed. It was a very strange and difficult time for me, as I was a student with both, benefiting a great deal from both of their teachings.

A fervent Francophile, Estrada provided a rigorous and efficient education of counterpoint. My two years spent at the conservatory had made me respect him greatly, as he was a true master. Although my first encounter with him had been catastrophic. As a young boy, I had gone to his office to ask advice on my future career as a conductor. His answer had been sharp: "Don't you worry about that. There is no room for another conductor in this small country. So, who are you going to conduct?"

When I was sixteen, I was hoping to conduct the SODRE orchestra. Around that time, I read in the newspapers that SODRE was organizing a competition for a new orchestral work. Furthermore, the winner would have his score performed by the SODRE Symphony Orchestra. Straightaway, I started thinking that, if I happened to be the winner, they might allow me to conduct my score. But there was a snag: we were only six days out from the deadline, which had been announced at the last minute. It never crossed my mind that a winner might have already been preselected, as only allowing six days to write a score for orchestra seemed to me rather unusual. Unabashed, I started composing an overture, the *Legend of Faust*, inspired by Thomas Mann's famous book, which had impressed me so much. I worked tirelessly, night and day, over five solid days and nights, without sleep. My mother would get up in the middle of the night to warm me some soup so I could keep my strength up and carry out the insane task I had undertaken. Her support was crucial to me. My family was bewildered but at the same time delighted to see me so committed and disciplined in writing that composition.

Then came Saturday, the deadline. The composition had to be handed in to the jury no later than noon, but I still had a few pages to finish. At eleven o'clock, I jumped into a taxi. I lived half an hour away from SODRE. I stopped for a moment on the way to properly seal the envelope that contained my name—in no way should the jury be aware of the composer's name beforehand, of course—and to finish the last pages of my composition in the taxi. In fact, it was a false coda, as I knew that I could replace it eventually with another more elaborate one. I don't remember showing any sign of surprise when I was announced as the winner of the competition. Unfortunately, I was not allowed to conduct my overture, as I was too young. Eleazar de Carvalho was chosen to conduct the score. A few months later, he became my first orchestral conducting teacher, at Tanglewood. As with Leonard Bernstein, Carvalho had been a protégé of Serge Koussevitzky, who had advised him to concentrate in modern music. When he was named music director of the St. Louis Symphony, he immediately took Koussevitzky's suggestion and excessively programmed contemporary music. One day, he paid for a full page in *Time* magazine to advertise an outdoor concert entirely composed of "music happenings" and performed works by composers like John Cage, forcing the conservative public of St. Louis to follow the concert in a sort of procession, as indicated in Cage's score. Before long, Eleazar de Carvalho was back in Brazil. He was a wonderful teacher of conducting technique, and I never understood why my colleagues and friends like Seiji Ozawa—who was my roommate at Tanglewood in 1957—Zubin Mehta, and Claudio Abbado usually didn't mention Carvalho in their biographies.

Spurred by my success with the *Legend of Faust*, I decided to carry on in that field and entered another competition, this time for a chamber-music composition organized by the Student Musicians Association. This time I had a few months to compose it. It was a saxophone quartet, and I won first prize.

You organized and directed, in Montevideo, the first festival entirely devoted to American twentieth-century music . . . You were sixteen years old.

I don't really know what motivated me to set up an American music festival in Montevideo that year. Anyway, I made an appointment with the US ambassador, and in less than a week I had drawn up programs and found players for a series of concerts, radio broadcasts, and conferences to cover a six-month period. All the material I needed came from the library of the Uruguay-American Institute.

I designed the brochures and the advertising inserts, and the American Embassy oversaw the printing, which was superb. In special recognition of their support, I composed a hymn for the Uruguay-American Institute to be used for their various local events. In short order, I had managed to master the art of conferencing and radio broadcasting, which proved to be very useful throughout the rest of my career. I had managed to convince the best artists in the country to take part voluntarily and persuaded SODRE's national radio station to broadcast the entire series of events.

It is thanks to that festival that I discovered the music of Aaron Copland, Samuel Barber, Walter Piston, and Roy Harris. The nonstandard and unconventional scores by Edgard Varèse and Carl Ruggles fascinated me as much. I broadcast *Ionisation* by Edgard Varèse dozens of times on the radio during the festival and received many violent protestations from scandalized listeners. *Sun-Treader* by Ruggles literally enchanted me. It was right at the beginning of the fifties, and the score from a certain Charles Ives had hardly been covered in the media and performed in the halls. Carl Ruggles owed a lot to him.

What role did Virgil Thomson play in your young career?

We were in the middle of the festival when Virgil Thomson started his South American grand tour, which had been sponsored by the State Department in Washington. I was at Hugo Balzo's when I heard about it. A great pianist, Balzo was also SODRE's artistic director. He showed me—not without contempt—piano scores by Thomson that to him, at the time, seemed naive. Today I better understand what Thomson was attempting to achieve, possibly in reference to Satie: a simple but very delicate and refined music. This, to Balzo, seemed useless and stupid. And there was no way that Thomson would ever conduct his own score at the SODRE, even if the American Embassy was putting on the pressure. He flatly refused their request, and so Montevideo was the only Latin American capital to refuse Virgil Thomson.

Thomson had just given up writing his acclaimed and influential critic's column for the *New York Herald Tribune*, and the American government had organized this special tour for him. When Thomson landed in Montevideo, it was winter. The rain was pouring down. The only event planned for him was a lecture at the Uruguay-American Institute auditorium, a small room, and his audience consisted of only my parents and me. Thomson was furious. After a short speech in English lasting just a few minutes—of which I did not understand a single word, not having mastered the language at the time—he stopped talking and refused to utter another word. Just before he left, I was introduced to him by the cultural attaché to the American Embassy; I had been hoping to pass my scores along to him. He refused to take them, saying they were too heavy to carry. The cultural attaché picked them up and whispered that he would have them sent to Thomson's hotel room. I wasn't very hopeful. So, it was to my surprise the next morning that I received an early phone call from Thomson. He was at the airport in the departure lounge and informed me that he had taken a look at my work and was bringing my scores home with him. He promised me that he would show them to Aaron Copland and that he would do everything in his power for me to go and study in the United States. I could not believe my lucky stars.

A few weeks later, I received a phone call from the American Embassy. Not only had he fulfilled his promise, but he had done even more: he had personally gone to Philadelphia to show my music to Efrem Zimbalist, head of the Curtis Institute of Music, one of the most prestigious music schools in the world. Zimbalist had instantly accepted me as a student, awarding me the maximum scholarship. Thomson had previously showed my scores to Eugene Ormandy and convinced him to contact Zimbalist. I needed neither to apply nor to audition. As a precaution, he had also forwarded my scores to Howard Hanson, head of the Eastman School of Music in Rochester, and he too had accepted me on a full scholarship. I was faced with a difficult choice: I absolutely loved Howard Hanson's music, but in the end, I opted for the Curtis Institute, partly motivated by the fact that the entire Russian side of my family was now living in Philadelphia. The other reason was the letter that I received from Bohuslav Martinů, the most beautiful welcome letter ever written. Unfortunately, I never got the opportunity to meet him. By the time I started there, he had moved to Switzerland for work and settled there, thanks to a comfortable fellowship from the Guggenheim Foundation, the same one I would receive two years later.

Aware that I was not so sufficiently well-off to go and study in the United States, Thomson did everything in his power at the State Department and managed to get me a backdated scholarship, via a special government dispensation. I left for Philadelphia. I was seventeen. It was my first trip outside the family nest and out of the area, apart from an excursion to Buenos Aires the previous year for a weekend at the invitation of Alberto Ginastera. My family never traveled abroad. In those days we didn't have a phone line, which at the time was a sign of luxury. Our only contact with a phone was at the local grocer's shop. It was there that I had received Thomson's call from the airport and the one from the American Embassy informing me about the scholarship—renewable—from the International Institute of Education by intervention from the Department of State meant to cover my travel and my stay for a year. Going to America was like a dream. I left the wet and gloomy winter in Montevideo behind and arrived in Washington on one of the hottest June days in history.

I soon learned English, thanks to the accelerated courses reserved for foreign students. I had to live frugally and to stretch the fifty dollars that my parents had given me. A special dispensation had to be obtained from Congress before I could receive my scholarship under such unique circumstances; I had to wait for a few months. At long last, checks started to arrive on a regular basis, as well as my twenty-five dollars a month from my parents—a very appreciated bonus.

What did you study with Aaron Copland and Eleazar de Carvalho at Tanglewood?

From Washington, I went straight on to Tanglewood to study composition with Aaron Copland. Among my classmates was a tall and skinny Finn, ten years my senior—Einojuhani Rautavaara, who would become a very dear friend. Although we would only see each other occasionally thereafter, he opened a lot of doors for me in Finland. In the seventies, he also invited me to conduct and record some of his work in Helsinki, including *Angels and Visitations* with the Finnish Radio Symphony Orchestra.

In the four summers I spent at Tanglewood, I came across some exceptional people and gained considerable musical experience, although my English was not yet up to scratch at the time: Copland had welcomed me into his class, although I could only understand half of what he was saying. I felt good at Tanglewood; its landscape with green hills and its lake and its friendly campus enchanted me. The lessons were in groups of eight composers, and we also benefited from weekly private lessons. Copland was a wonderful teacher—exciting, full of energy, and always with a smile on his face. We worked mainly on orchestration, which to him was essential. Under his supervision, I composed a brief overture appropriately titled *Tanglewood*, although I never heard it performed. I had sent the score to Hugo Balzo, who had passed it on to Walter Goehr, one of the conductors invited to be part of the SODRE season, whom I unfortunately never met. The first performance received—so I was told—mixed reactions. At a later date, the SODRE main building burned to the ground, along with it most of the music library, including my overture. Some of my scores, previously written in Montevideo, were performed that first summer at Tanglewood: *Pequeña Música* for woodwind quintet and my *Suite Canina* for woodwind trio. This one was warmly received, especially by Lukas Foss. The following summer, 1957, I again joined Copland's composition and Eleazar de Carvalho's conducting classes. My roommate was a young Japanese, Seiji Ozawa, with whom I got along very well. We were kind and honest friends. He was way ahead of me, as he was four years my senior. He had just won the International Competition in Besançon and had been propelled to Tanglewood by Charles Munch, who had been one of the jury members in France, and Seiji had come highly recommended. He was awarded the Koussevitzky Prize for conducting. I received the composition award.

I remember, not without some emotion and a touch of nostalgia, the end-of-year student orchestra concert, when we played Tchaikovsky's Fifth Symphony: I conducted the *scherzo* and Seiji the final *allegro*. The following summer, I joined Hugh Ross's class to learn choral conducting. Ross soon became a friend and a mentor. He was a perfect gentleman. Among my friends at Tanglewood were Zubin Mehta and Claudio Abbado, both taking Eleazar de Carvalho's conducting course.

Which technique was Pierre Monteux using to teach you conducting?

Abbado won the Koussevitzky Prize at Tanglewood in 1958. I had chosen to go to Hancock, in Maine, where Pierre Monteux was teaching. He accepted seventy students, and they all had to play in the orchestra; imagine an orchestra made up of seventy conductors. Every morning, we gathered under a big tent. Monteux used to sit behind the viola section (he had been a viola player in Paris; he had even played in cafés and in cinemas). Monteux was famous for his brilliant mind and his wicked sense of humor. All of us had to get on the podium and learn by observing each other's mistakes. He had great experience, a will to clarify, and an in-depth knowledge of music. He rarely commented on practical technique or on arm movements. When he was making fun at our expense, it was always justified. His remarks were sudden, abrupt. We were learning on the job. Praise did not come easily to him. I was completely stunned when, after my first attempt, we could choose our own repertoire and I had opted for Schubert's Unfinished Symphony, and he told me, "This is not quite like we perform it in Vienna, but you have a valid and very interesting point of view of that score. You are producing a true Schubertian sound!" I nearly fell backward: I knew so little about tempo control or orchestral sound, my only basic approach having been with the youth orchestra in Montevideo. It was then Monteux's turn to select my next score: the Chausson Symphony, the one I had discovered and loved, thanks to Paul Paray's Detroit Symphony recording.

Carvalho's teaching method was different. He insisted heavily on the beauty of gestures. For a passage in *Night on Bald Mountain* by Mussorgsky he gave me the following instructions: "Keep the sound of the violins with your left hand high up so that the audience can see it; then open your right fist and let the flute take it over." It was always theatrical. Everything had to be planned, including the arrival on stage and the greetings. I was nevertheless convinced that I had learned a lot from him. I am surprised that he isn't more famous and appreciated. Some contemporary conducting stars owe him a great deal.

Like Bernstein, you were a pupil at the renowned Curtis Institute in Philadelphia, and like Bernstein you graduated in only two years instead of the required four . . .

My main reason for coming to the United States had been to enroll at the Curtis Institute in Philadelphia. In 1956, Philadelphia was a quiet and enjoyable town, where it felt nice to live and work. My classmates were all very talented, and I benefited greatly from their influence. I made great progress in the English language thanks to television. That was the first time I had set eyes on a TV set; it was only just arriving in Uruguay.

My composition teacher was Vittorio Giannini. He was also a teacher at the Juilliard School in New York and kept traveling back and forth. There were only a few of us in his class, three or four, and lessons were private. He was easygoing, and we became friends. As time went by, I would be invited regularly to join him and his wife for dinner at their house in New York, and years later I conducted his compositions as often as I could. He was a prestigious teacher, managing two important jobs, but he did not really teach me any more than I'd already known. I wrote, under his guidance, a piano sonata and other works just to graduate. I was bored. The desire to conduct gnawed at me and I was ever so keen to learn all there was to know about conducting. At the Curtis school I learned about composition, piano, and theory and history of music. That meant about a four-hour week of classes. I therefore took the initiative to go to the head of the school, Efrem Zimbalist—the legendary Russian violinist, who was married to Mary Curtis Bok, the patron of the institute—and bluntly expressed my frustration; I wanted to conduct. Unfortunately, the conducting class run by Fritz Reiner had been discontinued. Zimbalist replied, "Conducting cannot be taught . . . you do it by instinct. You learn by practicing. None of the great conductors in the twentieth century has been taught how to conduct. Toscanini, Stokowski are the most famous examples." I was not deterred. If that was to be the case, I would try to graduate as quickly as possible and then go somewhere else to study conducting. Leonard Bernstein had managed to graduate within two years instead of the required four, so I would try to do the same. Zimbalist and Giannini advised me on what I would have to do. I then wrote my piano sonata, a string quartet, and other pieces within a few weeks.

Through the International Institute of Education, I complained to the American State Department, explaining that without any conducting training I was not receiving the education for which I had come to the United States. The State Department agreed to pay my private tuition. Having discussed it with Eugene Ormandy, I opted for classes with William Smith, who was the pianist and assistant conductor with the Philadelphia Orchestra. Bill Smith was a true American. He was a professional, serious and vibrant, cheerful, laidback, but a rigorous and efficient teacher. He was the one to inculcate in me the very first basic conducting notions: how to separate the functions of the two arms and two hands, how to properly read and study a score. And there I suddenly realized that Zimbalist had not been completely wrong; all the great conductors had, in the past, no option but to learn on their own, as conducting had been a new artistic form and there had then been nobody who could teach them. Wagner, Berlioz, then Mahler had been pioneers, and a giant step had been taken by them. But then, why couldn't an experienced conductor pass on his knowledge and experience to newcomers? Why the need to reinvent the wheel when something could just be transmitted by a predecessor's experience?

Admittedly, as for creativity, talent cannot be taught. But the technical and psychological elements allowing this talent to express itself, to bloom, can be learned in books, by oral teaching, and by practice. One has to accept that conducting requires lifelong learning. There are so many subtleties in the personal and mysterious ways of practicing this art that years of experience are necessary to crystalizing a transcendent interpretation.

My unusual scholarship, still without any official designation from the US government, was renewed for a second year, and I graduated from the Curtis Institute within two years, not having a clue about what I was to do next.

How was your first meeting, which turned out to be so important, with Antal Doráti? What did you learn from him?

Pianist Hugo Balzo, who was then the artistic director at SODRE, spoke about me to Antal Doráti when he was in Montevideo to conduct. Doráti had recently decided to create a new position within his Minneapolis Symphony, selecting a student on scholarship in conjunction with the University of Minnesota. I received a cable from Doráti mentioning that, on Balzo's recommendation, he had agreed to invite me to do an audition the next day at eight in the morning in New York. My audition was to take place at the Salisbury Hotel, opposite Carnegie Hall—where he was due to give a concert—and he requested I be ready to conduct, by heart, a symphony of my choice.

To ensure that I arrived on time, I took the 4 a.m. train and arrived in New York just before seven. I took the subway to Carnegie Hall and stopped first at a cafeteria just opposite the hotel, the Horn & Hardart, for a coffee. At eight o'clock precisely, I knocked on Doráti's door, and he received me wearing his bathrobe. Straightaway, in just a few seconds, he described to me the incredible sequence he had worked out for my audition: I was to conduct (I had chosen Schubert's Eighth Symphony) without any music being played. If my expressions and my gestures could make him feel the music, I would get the job.

I was amazed. But before I could utter a word, off he walked to the bathroom to shave. He said, "Don't worry, I can see you perfectly in the mirror. Go on." I complied without protest and started to conduct an invisible orchestra. I was often disrupted: his wife crossed the room, looking at me with incredulity; her mother came and sat a few minutes by my side, never ceasing to observe me with curiosity; then Tonina, his ravishing eighteen-year-old daughter, kept coming and going, while eying me from top to toe, which appeared to me to be a sure sign of disapproval.

Finally, the maid appeared, carrying a large breakfast tray, at the exact moment when I was conducting the intense and dramatic passage of the second half of the first movement. Panicked, she dropped the tray with its entire contents—eggs, coffee, milk, jam, fruit juice spreading all over the floor. I was surprised but carried on my task 'til the end, pretending to look calm.

Much to my relief, Doráti suddenly appeared, roaring with laughter, while wiping his hands and face, still in his bathrobe. He then declared solemnly, "If you can conduct in this absolute mayhem and in such a hubbub without missing a single bar line and the slightest indication, you are the student I am looking for. You are hired. You'll be starting in September!"

Just as I was leaving, delighted, he stopped me, saying, "Wait a minute. Let me check if you have a good ear," and he played a note at random on the hotel's upright piano. He was surprised when I answered him, smiling, "B natural," which was the right answer. He had been really taken aback by the speed at which I had given my answer, but he relaxed when I added that the test was easy, as B was the key for the Unfinished Symphony. As great a musician as he was, Doráti did not have perfect pitch, and he was very conscious of the fact. He was not the only famous conductor who had some difficulty identifying the right note; he had difficulty recognizing a difficult chord. That limitation did not seem to bother him in the least, as he could compensate with other more important abilities. An absolute pitch and an infallible memory were invaluable tools but apparently not necessarily essential.

Doráti was an extraordinary teacher. Our private lessons were on Monday evenings at his house in Minneapolis. We worked on the compositions he was to conduct each week. The gestures, the technique, were not part of the lessons. Rather, Doráti would study the structure of each score, its harmonic subtleties, which instruments to emphasize—all that he had learned through many years of experience. After working for long hours, we would then join his family downstairs for supper.

Score in hand, I used to wait impatiently for rehearsals to begin. With me was David Zinman. Having only recently graduated from Oberlin, he'd applied too late for the Doráti scholarship I'd already won. Having no other plans, he still chose to come to Minneapolis. We struck up a friendship straightaway. His strong will, his genuine desire to become a good musician, his infallible sense of humor did not fail to impress me. He was bound to have a major career.

My two years spent in Minneapolis brought me invaluable experiences. More so, school life had been all I had wanted it to be: no restrictions, real freedom, and . . . many girls!

I rented a room in the neighborhood called "Dinkytown" (noisy town). I organized concerts with the university orchestra. For the first time, I faced a large, professional orchestra when Doráti invited me to conduct my *Elegy for Strings* at the subscription concerts the following season. The second time was a few weeks later in Mexico, when Luis Herrera de la Fuente asked me to conduct the National Symphony Orchestra of Mexico for several weeks. Those were my first real concerts. I was nineteen.

If the Curtis Institute diploma I had earned was leading nowhere, the University of Minnesota would give me the chance to study for a Master of Arts degree, in case I needed it in the future for a teaching career. I did the same as I had Philadelphia and managed to qualify for my Master of Arts in composition in two years instead of four. Apart from music, I also studied Latin American literature. My thesis was my *Partita*, Symphony No. 2. Apart from what Doráti taught me, which was essential, the rest was negligible.

Doráti was constantly at odds with Sokoloff, the orchestra manager. Sokoloff had the upper hand in the end, and Doráti was forced to resign. As a departing gift, he prepared a special recording of screams for Sokoloff. Doráti had a terrible temper. His was, in any case, a typical example of conductor's behavior in those days. He was a dictator while being recognized as an excellent conductor. I was his last student. He had in fact declared to the Minneapolis *Tribune* that he would not take any more students after me. I was lucky to have benefited from the teachings of one of the last great masters of a disappearing tradition—a rare privilege and an extraordinary opportunity that I never took for granted.

During my second year in Minneapolis, I met Mrs. Faith Smyth, a patron of the arts who seemed to cultivate a complex sometimes known as the "von Meck"—the lady who had supported Tchaikovsky without ever meeting him. Faith Smyth had helped further quite a few careers, including Leontyne Price and Jorge Bolet. She took me under her wing, commissioning me to write a composition for large orchestra—*Partita*, Symphony No. 2, which not only was used as my thesis to obtain my Master of Arts degree but also, thanks to her, I conducted with the Washington National Symphony Orchestra. I introduced Mrs. Smyth to Doráti, and she agreed to sponsor the recording of his symphony, his last recording in Minneapolis.

Now that my studies were finished, and Doráti was leaving Minneapolis, my future once again seemed uncertain. But my biggest experience was yet to come down the road, as I was eventually to become associate conductor for Leopold Stokowski, with the newly formed American Symphony Orchestra at Carnegie Hall in New York.

You seem to possess an instinct, an inborn intuition, for conducting.

It came to me in the most natural way when I began conducting at age eleven. I learned in the same way that a child learns to walk, with experience and avoiding the same mistake twice. I was convinced that it was the most natural thing to do. This is the reason I don't remember my first experience working with a large orchestra—not even recollecting any fear or emotions linked to this event. Nevertheless, I think it was in Minneapolis, in 1958, when Antal Doráti had asked me to do my first orchestra reading, the entire second movement of Tchaikovsky's Fifth Symphony. I'd had an idea of how it was supposed to be performed, but it seemed to me then that I couldn't get the orchestra started together, that I was trying in vain to move a herd of elephants. Something good must have come of it, though, as a few players came to congratulate me at the end of the performance. I was devastated. True to form, Doráti made no comment. But the following day, he invited me to conduct my *Elegy for Strings* in one of his own regular subscription concert series of 1958 and 1959.

A year later, my attitude when facing a large orchestra had completely changed. I had overcome the problem of getting a large symphony orchestra started and controlled. I was now in full control. The benefit of many experiences with highly professional orchestras had refined my technique, especially as guest conductor for the National Symphony Orchestra of Mexico and conducting the university orchestra in Minneapolis.

It was at the end of my second season with Doráti that I went back to Uruguay after a four-year absence and conducted the SODRE Orchestra for the very first time. We performed Rimsky-Korsakov's *Russian Easter Overture* and Beethoven's Eighth Symphony, and critics judged my interpretation too strict and square. I believe they were right. Later I allowed for more freedom within a strictly classical framework, thanks to experience and to subtleties taught me by Pierre Monteux and other great masters. Years later, the Eighth Symphony would become one of my major successes in concert halls and on recordings.

It appears that conducting can carry some unexpected risks.

In 1975, I was invited by UNAM, Mexico's university—probably the largest in the world—to organize and run a festival of contemporary music. Soloists came from the United States, and the chorus was Mexican. The festival was a complete and popular success. During the final concert, while I was conducting a large choir and orchestra with music by the Spanish-Mexican composer Rodolfo Halffter—Ernesto's brother and uncle to Cristóbal—I had an accident that landed me on front pages around the world.

I had just arrived from Pittsburgh, and my luggage had been lost. Therefore I urgently needed to buy clothes and other things and to get hold of a baton for conducting. The driver, who had come to pick me up at the airport, informed about the problem, reassured me, saying, "Batons? In Mexico, you can buy one on every street corner!" And this was my immediate task at our first stop. But instead of being made of wood, the baton was, unfortunately, made of fiberglass, obviously made for band conductors. When wood breaks, it's not a weapon. In the case of fiberglass, if broken, the baton becomes a sharp and formidable weapon. There was some risk of the baton breaking during the concert, hitting the metallic music stand, and becoming a sharp blade. Halffter's score has a huge choir literally surrounding the audience. As I was frenetically trying to get them to sing, doing a full circle on the podium, my clumsiness and speed made me pierce my left hand. The baton broke in half. One half went straight through my left hand, a tiny piece of the other half still embedded in my right fist. Possessed by the intensity of the music, in total osmosis with the work, I felt no pain, no surprise or shock. I conducted 'til the end of the piece. Toward the end, as I was beating time with my right hand, I tried my best to remove the piece of baton from my left hand without missing a single beat. The players were watching me in horror, stunned. The ovation that followed was so thunderous that you would have thought they were watching the end of a bullfight. And then came the pain. I was quickly rushed to the American Hospital for a tetanus injection, which I refused when I noticed that the nurse was trying to decipher the instructions on the box containing the needles, slowly and with great difficulty. There was no infection.

The news made Mexican headlines, which were then picked up extensively by various American newspapers, including the *New York Times*, and made their way around the news agencies. I was also interviewed by *Time* magazine about the dangers of conducting orchestras. The following week, Sir Georg Solti suffered a similar mishap while conducting Mozart's *Don Giovanni* at the Metropolitan Opera in New York. It was a slightly different situation this time, as he was using a short wooden baton and had accidentally pricked his eyelid. The curtain had to be dropped, and the performance was interrupted. Solti was treated and made comfortable. This time the media were totally indifferent and didn't even report the incident. Solti told me not long after that "they must think that conductors do that sort of thing all the time." Unfortunately, the accident had annoying consequences for me: one of the nerves in my left hand had been seriously damaged, and I had to give up playing the violin. It was no tragedy, as my profound passion for music was more about composing and conducting.

· 2 ·

The Uncertainties of a Double Career

**As a young composer, was it challenging to
get your compositions performed and published?**

It was in 1956, following my first summer at Tanglewood—a sublime summer during which I fell in love with an adorable girl (whose feelings were
mutual)—when my American career took off. To my despair, weeks into
our romance that wonderful girl became infatuated with a weird and lanky
character, a specialist in pantomime, a sort of Marcel Marceau, his idol. He
fascinated her, literally hypnotized her. I was heartbroken! Oh, no—I was
not going into pantomime to get her back! At the end of the wonderful first
Tanglewood Summer I buried my regrets in a small room in the heights of
Manhattan, waiting for my first school year to begin at the Curtis Institute
in Philadelphia, and writing my first symphony, which took me two weeks!
A work in one movement, profoundly steeped in my sadness. The piece was
supposed to tell, in romantic tradition, a tormented story. I submitted that
score as well as one of my earlier Montevideo essays that had impressed
Virgil Thomson so much, my saxophone quartet, to the BMI Student Com-
poser Award competition and won the prize. I was completely surprised.
An international prize—surely a good omen for my American beginnings.
But some other great surprises awaited me that summer. The famous New
York Woodwind Quintet, having heard my wind compositions during my
stay at Tanglewood, had chosen to include *Pequeña Música* in their first
South American tour, officially sponsored by the US State Department. I
was notified by their famous flutist, Samuel Baron. At about the same time,
Guillermo Espinosa, a Colombian musician who was then head of the music
department at the Pan American Union in Washington, announced that he
had decided to publish my *Elegy for Strings*. That was my first-ever published

25

composition and the first to be played worldwide, conducted in Brazil and Uruguay by my ex-teacher Guido Santórsola, by Juan Protasi in Paris with the ORTF orchestra, and later on by Leopold Stokowski, on December 3, 1958, at Carnegie Hall in New York.

I had only been in the United States for three months. I was amazed. Espinosa explained to me, "We really want to see you start out in the United States under optimal conditions. Every year we publish a new composition that has great merit, as an award, and this year we chose your *Elegy for Strings*." Their choice suited me perfectly! Pan American Union music publications were managed by Peer-Southern, and this is what brought me to the attention of their classical sector director, Vladimir Lakond. We met a few times, and I showed him some of my manuscripts, among them my *Canina Suite* for woodwind trio, also my very first piece, the Sonata for Solo Violin, and *Song of Destiny* for choir. He published every one of them. Within a few years, the whole of my chamber music had been published and produced. As for my orchestral music, that was a completely different matter. In those days Peermusic rarely printed compositions for large orchestra. I had to wait for some time before my *Poema Elegíaco* was published, and the same for *Fantasia*, eventually published in two separate versions—string quartet and string orchestra—and *Momento Psicológico*, a title suggested by Aaron Copland during my second stay at Tanglewood while attending his composition course. He maintained that the atmosphere in the music reminded him of a decisive psychological moment (hence the title). When Lakond retired and handed over to Ronald Freed, publishing opportunities with Peermusic increased a lot. Freed had started as a trainee with Lakond after graduating in voice at the Juilliard School. He soon became one of the most prominent and dynamic publishers, with a flair, intuition, and expertise that enchanted everyone. He was an eternal optimist, full of humor. When he later stepped down to become president of the European American Music Publishers, it was hard for classical composers with Peermusic contracts. But it was a fabulous new opportunity for Freed. The European American Music Publishers had just been created and was the American branch for the biggest European music publishers. Unfortunately, for a while the classical music department at Peermusic remained static, especially because of Freed's successors. We had to wait until the arrival of Todd Vunderink, also a previous trainee in the company, for young composers to stand a chance of being appreciated. New ideas started taking shape as soon as Vunderink took command—for example, the recording of compositions as well as publishing them. Behind what was at the time an audacious project was Ralph Peer, son of the organization's founder. I never had the pleasure of meeting his father, who had been a legendary figure in the music world. But I was very well acquainted with Ralph's mother. She was a fine, original, brilliant lady. One of the many and pleasant surprises she gave me was when she invited all her company executives from around the world to New York to attend the premiere of my ballet, *Orpheus Times Light*. It was adapted for the Joffrey Ballet on a special commission from the National Endowment for the Arts, using an expanded version of my harp concerto *Colores Mágicos*. I conducted the premiere of the ballet at the New York City Center theater. The subsequent performances and the national tour were conducted by Seymour Lipkin, famous pianist and music director of the Joffrey Ballet company. Mrs. Monica Peer arranged an elaborate affair after the premiere, with all the Peermusic directors from around the world, at the best discotheque in Manhattan. It was a revelation for me, as I had never experienced anything like it.

When no other music publisher would represent the music of Charles Ives, considered too radical and eccentric in the early part of the twentieth century, Peermusic was the first to accept it. I was amused when the Boosey & Hawkes library showed me a framed, never-cashed check from Charles Ives, which he had offered to cover the expenses of publishing one of his works. Peermusic planned for the long term. Not only did they uncover some of the greatest Latin American popular musicians but also many classical composers before anyone would even consider showing any interest in their work. Under Freed's direction, my scores, including risky ones, got published: harp concerto *Colores Mágicos*, Concerto for Accordion and Orchestra, and a luxurious and impeccably designed brochure consisting of a good number of worldwide reviews.

Leopold Stokowski premiered your First Symphony when you were just seventeen.

I was walking through the streets of Philadelphia on my way to school, with my symphony score tucked under my arm, with a friend who was attending the same course with Vittorio Giannini, when a corpulent and very friendly cellist, Harvey Wolfe, bumped into us. We were all running—me and my friend late for classes at the Curtis Institute, Harvey rushing to get to the airport for his first job, the Houston Symphony with Stokowski. Both my large score and his cello fell to the floor. I talked to Harvey briefly and hurriedly about my symphony, and he proposed to show my score to Stokowski. Without hesitation, I handed it to him. I didn't stop to consider if a famous conductor would even contemplate listening to a new young cellist and if he would even glance at an unknown seventeen-year-old composer's new work. The encounter had completely left my mind until a few weeks later, when the doorman at the Curtis Institute handed me a note: "Call Houston, Texas, immediately! Maestro Stokowski wants to speak to you urgently."

At the time, I was convinced that it was all a prank, like students frequently used to play on one another, sending pretend messages signed by famous impresarios or film stars, urgently requiring our attention. I therefore ignored the message, even on the following day when it was repeated, more urgently. Then, Efrem Zimbalist, president of the school, asked to see me urgently. He was shocked: "Have you gone mad? Ignoring a personal call from Stokowski! His secretary had to call me to ask how to contact you." From Mr. Zimbalist's office, we called Houston at once. I had the maestro on the line. He spoke in a jerky manner, sparing words, omitting all adjectives, and with a strong central European accent: "I cannot give first performance of Ives's Fourth Symphony next week. Too difficult; impossible for the orchestra in a short time. Need another premiere. Musician from orchestra gave me your First Symphony yesterday. That is what we will be performing in place of Ives's Fourth. Need your orchestral parts at once. Goodbye." I remained speechless. When I came to my senses, I realized that I didn't have any money to pay for the trip. I had forgotten to ask him to cover my traveling expenses—a mistake I would not make again! Zimbalist and his wife, Mrs. Mary Curtis Bok, paid for my airfare without a fuss. In cases like this, the Curtis school was tremendous. A huge problem remained: I did not have individual musician's parts for the symphony, only the conductor's score. Photocopiers had not been invented yet, so my classmates helped me copy the required instrument scores, night after night. We received a lot of help from the Fleisher Collection of Orchestral Music in Philadelphia, which took care of printing the parts, a very dirty task that left hands blue with ink. I am ever so grateful to Mr. Seder, chief of the Fleisher Music Collection at the Free Library of Philadelphia, for saving my life on that occasion. I arrived in Houston, fully prepared, on October 3, 1957, just in time.

Unforgettable musical memories from Houston. Stokowski made the orchestra sound like the Philadelphia orchestra of his recordings, which I had been collecting. The powerful sound of the strings was overwhelmingly full and warm; never did the brass cover them, and the woodwinds were perfectly audible. So brilliant and so musical. After the first rehearsal, the maestro seemed pleased and joked to the orchestra manager, "What we need at the end of the symphony are real bells, like church bells. We need bells . . . and especially many girls" . . . All this while observing me, on the sly, as I was entangled in whispered conversation with a young girl in the orchestra.

After my symphony, the program included Prokofiev's Piano Concerto no. 3, which I was hearing for the first time, with soloist Leonard Pennario, and it finished with Mussorgsky's *Pictures at an Exhibition* in an orchestration by Stokowski. An encore had also been planned but was not played on either of the two evenings. I was amazed when the *Houston Chronicle* critic wrote about the "encore" as one of the best performances of the evening. That same critic loved my symphony (which suggests he had probably been present at the concert) and made the remark, "The young composer expresses himself with his heart on his sleeve"—a weird expression that I was hearing for the first time. Retrospectively, I completely agreed with him. The other newspaper, the *Houston Post*, published the interview that I had given them and added all sorts of amazing predictions for my future career.

That a conductor of Stokowski's stature had chosen my symphony, over and in place of Ives's Fourth, represented an unparalleled opportunity. Moreover, my music was exactly the sort that made the maestro salivate. For him, it came from Heaven. And he conducted it as if he had written it himself. He had found himself trapped when the orchestra had been unable to get past the very first notes of the Ives. Having invited all the American music press to the "historic premiere of the most difficult composition ever written," he could not cancel the reporters and music critics from *Time, Newsweek, Life,* UPI and the AP, and *Musical America,* who had been invited for weeks. With all those reporters present, I thought I was becoming famous overnight. I was interviewed around the clock. All the critics surrounded me. *Time* magazine prepared a long article. *Life* magazine had their photographers follow me everywhere, including to the hairdresser. But then, just a few days before the premiere of my symphony—October 8, 1957—the USSR sent the first Sputnik into space, ahead of NASA. This was a considerable event that monopolized the interest of all the newspapers and media. For months music, ballet, theater, literature, plastic arts had no place in the important publications. Every single page was dedicated to Sputnik's scientific impact. The USSR was winning the space race! Nothing was published apart from the local press articles out of Houston. The orchestra sent telegrams to all the daily newspapers but to no avail. When that media space boom dropped, like a soufflé, I called *Time* magazine's critic, who had seemed so interested in and satisfied with the concert, to inquire about the publication date for his article. I took a slap in the face that I am still not ready to forget: "News is only interesting news when it happens. After that, it's old news. Nobody is interested in old news. Of course, if another event puts you in the limelight, we could use this article, but at this moment no musical subject is planned for the foreseeable future. For now, only science is dominating the news."

My first symphony is just a single movement because the idea of writing a symphony in various unrelated movements didn't make much sense to me at the time. I had been carrying this music in my head for a long time, and it had only taken me twelve days to give birth to it, in a fever, as if my life depended on it. The small digs I had been renting with a few of my pals from a Mrs. Nussbaum, on 156th Street in Manhattan, practically in the heart of Harlem, were poorly lit, and we had no kitchen access. But financially it was within our means. Many South American students at Tanglewood had decided to spend their remaining time that summer in hot and damp New York. Among them were flutist Gerardo Levy, clarinetist Efrain Guigui (who spent all his time studying theory), and the excellent violinist Alberto Lysy, protégé of Yehudi Menuhin, all three originally from Buenos Aires. Looking back, I find it difficult to understand how, before I had even started composition classes at the Curtis Institute, I managed to compose the symphony over the summer of 1956, which turned out to be an excellent passport for my entrance onto the American musical scene.

My first encounters with Stokowski were brief. At the end of my first rehearsal, he asked me if he could change the orchestration in one section, adding his favorite tam-tam to a percussion sequence and adding another trumpet. Wishing to prove to him that I knew what I was doing and that I could not be easily led, I refused. He respected my decision and stuck to what I had written. A seventeen-year-old composer refusing a change to a world-famous musician like Stokowski was very daring on my part! Later on, after listening to the recording, I realized that he had been right. I had been wrong to not have heeded his advice, because he was a master of orchestration.

Before leaving Houston, I asked him a simple question, one so crucial to me. I wanted to become a conductor; would he be so kind as to give me some advice? His answer came as a true Stokowski sarcastic remark but nevertheless containing a good part of truth: "It's quite simple. All you need to do is travel the world and observe all the bad conductors. You'll then learn what *not* to do!" It is true that one always learns from other people's mistakes. Nevertheless, I learned much more by watching him at work during my five fabulous years with the American Symphony Orchestra in New York as associate conductor.

In Houston I heard my symphony rehearsed then played in public two days in a row. To my great amazement, it sounded just as I had imagined it. Working from my desk and not from a piano, I had assumed that there would be a few differences between what had been in my mind, on paper, and the live orchestral sound. Some composers, like Stravinsky, compose at the piano, while others seem comfortable writing at a desk.

Your Piano Sonata and Second Symphony
use Latin American rhythms . . .

Back at the Curtis Institute, I started work on a piano sonata, the first of my compositions in which I introduced, knowingly, some Latin American elements, as if it were a duty. I used the most common rhythms. It was at the time—1957 and 1958—when Heitor Villa-Lobos was reigning supreme, and I had taken his exhortation seriously: "Never forget about your South American roots. Do you ever feel nostalgic"—*Saudade*? "Do you ever miss the beaches and the girls from Punta del Este?" He was a great musician and a colorful character. I followed his advice. The following year, as I was working on my most ambitious project, *Partita*, I went even further, mixing rhythms of Brazilian conga and authentic Uruguayan candombe, the entire composition filtered through a jazzy semi-improvisation on drums at the end.

After this, I gave up any claim on Latin Americanism. I had been sincere when I'd written that music, but I really preferred finding my own language, writing a score that would be truly mine. And it came to me, naturally, probably by instinct. When my Piano Sonata was played in public, during an evening at Curtis Hall, I felt for the first time that, for that conservative institution, as if I were the bad boy in the house—a little too modern, and free in a very traditional and conventional school in which Giannini, the very essence of conservatism, represented the establishment. That is when Mrs. Faith Smyth came into my life and commissioned my *Partita*, Symphony No. 2. I had been introduced to her by pianist Jorge Bolet, whom she had sponsored for Charles Vidor's 1960 film *Song Without End*. Bolet was engaged to play the piano but also to do some cameo acting. Unfortunately for him, only the sound part of his work was used in the final edit. He was the dubbing pianist for Dirk Bogarde in the role of Franz Liszt. The film was, nevertheless, the catalyst that enabled Bolet to return to the concert halls, and thanks to Mrs. Smyth his career took flight again. Bolet performed with me several times in Australia, just after his musical accident in Mexico City: Bolet had inaugurated a new concert hall in Mexico with a solo recital, and the stagehands had neglected to secure and lock the piano legs. The staged being raked, as soon as Bolet played a first chord with eyes closed, the piano rolled all the way down the stage, falling into the orchestra pit with a huge racket. The news went around the world, some with the picture of an incredulous Bolet standing onstage alone, staring at the remains of the grand piano.

Leontyne Price received an invaluable helping hand for her incipient career when Mrs. Smyth commissioned a composition to be written especially for her, procuring her many bookings and opening many doors. Mrs. Smyth also facilitated the production of an off-Broadway show, *The Fantasticks*, a magnificent musical by Tom Jones and Harvey Schmidt, which opened on May 3, 1960, in Greenwich Village. It became a big success. Faith Smyth was a decisive and energetic lady. One day, toward the end of my two-year stay in Minneapolis, I introduced her to Antal Doráti. They became friendly straightaway. She then financed his last Mercury recording in Minneapolis, his own symphony.

Although he invited me to conduct my *Elegy for Strings* with his orchestra in Minneapolis, Doráti was not encouraging when we discussed my future as composer. He told me, "Just be happy to compose, or just let it go. Conducting is more practical. Other conductors will not perform your music because you are competition. When Mahler was still alive, very few colleagues conducted his music other than himself." All talent consideration aside, he hated talking about it. He himself was an above average composer but terribly bitter that nobody would perform his music. I was privileged to have conducted the world premiere of his difficult *Missa Brevis* for choir and percussion at a concert that I had organized in Minneapolis. If he was grateful, he never acknowledged it.

Unlike my First Symphony, which had a single movement, my Second Symphony, *Partita*, was constructed in four distinctive parts. The first movement, prelude, uses rhythms and brilliant colors from Latin America. The second movement is a funeral march with Slavic inspiration, a piece with violent contrasts and a dark and tragic feeling. The third movement is an interlude, a transition allowing access to a grand finale, a complex fugue in which the funeral march theme slowly but inexorably transforms itself into a very irreverent conga-candombe, and the piece ends on a jazzy sequence, based on the same Latin mold that had shaped the rest of the work.

I felt quite sure that Mrs. Smyth had a lot to do with the invitation that Howard Mitchell sent me. Mitchell was the music director for the National Symphony Orchestra in Washington, DC, and I was surprised when he invited me to conduct my *Partita*, Symphony No. 2, with his orchestra. In 1960 the Kennedy Center was not yet in existence, and the concert was performed in the gigantic auditorium of the Daughters of the American Revolution, the usual residence for the orchestra. It was a great success. Paul Hume, the famous and feared *Washington Post* music critic, was assigned to review the concert. Hume had become famous for daring to criticize President Truman's daughter for her vocal recital, which had led to angry letters of complaint from President Truman to the *Washington Post*, making Paul Hume a household name across America. The president had written, among other things, that the music critic surely wished he could sing as well as Margaret Truman. Having made the best of his fearsome reputation ever since, Hume used to strongly criticize all who dared perform in the federal capital. His criticism of my *Partita* was no exception. I have kept, etched in my mind, the moment we met, the next day, during the sumptuous lunch organized for the sponsors, lady friends, and supporters of the orchestra. Hume was surrounded by board members of the orchestra when I was introduced to him. I held out my hand to him. He said to me, "You are shaking my hand after what I wrote about you in the *Washington Post?*" My answer to him was, "Yes, of course." At the time I had not yet set eyes on his review, everything being a novel experience for me. At the luncheon, Hume was put in charge of the keynote speech, and he started it by reading a dozen reviews by music critics of the past for works that eventually became great staples of the symphonic repertoire—Beethoven's Ninth Symphony, Berlioz's Symphonie Fantastique, Tchaikovsky's Piano Concerto no. 1, and so on. All the reviews Hume read seemed scathing, sarcastic, devastating. That was his way of praising my work, he explained, because having negatively reported on it was the sign that time would take care of itself, perhaps rectifying his original review. His declarations had the benefit of making my piece somewhat controversial and did not fail to intrigue the guests who had not listened to it yet, and one fortunate outcome was that the next concert was completely sold out.

It had been a special evening for the Washington premiere of my Second Symphony on November 8, 1960, as it was the day of the election of J. F. Kennedy as the new president of the United States. TV sets had been installed backstage, in corridors, in dressing rooms, in the foyer, and the public, in small groups, was coming in and going out nonstop to check on the outcome of the results, as it seemed to be a close election. About 10 p.m., Nixon and JFK were still neck and neck, and no winner had yet been named. The following evening, the concert hall was again full. And, surprise, Hume reversed his criticism and declared that each hearing made him better appreciate my *Partita*. I must admit that I was quite astonished by his rapidity in retracting his earlier comments, but I had not been upset by them.

Months went by. I was teaching temporarily as a substitute professor at Swarthmore College in Philadelphia when I received a phone call from Robert Whitney, music director of the Louisville Orchestra in Kentucky. He had decided to record my *Partita* but had encountered a problem: it was too long for one side of an LP (long-playing in 1961). One of the movements would have to be sacrificed, and he had decided that the "Funeral March" would be excluded from the recording. He was asking my permission. I agreed, as it was the first time that one of my compositions would be recorded, and I could not miss such an opportunity. It was a shame because I believed that the "Funeral March" was the best movement of my *Partita*, and Copland's favorite.

Whitney was a visionary. He and his orchestra were the most imaginative and most progressive in the American symphonic music world of the time. He had received many grants and had changed the routine by playing and recording dozens and dozens of new scores. He gave, from my shortened *Partita*, an extraordinary performance. The critics welcomed it: "It is an explosion of sounds, a sort of South American *Rite of Spring*" (Alfred Frankenstein, *San Francisco Chronicle*). The recording became one of the best sellers of their series: "Louisville has finally given us a contemporary composition that the wider public can understand and love!" (*Louisville Courier-Journal*)

What was your first position as conductor or music director?

I had read in an article in the *New York Times* that Stokowski would be performing the premiere of my *Elegy for Strings* on December 3, 1959, at Carnegie Hall, presented by the Contemporary Music Society. I was thrilled, as not only was it the second time that Stokowski would be conducting one of my compositions, but December 3 would be my twenty-first birthday. Unfortunately, I was not able to attend the concert, as flights from Minneapolis to New York were too expensive for me at the time. Three months later, in the spring of 1960, Doráti left Minneapolis, and I found myself in a difficult situation. Until then I had been lucky: after leaving the Curtis Institute for Minneapolis, I had received two consecutive fellowship awards from the Guggenheim Foundation and in addition two simultaneous scholarships from the University of Minnesota and the Doráti Fellowship to cover some of my expenses. Both had been renewed the following year, but now I was at a loss. It was not possible for me to go to Europe like David Zinman, who had followed Pierre Monteux from concert to concert. I did not have any plans. My wish was to conduct and compose on a regular basis. Leaving Minneapolis by car, heading for the East Coast, I stopped at a café in a small town in New York State. There I had a quick look at the local newspapers. Their orchestra, the Utica Symphony, was advertising for a conductor, and public auditions were due to take place that same evening. I managed easily to edge my way between candidates, and, to my surprise, I was selected for the position. Nothing to brag about, as after all it was a semiprofessional ensemble and the future of my appointment depended on the goodwill of the local politicians . . . something I was not at all prepared for!

I may have impressed the members of the orchestra with my knowledge of solfège and music theory, acquired thanks to Santórsola during my early student days in Montevideo. Orchestras—apart from those from the Latin countries where solfège is current practice—were often amazed by its mere use, as if it were sheer virtuosity. They were convinced that anyone who could sing naming the individual notes at high speed must be a talented musician (which is not always the case!).

The pay I was receiving from Utica was small, barely covering the cost of renting a small room at the YMCA. The fee was about two thousand dollars a year. Fortunately, the position as music director was also paired with an assistant professorship, part time, at the local Utica College of Syracuse University to teach violin and composition. The college was brand new and the classes held in improvised classrooms. The administration was attached to the University of Syracuse. All the same, I had a private office with a desk and a telephone, as well as access to their library, where I was free to study and compose. It was in that library, which was also used as a cafeteria, that I composed my *Fantasia* for string quartet. The noise made by the cutlery and all the talking could not distract me from my task. I took so much pleasure in writing that piece, commissioned by the Harvard Musical Association. I had won the competition organized by this venerable institution, and part of the award was to have members of the Boston Symphony Orchestra perform the premiere of the winning work at the magnificent lounge of the association in Boston. It was spring 1961. The Aeolian Quartet gave the second performance, in Washington, during the Inter-American Music Festival, which I could not attend. I was pleasantly surprised by the *Washington Post* review in which they referred to *Fantasia* as "a blaze of glory, the *1812* of string quartets." That had not been my intention when writing this piece, but I was delighted with its success. Vladimir Lakond at Peermusic suggested a version for string orchestra, and he published the two versions. The more that time goes by, the more attached I become to this piece that I composed in less than a week among constant student chatter . . .

I spent two rather difficult years in Utica. All the musicians needed another job. The first violin was the local bank's vice president. He was not—far from it—a good instrumentalist, but it was clear that he was indeed the best one in the orchestra. And he had a strong personality and was appreciated by his colleagues. As soon as I was nominated, I received an invitation for dinner at the home of a local violin teacher who was also a conductor and whose ambition was to become either the first violin or the orchestra's conductor. With that aim in mind, his wife had just become vice president of the governing board and president of the powerful woman's committee of the Utica Symphony. That couple had probably supported my application because at twenty-two I still looked like a boy, so they thought that I would be easily manipulated and eventually replaced. It was not long before I was made to understand by them that it would be a good idea if I got rid of the first violin and replaced him with the outsider, the husband. I did nothing of the sort. The couple put pressure on me during the two consecutive seasons. In private, all members of the orchestra supported my position and were suspicious of the pretender, who was incompetent according to them. The couple then started using their influence on the orchestra's administration, intrigues for which neither Doráti nor the other conductors with whom I had studied had prepared me, and it seemed to be a music director's daily ordeal. As my new contract—five hundred dollars more per year—was on the verge of being signed, the private invitations to dinner, usually frequent from the members of the administration committee, became rare. Some plotting was going on. I was then invited to come along to a committee meeting, during which I was ordered to dismiss the first violin with immediate effect. And I was to appoint immediately, of course, the vice president's husband. I said that I was going to think about it, but it seemed obvious that I would be doing nothing of the sort. The committee therefore voted for the change of the first violin and informed me that I just had to accept their decision. All the members of the orchestra and myself sent a letter of complaint. It ended up in a public meeting. As soon as it started, the vice president came to see me and asked me to show my still-unsigned contract renewal, which I had on hand, and he announced, "Your contract won't be renewed; we are retracting it." The musicians present were speechless. I left. I heard later that the orchestra rebelled against the imposed violinist. A compromise had to be reached, and another concertmaster was appointed. The orchestra no longer exists.

During my stay in Utica, I gave the premiere of Howard Hanson's *Elegy in Memory of Koussevitzky*, the American premiere of Alberto Ginastera's orchestral suite *Panambi*, and several world premieres of works by the Spanish composer Carlos Suriñach and the Brazilian Camargo Guarnieri. I also organized a school for choirmasters to which I entrusted Hugh Ross—who had been my choir teacher at Tanglewood—initiated a national competition for composers, and performed a stream of new works by local composers who rarely had the opportunity to have their music heard. Nowadays, with more experience, I might be more apt to extricate myself from a situation like the one I encountered in Utica. But respect for certain principles—my refusal to compromise in dubious and frankly dishonest situations—has remained for me an ideal to be defended at all costs. That painful experience helped me forge my resolution to only perform as guest conductor and never to accept full-time positions (I was offered a few) in order to avoid being implicated in any political-administrative situation that has nothing to do with music. After a week of guest conducting in New Mexico, the managing director of that orchestra drove me to the airport and offered me the position of music director, starting immediately, with two caveats: I was to dismiss the concertmistress and the first trumpet. Memories of Utica! I noticed that when the first violinist walked on stage, the entire audience had cheered and the musicians in the orchestra had tapped their feet. Removing her would foment revolution, and she seemed perfectly adequate. The trumpet player was the head of the local musician's union. Sensing that I might be offered the position as music director, he had driven me around the beautiful city and given gifts to my wife and little daughter. The city mayor had given a reception for me. I sensed a political situation and declined the offer. The management engaged a new graduate to direct the orchestra, who did what was expected, and the orchestra went on a long strike that threatened their continuity. Another orchestra of the same size and budget, this time in beautiful San Antonio—after several concerts and after I had taken them to Mexico City to inaugurate a new auditorium—also decided to offer me the music directorship. The president of the orchestra took me and my wife to dinner and laid out their two conditions. She explained, "You would have to stop this guest conducting all over the world." I asked, "Why?" Her reason: "If I have a valuable painting, I want it hanging in my house all the time, not lent around the world." Trying not to smile, I continued: "What is your second condition?" Looking at Carole, she said, "The wife of the conductor is an essential presence here, to inspire the woman's guild on which we depend so much for fundraising. Carole will have to be here all the time, not singing all over the world." We bid her goodbye.

The future looked rather bleak after Utica until I received an invitation from Luis Herrera de la Fuente, music director of Mexico's National Symphony Orchestra, to spend two weeks in Mexico conducting their orchestra. From Mexico City I took a few days' break in Acapulco, where I wrote to Stokowski to inform him that I was free. At age eighty-two, he was about to start a new venture with a new orchestra put together especially for him, in residence at Carnegie Hall. Just hours later I received a telegram from Stokowski: "Dear Maestro—do you want to become my associate conductor? Starting in September. Would you be willing to audition some of the musicians? Are you interested? Call me if you accept!" I could not believe my eyes.

What did five years as associate conductor to Leopold Stokowski represent to a not-quite-twenty-one-year-old musician?

I spent five amazing years as Stokowski's associate conductor at Carnegie Hall. On the artistic side, these were invaluable years that left their mark on me. On the financial side, it was a homeopathic treatment, and I had to seize all opportunities to earn a decent living. I accepted all the teaching jobs available, wherever I was wanted. I gave lectures at the Jacques-Dalcroze music school in Manhattan, and I temporarily stood in for composition teachers in nearby universities when they were on sabbatical. During the summers I worked in children's summer camps. During 1962 and '63, as I was officiating with the maestro and his new American Symphony Orchestra, I took charge of the composition class and conducting the student orchestra at Swarthmore College in the Philadelphia suburbs. I substituted for the entire season for Claudio Spies's classes—a wonderful time of learning, among students about my age or slightly younger, whose IQs were very high. Furthermore, the campus was wonderful. It was during that very busy period that I started receiving my first invitations to conduct in Europe, from Harmonien (the Bergen Philharmonic) in Norway, and from Kol Israel Orchestra in Jerusalem. The Norwegian invitation had much to do with the composer Harald Sæverud, whom I had met the previous year in Minneapolis. He had written a symphony—the *Minnesota Symphony*—commissioned by Doráti, and it had received a triumphant welcome upon its premiere in Minneapolis. Sæverud had come to visit me during his stay to observe me conducting the university orchestra and had recommended me to the Bergen Symphony Orchestra.

I was so engrossed in conducting and teaching that I had no time for composing for quite a while. Then Stokowski asked me to write a piece for the opening of the second season at Carnegie Hall. As he was late in his request, it put me in a difficult situation, as there was little time left to create something substantial. After a few unsuccessful attempts, I decided that I would offer him the second movement of *Partita*, the "Funeral March," which had been removed from Whitney's recording due to space constraints on their LP. It was the type of music that Stokowski loved. He accepted it immediately and asked me which title I wanted to give the piece. I tried to find a title that would be more appropriate to his personality, because to put a man of his age in charge of conducting a funeral march might have been in bad taste. I entitled it *Poema Elegíaco*. When I wrote that movement for *Partita*, I had in mind the idea of expressing the death of the spirit in our highly materialistic and pragmatic times, not human death. Harold Schonberg wrote a glowing review in the *New York Times* of the first performance conducted in a masterly fashion by Stokowski. It was the third time that he had conducted my music. Almost immediately, some of the best musicians in the orchestra asked me to write new music for their instruments. Paul Price was already one of the most famous percussionists in the United States when had he joined Stokowski in New York. He had created the Manhattan Percussion Ensemble, which had rapidly become a real institution with its significant annual series of concerts. I composed for him my *Symphony for Percussion* in three movements, for five percussionists, inspired in structure and choice of instruments by Carlos Chávez's *Toccata*, which I knew by heart, having conducted it often. But that is where the similarities ended. My piece had a totally different approach to the sound of the percussion instruments. My next ASO commission came from the first trombone, Davis Shulman, for whom I composed *Variations on a Theme from Childhood* for trombone and string orchestra. A version for bassoon and strings was recently recorded.

Having heard about a competition given by the American Accordionists' Association, I wasted no time in requesting to participate, and I ended up winning! It was a real challenge for me to write for an instrument that I did not know at all. They lent me books, music, and an accordion. Within a few weeks, I was ready to present them with not only the expected concerto but also with a bonus, a virtuoso *Moto Perpetuo* for solo accordion. Not long after that, as I was passing by the front window of the Patelson's Music House behind Carnegie Hall, I noticed on the window display my new composition published by a company I didn't know, and it was on sale. Surprised, I walked into the shop to buy a copy, and then I called the publisher, a company called Pagani. The owner himself answered my call and kindly informed me that he was about to send me the publishing contract. I contacted Mr. Lakond at Peermusic. Admittedly, I had no exclusive contract with them, but I had never given any of my compositions to any other company. Lakond wrote to Pagani, and we came up with a suitable agreement, and Peermusic quickly published my concerto. The explanation was simple: The American Accordionists' Association always gave Pagani the scores that they wanted published, and Pagani exclusively published music for accordion. Therefore, things had happened as usual for them. A separate institution from the publisher Pagani, the American Accordionists' Association is wonderfully managed. On my opening night conducting the opera *Manon* by Massenet with the New York City Opera, I was thrilled to see Elsie Bennett seated in the first row. She was the heart and soul of the Accordionists' Association.

How did you become composer-in-residence of such a prestigious organization as the Cleveland Orchestra?

The road that led me from New York to Cleveland—otherwise known as the road from Leopold Stokowski to George Szell—was the fact that I won the American Conductors Project award, a national conductors competition forged by the collaboration between the Ford Foundation, the Baltimore Symphony Orchestra, and the Peabody Institute. That competition was a superb project, initiated and developed by the president of the music school in Baltimore, the composer Peter Mennin, who was to become president of the Juilliard School in 1962. Not only would the winner be receiving a financial reward, but he or she would also be benefiting from a three-month stay, all expenses paid, with the Baltimore Symphony to conduct every day under the supervision of senior conductors like Fausto Cleva for opera repertoire and Max Rudolf and Alfred Wallenstein. The jury consisted of the previously mentioned conductors and Leonard Bernstein, George Szell, and Peter Mennin. The year I won the prize—1964—there was a tie between myself and James Levine, who had just graduated in piano from Juilliard. To spend three months in Baltimore I had to apply for a leave from the American Symphony Orchestra. By the end of these months' rewarding experience, Szell proposed that Levine and I both become his assistants in Cleveland. Levine accepted on the spot. I declined Szell's wonderful invitation because in New York I had the opportunity to conduct every year at Carnegie Hall, often sharing the podium with Stokowski. Also, I saw that the Cleveland Orchestra had a large conducting staff. It included Pierre Boulez as principal guest conductor, his first conducting job; famed choral conductor Robert Shaw as associate conductor; Louis Lane as first assistant conductor; and Michael Charry as another assistant conductor. I felt that with such staff—and now with Jimmy Levine and myself added as assistant conductors—neither of us would have much opportunity to conduct, only observe rehearsals. When Szell contacted me again the following year, he added the extra responsibility of conducting the Cleveland Philharmonic as well as the position of composer-in-residence with the Cleveland Orchestra with a grant from the Rockefeller Foundation. I did not hesitate to accept the offer. Stokowski had already announced his intention to move back to England. It was during that time in Cleveland that I started touring Poland. I conducted every orchestra in the country, going from one town to the other. It was, without a doubt, my first real experience in rehearsing, again and again, a wide range of scores, and with all sorts of orchestras, until the basic repertoire became an integral part of myself. An exceptional experience. My first tour of Poland only lasted a few weeks. Then, as the years went by, tours lasted much longer, sometimes a few months at a time. Poland was the first European country to open its musical doors to me. Maybe because it was my mother's birthplace, I felt at home in that country of great musicians, despite the deplorable, harsh life conditions during the time of the communist regime. Later Poland became the first country behind the Iron Curtain to rebel against Soviet domination. I could feel the first cracks while on tour, and, surprisingly, it was in the music and media world that it started brewing. Under the Soviet model, the Polish state had absolute monopoly and used to firmly control all sectors of activities. At the beginning of the eighties, some audacious and brave employees at the state-controlled radio and television decided to create their own independent company, an act incompatible with the ruling communist orthodoxy. And within this new private radio and TV company they simultaneously founded an artistic management agency, putting themselves in direct competition with PAGART, an old-fashioned state monopoly. PAGART was at that time Poland's only music-management organization, and it was compulsory for artists to join if they were seeking work in or outside Poland. It was the exact equivalent of Gosconcert, the sole artists' agency in the USSR. When Polish artists wanted to perform abroad, PAGART, or its equivalent in the Eastern countries, would assume their earnings and pay them a small fraction of that income. Same thing if Western artists wanted to perform in those Eastern countries: they would have to sign agreements with the powerful state agencies. When Poland broke from custom—which the Soviets ignored—it was the warning signal to their stranglehold. Not long after that, Poland started to witness the birth of independent unions, which ended with strikes and a surprising and unexpected feeling of freedom.

From Poland, I then started my Australian career, sometimes spending six months working with all their orchestras, performing hundreds of concerts, covering a vast repertoire. The Australian Broadcasting Corporation offered me the position of principal conductor of the Adelaide Symphony Orchestra. I refused but gladly accepted the role of principal guest conductor. Simultaneously, during a few seasons I was also responsible for running the oldest music festival in America, in Worcester, Massachusetts. This meant I could hardly find time to compose. And in addition, I now had a new family and was often accompanying my wife, Carole Farley, on her tours performing in opera houses around the world.

Under which circumstances did you write your experimental concertos—*Nueve* for double bass, and *Colores Mágicos* for harp?

The second orchestra of which I agreed to be music director, after the one in Utica, was the Plainfield Symphony Orchestra, the oldest orchestra in the state of New Jersey. As in Utica, it was a semiprofessional ensemble. Out of economic necessity, I remained with that orchestra for six or seven years, traveling by bus from New York to Plainfield every Monday for the weekly rehearsals. For its fiftieth birthday, the orchestra commissioned me to write a composition, and my choice was a concerto for double bass for Gary Karr, who was living in Plainfield. Karr was a musician unknown to me before Stokowski mentioned him with reverence. I took the time to listen to him and soon realized he was a phenomenon. He played the double bass like many cellists only dream of playing their instruments. Gary mentioned that he was the eighth generation of double bass players in his family. To write a concerto for such a virtuoso was an absolute feast. Gary was very extroverted and had exceptional stage experience. By way of cadenza I had him recite some poetry. I used the brass in an unconventional way, by placing them around the audience, therefore creating unusual sounds. It was a huge success. Soon it was performed in Cleveland. Years later I conducted this piece all across South Africa with their National Radio Orchestra and with Gary Karr as soloist.

I titled the bass concerto *Nueve*—number nine—because I only used nine different notes in its composition, which I believed at the time would be the finest idea, a self-imposed discipline. There were nine variations and other elements around the number nine. Why nine? Maybe because my apartment in New York is on Ninety-Ninth Street, on the ninth floor. Much later, a triumphant comedy on Broadway was entitled *Nine*. I was somehow peeved. After all, I had been the first to come up with that title. *Nueve* was my second score to require space distances between instrumentalists. The first one had been *Erotica*, a twelve-tone piece for woodwind quintet, whose members were placed around the audience, and a soprano, singing backstage with no lyrics. I had written it especially for Carole Farley, my future wife, who had just graduated from Indiana University and was about to depart for Germany to continue her vocal training after winning a Fulbright Grant.

I have never quite understood why *Erotica* did not work out as well when all the instruments were played close together. A reasonable distance between them was necessary to reflect the piece's potential and its meaning. It was magical! For the recording—with RCA—made by the Australian Wind Virtuosi, the technicians from the Australian Broadcasting Commission recreated the illusion of distance by cleverly positioning the microphones. The soprano part can only be performed by an opera singer who has perfect pitch because she is far backstage, and there is a semitone's difference between the soprano and the flute—extremely hard to do. The spaced musical experiences with my concerto for double bass and for the woodwind quintet piece were a platform for my following work, a harp concerto I called *Colores Mágicos*. A member of the Cleveland Orchestra introduced me to Stanley Elliott, inventor of a device called the Synchroma—an extraordinary object structure, resembling a TV set, that somehow heard the music and transformed it into bright, vivid colors that kept changing and were projected on a screen. This bizarre machine would react to the volume of the sound, as well as its speed and tone. Elliott had also invented another smaller machine into which you could insert photographic plates and kaleidoscopic abstract pictures. When the music started, the pictures would come to life and follow the music. A fantastic process! I was fascinated by these inventions. Around the same time, Colonel Samuel Rosenbaum from Philadelphia commissioned me to write a concerto as a gift to his wife, harpist Edna Phillips. Not long before that, he had commissioned Alberto Ginastera to write a harp concerto; I was in very good company. Rosenbaum was a prominent member of the board of the Philadelphia Orchestra, and his wife had recently retired as the orchestra's star harpist. Composing that score was an exciting and passionate adventure. I included multimedia, unusual use of space, polytonality. It became a series of variations, without bar lines, with the sounds setting off surprising visual effects thanks to the Synchroma. The harp soloist was alone on stage, with the chamber orchestra performing in the pit, similar to an opera. Images were projected on the stage's background screen, like in a movie. The harpist was dressed all in white, becoming a living screen for the small machine, her playing giving life to the images that had been introduced beforehand. The premiere took place during the Inter-American Music Festival in Washington. Carole Farley bravely sang backstage, the singing opening the score with a mysterious atmosphere. Harpist Heidi Lehwalder, chosen by Rosenbaum, replaced Edna Phillips, who had just retired, and I was conducting. It was an immediate success! Rosenbaum was truly overwhelmed. However, he warned me about future performances if they were to rely on these machines, and he was right. Many performances had to be canceled because Elliott wanted to charge astronomical fees for the use of his inventions, and one could only use them if he was the operator. Strangely enough, those devices were never commercialized. They were used a few times in nightclubs or at congressional meetings, but they were soon forgotten. *Colores Mágicos* had a second life when Gerald Arpino used it to create a ballet, which he entitled *Orpheus Times Light*. It was he, star choreographer of the famous Joffrey Ballet, who informed me, calling me from New York to Strasbourg, where I was staying with my family, at eight o'clock one Christmas morning. (It was two o'clock in the morning in New York!) He explained that he was just wrapping Christmas presents when the silver ball of string rolled under the bed. He was bending to pick it up when he discovered a magnetic tape that may have been lying there for some time. As he did not know what it contained, he listened to it and found the music fascinating, so he decided to use it for a new ballet. The only name on the tape was Jean Dalrymple, a famous public-relations representative for artists. Arpino called her in the middle of the night to ask about the origin of the tape, and she explained that it was my concerto for harp, *Colores Mágicos*, and that she had given him the tape a while back.

Jean Dalrymple considered me as her fourth José. The first two had been José Iturbi and José Ferrer. Another, José Limón, would also soon have a place. Arpino was hoping to ask me if I could add more music to my score—twelve more minutes—to create a full ballet in just one act. He needed nearly twenty-five minutes. I told him that I was flattered by his proposition but that my concerto was nevertheless completed and finished, that it was an entity, and that nothing could be added. Still, when I was back in New York, I attempted to take up the impossible challenge and managed to increase the time for the score to twenty-three minutes. *Orpheus Times Light* became a complete success. Its genesis had been traumatic. During the final rehearsal I noticed, with amazement, that the dancers were still performing for a few minutes after the music had ended. Noticing my astonishment, Arpino told me, "Could you manage to prolong the last note for another two or three more minutes?" Furious, I rushed outside. Arpino followed me out to the street, apologizing and proposing instead to pare back the end of his choreography so that it ended perfectly with my already-increased performance time. I calmed down, and the dancers appreciated my outburst, telling me candidly and spontaneously, "If you had allowed him, he would have increased it by another twenty minutes. Thanks to you, it will now be be much more concise!" What surprised me most was that the choreography, as far as I could understand, had absolutely nothing to do with the music. Had I replaced my concerto with a Bach fugue, the result would have been the same. And apparently this dichotomy was intentional, Arpino having no intention of imitating, illustrating, or following the score; they were two entirely separate elements. I was left perplexed by his choreography. I agreed to conduct the premiere at the New York City Center. All subsequent performances were conducted by the music director of the Joffrey Ballet, the wonderful pianist Seymour Lipkin, who also conducted the American tour. It appeared to be a ballet loosely based on the legend of Orpheus but with some obvious homosexual undertones. I never understood what this had to do with my harp concerto. It turned out to be a great popular and critical success. The Joffrey had become an immensely beloved ballet company, regularly touring the country. Arpino respected several of my concerto's scenic requirements, placing the harpist beyond the stage, not far from the dancers, and placing the orchestra in the pit. The offstage voice that opens and closes the concerto was prerecorded, and Arpino and I agreed that we would start without a curtain, only with a slow lowering of the house lights. I was asked by the choreographer to sneak into the pit without being noticed to avoid applause. As the house lights were starting to be lowered and the stage lights slowly came up, the voice of the soprano would be heard in the distance. My signal to enter the pit was going to be a green lamp, before the voice started. But on opening night, the signal lamp never lit up! We all completely panicked backstage when we heard the voice and the dancers on the stage floor! Someone in the production room had completely lost it! It was opening night. I immediately rushed to the pit in the darkened house, conducting right and left until I finally reached the podium. The audience didn't notice, and the musicians must have thought it was planned. Even after the technical team had apologized, my heart was still racing! It had been a close call.

Mrs. Peer, widow of the founder of the Peermusic publishing empire, usually took premieres like this one seriously. She had sent invitations to all the directors from her agencies. They had come to New York from Santiago de Chile, Sydney, and Hamburg. She arrived from Los Angeles with her new husband. The evening ended with supper at a newly opened discotheque, Régine's; it was the noisiest place on Earth. I was profoundly touched by her attentions and her sincerity. The Joffrey Ballet went on tour with *Orpheus* across the United States, and my harp concerto remained in their repertory for several seasons. Although it was a success in concert and as a ballet, *Colores Mágicos* was not my main concern at the time. Instead of composing new music, I accepted all offers to conduct. I went on annual tours to Poland, remaining there for months and conducting all the orchestras in the country until I came across the orchestra in Katowice, the best of all. I then dropped all the others. This is the orchestra that I conducted on my own, just a week before we started recording with the London Philharmonic, Charles Ives's Fourth Symphony. The film of this performance was broadcast on American TV dozens of times via NET—PBS's predecessor.

The only composition that I wrote during that period was a commission from the University of Mexico, UNAM—*Preludio Fantástico y Danza Mágica*, for five percussionists, trying to recapture the success of my *Symphony for Percussion*. But in the newer work, the musical language had become more elaborate and original. For the first time I used graphics instead of notes, and these could be interpreted at random by the performers.

Meeting George and Muriel Marek brought you back to composing . . .

The first compositions I wrote, after years of silence, were rather short: *George and Muriel* and *Dorothy and Carmine!* When I was commissioned to write a violin concerto later, I was quite ready for a more personal, deeper, more elaborate score. By that time, the music that was expected of and accepted from composers had become more permissive. Krzysztof Penderecki had abandoned sound effects and had become almost tonal. I no longer felt under any pressure and felt comfortable to write music that reflected my instincts. Constraints had disappeared, and from now on I could just write my own music. What is my own music? Who are the composers who presided over my training? Who influenced me? I honestly cannot give an answer to that. I simply do not know. Some influences are subliminal, beyond our control, consisting of unconscious recollections and faded memories. I am fully aware of being influenced by Slavic but also by French music. But it is obvious too that two of my compositions—*Partita* and Piano Sonata—display an influence of Latin American music, which I have been assimilating since early childhood. But I believe that I possess my own language, while it is likely that other influences are noticeable, which can always be said of composers. The origins of some of these influences are a real puzzle. Here is an example: in my 1954 *Suite Canina* for woodwind trio, I wrote sequences in Charles Ives's style, but that was well before listening to any of his compositions or having heard his name. My suite unconsciously expressed a true passion to go to the United States to study. I included a few famous military marches, sometimes in counterpoint with one another, as Ives used to do, and with his same sense of musical humor. It was pure intuition, total coincidence and quite a mystery, since at the time I had practically no knowledge of any contemporary music, much less of Ives.

My creative silence broke for George and Muriel Marek's sixtieth wedding anniversary. I had bumped into George while walking on the beach at Fire Island, their holiday resort. For decades, he had been one of the directors at RCA and had contracted and worked with many of the great artists of the day—Reiner, Heifetz, Toscanini, Rubinstein, Monteux. When George Marek and I met, he had just retired. We became friends straightaway. He recognized me while walking on the beach and invited me to meet Muriel. At the time, under the patronage of the University of Miami, I was in the middle of organizing my new festival and busy looking over every detail. The enthusiastic double bass teacher at the music school, Lucas Drew, wanted Festival Miami to commission several composers, including me, to write new double bass pieces. I combined both projects, his and mine, as a wedding-anniversary present to my new friends, George and Muriel Marek, by composing *George and Muriel* for double bass, bass ensemble, and choir. The premiere at the festival was such an absolute success that I really felt reborn as a composer. The following year, I wrote *Dorothy and Carmine!* for a beloved elderly couple I knew who had finally decided to tie the knot after decades of living together. I was pleased with that piece, in which I was once again experimenting with sounds and motion. A flutist had to unexpectedly walk from the audience to the stage while performing a solo line, while a second flutist played a ghost echo behind the audience, from the balcony, and the stage and house lights slowly lowered until we were in complete darkness. Again, it was an absolute success. I then composed a third piece of that sort, also as a wedding present, for violinist Michael Guttman. A short piece for solo violin called "Michael and Emmanuelle." I did many recordings with Michael Guttman—the violin concertos by Dvořák, Bloch, Hindemith, Milhaud, and Rodrigo, among others. I had first been introduced to Michael's parents by flute virtuoso Jean-Pierre Rampal after one of our concerts together in Brussels. It had been eight years of silence for me as a composer when Guttman commissioned me to write a violin concerto. His brilliant idea was to produce a recording called *Four Seasons* (not by Vivaldi!). He had been one of León Ara's students. Ara was Rodrigo's son-in-law, with whom he had studied the *Concierto del Estío* (Summer concerto) for violin and orchestra, composed by Rodrigo in 1943, a few years after his triumphant *Concierto de Aranjuez* for guitar, written in 1939. There was a spring concerto by Darius Milhaud—*Concertino de Printemps*—but no autumn and winter concertos. I explained this problem to everyone I knew until composer and music critic Robert Matthew-Walker suggested a salon piece, *Automne* by Cécile Chaminade, and we asked Michael's Brussels friend Paul Uy to do the orchestration. We asked many composers if they would consider, on short notice, to write a winter-inspired violin concerto, but no one seemed available at the time. My next task was to compose a winter concerto so the recording project could move forward. I only had four weeks to write it, as the Royal Philharmonic Orchestra had already been hired by ASV Records. I started sketching the new work, my first large composition in a long time, while I was busy putting together Festival Miami. I finished the concerto in London while on tour and put in the final touches in Bloomington, Indiana, where I had been invited to conduct their chamber orchestra at the school of music. I was excited to listen to the result. The premiere of *Winter Concerto* took place at the Lincoln Center in New York, Guttman accompanied by the New Jersey Symphony, conducted by Lawrence Smith, the last concert in a series sponsored by Absolut, the vodka company. It was a huge success. My concerto was then played in Florida by the Miami Chamber Symphony, in London by the Philharmonia Orchestra, in Madrid by the Orquesta Sinfónica Nacional. The recording became a best seller. It has since been recorded twice with different soloists and orchestras.

Your relationship with Hollywood?

I am not sure how it all happened, but I recall that a TV executive called me to invite me to compose and conduct the music for a made-for-TV film based on the play *The Star-Wagon* by Maxwell Anderson. I accepted before I found out any details, and I signed the contract. The main role was to be played by Dustin Hoffman, his first big role, not long before *The Graduate* made him a household name and launched his movie career. I devoured Anderson's book, which appealed to me at once with its complex personal relationships and science-fiction undertones. Dustin and I lived near each other in Midtown

Manhattan, and we both went with our respective girlfriends at the time to watch the final edited version of the two-hour film. The budget I was given was amazingly low, and it included all expenses, even the fees for the orchestra. I realized it would have been prohibitive to record it in the United States, so I flew down to Montevideo and asked a musician to put together an orchestra. I copied by hand all the musician's parts, and we recorded the music in one three-hour session. To this day I continue to receive e-mails from people in the industry imploring me to revive the music, perhaps with a concert suite. Having heard that the film was available as a commercial DVD, I purchased it and enjoyed the memories. We also discovered that it is available on YouTube as well. Alas, like many Hollywood film scores of those days, the music is lost. I could write it from memory, watching the film, and that is something perhaps for the future. Seated at a restaurant near my London apartment a few years ago I saw Dustin walking around, looking for someone. He recited the exact date of the film, both our addresses in New York, and other details. Actors, like singers, tend to have such great memories.

Years later, while working with Stokowski and the American Symphony Orchestra at Carnegie Hall I was approached by John Duffy, who had been a classmate in my composition class at Tanglewood with Aaron Copland. Duffy invited me to become music director of the American Shakespeare Festival in Stratford, Connecticut, for an extended spring-summer period, an experience I enjoyed on many levels. The theater was required by the musicians' union to engage an orchestra, and since some Shakespeare plays make musical references the festival agreed and commissioned music to be interpolated among the scenes. The orchestra of some eighteen musicians and I were hidden on an adjacent balcony. I had to follow the plot carefully, eventually memorized, so that the musical interludes were performed at exact moments. When David Pressman was invited by the festival to rescue a production that had developed staging problems, he and I became instant friends. He and his wife, Sasha, had me over for dinner regularly, and the friendship continued after the Stratford experience. Pressman was asked to direct three excerpted Shakespeare plays for national TV, and he commissioned me to compose and conduct the music. Due to budgetary reasons, it had to be for a total of six musicians. There is a wonderful letter from Leopold Stokowski with his reactions to the music, included among his letters, in this book. The music later on became the basis for a concert work I called *Six on TV*, a title inspired by the Silvestre Revueltas work, "Ocho por Radio."

Meeting British composer John Powell while conducting his oratorio *A Prussian Requiem* around the world, and recording it in London with the Philharmonia, led to the invitation to conduct the Hollywood Orchestra in Powell's music for the 20th Century Fox film *Rio 2*, a wonderful learning experience. Performing Powell's oratorio in places as distant as Montevideo's Metropolitan Cathedral, Lima's wonderful new theater, and London's Royal Festival Hall was a moving experience every time, as was the recording with the Philharmonia in London, both with the extraordinary tenor Javier Camarena. The London performance was an instant success but marked by tragedy. Powell e-mailed me and David Whelton, managing director of the orchestra, barely twenty-four hours before the concert to express his regrets at not being able to attend the premiere in his home country. His beloved young wife, Melinda, who had been ill for some time and undergone various medical procedures, seemed to be entering the last hours of her life. Powell's assistant, composer Batu Sener, attended the concert and e-mailed John after each segment of the oratorio, indicating the intensity of the performance and the hushed public attention. Toward the end, John e-mailed Batu, "Do not write any more comments; Melinda just drew her last breath."

Recently, while on a long flight, I looked at a new movie and was excited when the opening scene featured a humanoid robot playing a piano reduction of Wagner's "Entrance of the Gods into Valhalla" from *Das Rheingold*, and as the film continued, I realized that this music was not being used as background but was an integral part of the plot. My biggest surprise came at the climax of the film, when the evil android David, finally entirely alone in the spaceship, asks the ship's computer to play the Wagner excerpt, which is then heard at top volume. I recognized my performance, recorded with the Bournemouth Symphony Orchestra, which several fans had posted to YouTube, and one of these postings with elaborate visuals had already exceeded half a million hits. When the film credits came up, at the very end, there it was, the credit to the orchestra and me in a separate and larger space. I was happily surprised by it, since I had no prior information about it. I asked Naxos of America, and it was explained that the film director had requested this performance of the music, and it was licensed as a routine agreement. I was even more amazed after I looked up the large number of other available versions of the music and never learned why mine was chosen. I saw the film a second time on a subsequent international flight but never got to see it on a large movie screen. *Alien: Covenant* (2017) made a deep impression. Ridley Scott, director of the film, is a classical-music lover.

I met Michael Kamen at a Canadian music camp in the lake region near Toronto, where I went for a week to conduct their student orchestra. It was during my American Symphony years, during which I had to take on short summer jobs. Michael and his girlfriend attracted my interest at once, perhaps by intuition. No one could predict that the thirteen-year-old boy would become one of Hollywood's most successful composers one day. He seemed rather bohemian and easygoing. I thought enough of the couple that I composed a duo for them and gave it the title of the region, "Manitowabing." It has been recorded a few times. Years later I encountered Michael in the street and realized he lived nearby. We also saw him and his wife and daughters regularly in Fire Island, where the family spent long summers. Eventually I realized that Michael was heir to a large family fortune, which made it possible for him to rent a castle in London. Michael had an amazing musical intuition and ability, which led in time to his being invited to compose the music for a movie, *Brazil*. He called me to ask if I knew the tune by the same name and how to get ahold of it. I put him in touch with my publishers, Peermusic, and he had the music the same day. That started an amazing career in the industry. Years later, while conducting in Germany, I got a message from Michael asking for help with one of his movie assignments, *Event Horizon*. The director felt that the music he had provided for the scenes on the planet Mars did not sound like Mars . . . and could I come up with something that sounds like Mars, overnight? I took the hotel stationary and improvised music manuscript paper. The assignment was to write music for two short scenes, and I wanted to avoid any influence from Holst's *The Planets*. The finished music was faxed from my hotel late that evening, copied for each instrument, and recorded in London in the morning. Other surprises included seeing listings of the film *Children of the Revolution*, but to this day I do not know which one of my recordings was used for it. Another film, *Bad Boy Bubby*, listed my name in the music credits and specified the use of "Largo" from the opera *Xerxes* by Handel, included in my recording of Baroque classics. I never saw either movie.

Your *Winterreise* was very particular . . .

I wrote *Winterreise* (*Winter's Journey*) in 1999. The genesis of this seven-minute piece goes back to 1991, at a time when I had received the commission to write a violin concerto. Although the title was borrowed from Schubert, there was absolutely no reference to his work in my piece, which has, at its climax, quotations from Haydn's "Winter" from *The Seasons*, Glazunov's "Winter" from the ballet *The Seasons*, and a counterpoint using the theme from the finale of Tchaikovsky's first symphony, *Winter Dreams*. If you listen carefully, you can also hear at the end the "Dies Irae" developing from one of Haydn's quotes. This piece resembles a train rolling down the tracks: images becoming deformed, warped by the speed. One notices the snow-covered trees, frozen lakes, and streams. Small icicles smash onto the carriage windows. There is no sky. Only a blinding whiteness. Those are the undercurrent elements of *Winterreise*.

How did you meet your future wife, Carole Farley?

On a cold winter afternoon in New York in 1967, I received an invitation from Antal Doráti to attend his rehearsal at Carnegie Hall with the touring Royal Philharmonic Orchestra. I wasn't particularly interested in attending, since I had a date with a young lady I had met during one of my weekly flights to Detroit, where I was teaching violin at Eastern Michigan University while working with the American Symphony in New York. She was an stewardess. A violent and unexpected snowstorm hit Detroit, so she called me to cancel our date: all flights had been grounded! I was in a bitter and resentful mood when I went to Carnegie Hall to attended Doráti's rehearsal with the RPO. Entering the empty and darkened Carnegie Hall, I noticed straightaway a bright light, similar to a candle flame in darkness. It was a gorgeous, fair-haired young lady, the only person in the hall listening to the rehearsal. A few moments later I was sitting next to her and we were exchanging addresses and phone numbers. At the end of the rehearsal, Doráti wanted to introduce me to a young voice student from Indiana University, and it was precisely that young lady. I smiled and whispered, "We have just met . . ." Two weeks later, I was due to conduct the El Salvador Symphony Orchestra, one of the best Latin American orchestras at the time, which often had Pablo Casals as guest conductor. The soloist on the program for the *Four Last Songs* by Richard Strauss was the wife of a local senior clergyman who happened to be the orchestra's vice president. Without hesitation I called them to ask, in the most offhand way, if they would instead consider hiring a young soprano who would soon graduate from Indiana University and had just been awarded a coveted Fulbright scholarship to further her training in Europe and who was, on top of that, winner of a competition in the Metropolitan Opera. To my amazement, they accepted on the spot without any argument. It was the first concert that I gave with Carole Farley. Our wedding ceremony at the Plaza Hotel in New York, of course, included a concert. Carole sang one of J. S. Bach's wedding cantatas. I conducted the accompanying musicians. They had come especially from all over the United States. Gary Karr, the double bass virtuoso, performed *Bachianas Brasileiras* No. 5 by Heitor Villa-Lobos accompanied on guitar by Fred Hand. Argentinian star bandoneon soloist Alejandro Barletta came especially from Buenos Aires to perform Bach, sounding like an organ. He arrived in New York just in time to purchase a new tuxedo for the event, and there hadn't been any time for the long trousers to be hemmed. Carole had to mend them with needle and thread mere minutes before the wedding ceremony at the Plaza Hotel in Manhattan. There were some memorable moments for the 150 guests. There was someone behind the door who had not been invited—Wilma Salisbury, music critic at the *Plain Dealer*, Cleveland's principal newspaper. Having heard that a concert would be performed at our wedding, she had phoned me to request an invitation. As diplomacy was not among the best of my qualities, I argued that it was our private life and that she was not invited. Unfortunately, my hasty decision to not invite her far from vexing her had only aroused her curiosity. She engaged a photographer from United Press International news agency and probably bribed the receptionist at the Plaza, and the result was a full page in the papers, filled with our wedding photos, taken through a keyhole! In those days, long before the plastic keys, old hotels like the Plaza still used huge keys made of iron. United Press International was a vast agency, and these photos appeared in most of the American newspapers. The news seems to have been what was considered unusual, a wedding/concert, with a bride who sang and a future head of family who conducted, with an orchestra made up of top musicians from around the world. The young rabbi who married us, Mordecai Shreiber, ran into a few problems with the local authorities in the Jewish community of Cleveland. He had celebrated a wedding on a Saturday, on the Sabbath. Quite a sacrilege. Neither he nor I had been conscious of the fact. Our decision was the result of innocence. Carole and I spent our honeymoon in Bermuda.

On February 1, 1976, our daughter Lara was born in New York. Lara performed in the premiere of the opera *Marie de Montpellier* by René Koering in 1994 alongside her mother, who sang the title role. Lara sang under my direction in Washington in 1996 in a concert titled Classic Meets Pop, alongside Aretha Franklin, Sharon Isbin, and others, with the Baltimore Symphony Orchestra. Andrea Bocelli was supposed to have made his American debut at this concert but canceled at the last minute. He was still a complete unknown. Luciano Pavarotti had recommended him to me, and Bocelli had asked to sing "Nessun dorma." When Bocelli canceled, Aretha Franklin called me and begged to sing it in his place. She was quite disappointed when I turned her down, and agreed to sing her own repertoire, which she did outstandingly. Soon after I heard her sing "Nessun dorma" at the GRAMMY ceremony in New York, as a last-minute replacement for Luciano Pavarotti, and a few weeks later she sang it on the *Tonight Show*. I thought it was a most unusual interest on her part. Looking back in time, a simple snowstorm in Detroit happened to change my life.

What is your relationship with contemporary composition techniques and neoromanticism?

I have used a sort of dodecaphonic technique of my own in *Erotica* (1968), a combination of a series of twelve sounds with multiple sound sources in *Colo-*

res Mágicos (1970) and *Twelve Plus Twelve* (1969), in which every fragment can be performed as a beginning, middle, or end of the piece, sounding different at every performance. Even if these experimental compositions turned out to be successful, I was never quite satisfied with them. As time went by, I gradually stopped composing. For years, I did not write anything at all, immersing myself in conducting orchestras around the world, for which I was getting more and more requests. But the real reason was that, as a composer, I felt very isolated, contrary to when, in the early sixties, I was one of the five contemporary composers performing most in America (according to the League of American Orchestras in 1962).

We suppose that the promoters of the strict serial system had taken control of all key positions in the powerful cultural game, especially in the world of music. In the United Kingdom, the governing board of music for the BBC at that time, in the mid-sixties, turned down commissioned works that seemed too traditional. Academia was in control. Some composers stopped writing. My friend Jacob Druckman, one of the most prominent American composers, was appointed composer in residence at the New York Philharmonic in the eighties. But this was not the result of decisions by the Rockefeller Foundation, which had stopped awarding this type of position since they had awarded me my position in Cleveland for two consecutive seasons. It was now being sponsored by a new dynamic organization, created by my friend John Duffy, whose idea was to bring living composers and the public together. Calling itself. Meet the Composer, this organization was subsidized by both the public and the private sectors. I had first met John Duffy at Tanglewood, in Aaron Copland's class. He had contacted me when I was Stokowski's associate to offer me the position of music director for the Shakespeare Festival in Stratford, Connecticut, for which he was working as composer of the play's incidental music. I accepted the job for the year 1964, which turned out to be more than profitable for me. I learned some of the Shakespeare plays by heart. I soon received a request from a national television company asking me to compose and conduct the scores for televised performances of *The Taming of the Shrew*, *Romeo and Juliet*, and *King Lear*. This welcome opportunity arose because of David Pressman, one of the main producers at the Shakespeare Festival. Pressman had been a cofounder of the famed Actors Studio in New York, and the Shakespeare Festival had imported him to save a production that had run into some trouble. An amazingly talented stage director, Pressman had been sidelined like many artists for his leftist views and had taken refuge directing nationally broadcast television dramas. I took my score for the television Shakespeare shows and wrote a suite for woodwind quintet and percussion, "Six on TV." Although it had taken a lot of work to get it off the ground, John Duffy's organization performed miracles. It became so prestigious that he had to restructure it into various sections, founded right across the country. Many orchestras took advantage of this generous offer! Jacob Druckman's designation, under the sponsorship of Meet the Composer, as composer in residence with the New York Philharmonic was a considerable catalyst to the development of contemporary music in the United States. As soon as he started to work with the Philharmonic, with financial help from the organization and from the orchestra he organized an annual festival entirely devoted to new music. He took a substantial step forward, which had far-reaching consequences, by titling his festival The New Romanticism. This title, and all it was implying, was way ahead of its time. Nobody had even dared dream about it! Nevertheless, none of the scores selected by the festival could really be considered neoromantic. This title was one of Druckman's dreams as an intuitive anticipation of what was to come soon after. Some of the American composers did not approve of Druckman's approach, and at one of the parties one of them even resorted to physically attacking him for naming the festival "neoromantic." Partly unconsciously, Druckman had labeled future creations, opening the way to freedom in order to remove the upholders of a stifling and sterile system. In my case, it represented what I had been waiting for and really been looking forward to. He really was ahead of his time. As soon as this straightjacket was removed, my inspiration came back in force. Not to compare myself to them in any way, but in the past this had happened to certain composers who felt they could not continue to write after the styles had so drastically changed. It had happened with Sibelius, Rachmaninoff, Glazunov.

Which symphonic and operatic repertoire attracts you?

All Slavic music, not only Russian, is close to my heart. I can't explain why, because I could hardly listen to any music in my childhood as we did not own a record player. I also have a special fondness for Spanish music and a very deep feeling for French music, especially for Chausson and Ravel, whom I add to my programs as often as possible. If, without a doubt, the Slavonic, French, and Iberian works are a staple of my repertoire, I also am particularly interested in North and South American music. In 1979 I won the Alice M. Ditson Conductor's Award given by Columbia University in recognition of my efforts to promote contemporary music. This important award is given every year to the conductor who has performed the most contemporary music. I received it onstage at the Kennedy Center in Washington, DC, during the opening concert of my tour conducting the New York–based American Composers Orchestra. My concert was the inaugural event of the Inter-

American Music Festival. I also regularly program music by British composers Elgar, Holst, Britten, and Knussen and by Scandinavians Grieg, Sibelius, and Rautavaara. My basic repertoire remains Beethoven, Mozart, Haydn, Schubert, Tchaikovsky, Wagner, Dvořák, Schoenberg, Kodály, and Janáček. These were the composers I studied with Monteux and Doráti and while observing Szell conduct for two years in Cleveland. I learned from an exemplary tradition that I believe is, unfortunately, on the verge of disappearing.

I cannot say I have a favorite composer, a "desert island" favorite. On the contrary, isolating a single composer or a single composition, as great an idea as it seems, would be torture for me. I need diversity and richness in music. On that subject, the BBC released (in April 1999) a CD from a series titled "Desert Island Discs," on which they included "Tatyana's Letter Scene" based on text by Pushkin, from the opera *Eugene Onegin* by Tchaikovsky, performed by my wife, Carole, with the Melbourne Symphony Orchestra under my direction, from an original RCA Victor LP, then reissued on CD under other labels.

Contrary to what my discography seems to show, I have conducted a lot of operas. I conducted *La Bohème* at the Palacio de Bellas Artes in Mexico City, *Carmen* and *La Traviata* in Pittsburgh, the original Mussorgsky version of *Boris Godunov* and *Salome* at the Sydney Opera House. I conducted Massenet's *Manon* at the New York City Opera during two consecutive seasons, as well as many concert versions of various operas at Carnegie Hall in New York. I did *Traviata* in Cologne, *Don Giovanni* in Nantes. I conducted the American premieres of Tchaikovsky's *Iolanta* with the National Orchestral Association at Carnegie Hall and Massenet's *Chérubin* at the Manhattan School of Music. For the BBC I did a magnificent and unknown opera, *Le Pré aux Clercs* by Hérold. With the American Symphony Orchestra, *The Flying Dutchman* at Carnegie Hall. With many different orchestras in concerts, recordings, and films, I conducted *La Voix Humaine* (Poulenc), *The Telephone* (Menotti), and arias from various operas by Tchaikovsky, Prokofiev, Britten, Strauss, Delius. Also, at my Festival Miami, the American premiere of the only opera by Liszt, written when he was a teenager, *Don Sanche, or The Castle of Love* (1825), which had been premiered in Paris by the famous tenor Adolphe Nourrit. Then there was the modern premiere of the sublime *Macbeth* (written in 1910 by Ernest Bloch) in London at the Royal Festival Hall with the Philharmonia Orchestra. *Macbeth* had not been heard since its premiere at La Scala. The entire Bloch family came in from America for the event. Lorin Maazel became interested and did an entire concert of Bloch's music in Cleveland, televised nationally, and he invited me to conduct an all-Tchaikovsky concert with the Cleveland Orchestra.

Do you have you any special affinity with composers of Jewish origin, like Mendelssohn or Mahler?

I consider them as musical monuments, in the same way as Schubert or Haydn are. Mendelssohn (who lived from 1809 to 1847) was a fine, sophisticated, and elegant musician. Ardent too (he was a child of the Romantic era). Admittedly, he converted to Protestantism (and one can sense a change in his last symphony, *Reformation*), but he never put anything Jewish in his music. On the other hand, Mahler (who lived from 1860 to 1911) sometimes uses something that sounds Jewish in his scores: thematic elements, anguished rhythms.

I adore the music of Ernest Bloch (1880–1959). It's saturated with Jewish tradition. He almost always chooses Jewish or Hebrew subjects: *Baal Shem, Schelomo, Sacred Service, Trois Poèmes Juifs*, and so on. However, some of his masterpieces have absolutely nothing to do with his Judaism—for example, his opera *Macbeth* (premiered in Paris at the Opéra-Comique in 1910). I first heard about this sublime score when I met his family in New York—his daughter Suzanne and his son Boris. Suzanne was a teacher at the Juilliard School. Boris had remained in Portland, Oregon, where his father had spent most of his life teaching, but Boris had hardly any interest in music. I noticed that *Macbeth* had only received one production, at La Scala in Milan, since its Paris premiere and had since fallen into total oblivion. I decided it was time to revive that amazing musical drama and managed to set it up, in concert version (without decor or staging), at the Royal Festival Hall in London in coproduction with the BBC and the Philharmonia Orchestra, with excellent singers like Helga Dernesch in the role of Lady Macbeth and Ryan Edwards as Macbeth. The main support in this very expensive venture came from a friendly South African singer named Denny Dayviss. She regularly presented operas in concert version at the Royal Festival Hall, hiring high-class performers like Victoria de Los Ángeles, Montserrat Caballé, and José Carreras (who gave his first performances in this series).

Bloch's *Macbeth* in London was an absolute success. Unfortunately, it fell once more into oblivion. I think this is probably due to the simple fact that opera companies very rarely think of Bloch, since he wrote only one opera. However, in 1997 René Koering, then artistic director for Radio France and the Montpellier festival, presented it in concert or (form), conducted by Friedemann Layer with singers Markella Hatziano and Jean-Philippe Lafont. In 2018 the adventurous Manhattan School of Music did the American premiere, fully staged, in the original French version. Many years before, I had conducted there the American premiere of Massenet's last opera, *Chérubin*.

You worked with Salvador Dalí.

Not exactly, but the story is amazing and amusing. It all started when Doráti left Minneapolis in the spring of 1960 and moved with his family to Italy after his long and extremely successful tenure as conductor of the Minnesota Orchestra. Fellow Hungarian Lorenzo Alvary was a baritone at the Metropolitan Opera in New York, and Doráti told me that Alvary's wife had decided to give his friend Lorenzo a special wedding gift of his choice, and he chose producing an opera in Italy that would attract world attention. That it certainly did, but for the wrong reasons. Here is the amazing story. Alvary formed a production company that first engaged Salvador Dalí to design the costumes for the singers and, in place of sets, colorful backdrops for the stage. Once Dalí had been secured, Alvary commissioned a famous Italian musicologist and composer, Giulio Confalonieri, to reconstruct and enlarge a 1794 short operatic scene by Scarlatti. Confalonieri did an excellent job transforming the little scene by Scarlatti into an entire opera, keeping the original title of the scene—*La Dama Spagnola ed il Cavalier Romano*—and orchestrated it for strings. Next to be engaged for the opera production was the string ensemble Virtuosi di Roma, which normally performed without conductor; Alvary engaged his friend Antal Doráti. For the ballet scenes, Alvary secured choreographer Maurice Béjart, who was fast becoming known as the *enfant terrible* of the ballet world from his Brussels beginnings at the Opera. A special venue was required, and Teatro La Fenice of Venice was chosen and contracted. But Alvery still felt that something was still missing if they wanted to attract world attention. Arriving at the beautiful La Fenice to look it over, he felt that it lacked something—a beautiful scent, perhaps. He engaged Guerlain, the prime French perfumer at the time, to spray the entire theater just before and again during each opera performance. As with the other artists, Doráti felt sure that this unusual concurrence of artists would attract instant world attention and fame for each of the participants, way beyond their usual limited, specialized world. Little did they realize what was to come. Dalí, upon arrival in Venice, displayed his newly "invented" square bubbles, which of course only lasted a second, because bubbles are by nature round, but it got a lot of press attention. Besides providing the watercolors that the theater painters copied onto vast canvases to encircle the stage, Dalí had a woman ironing on the side of the stage all night long, and for added distraction he hung large carcasses around the stage, all entirely unrelated to the opera plot, but creating disbelief and cautious amusement.

Doráti asked me to assist him in Venice during the long preparation period before opening on stage. Rehearsals started and worked very well. I was also assigned to welcome Dalí when he arrived in Venice. It was an amazing scene, Dalí arriving on a gondola, dressed as a gondolier, wearing a flamboyant white gondolier's outfit. The paparazzi had a field day, and all the Italian newspapers the following day published the pictures on their front pages. We were all amused and believed that the publicity would help attract attention for the opera production. It only attracted attention for Dalí.

Opera rehearsals proceeded normally, except that Dalí never attended—not even opening night, which by a glitch in planning coincided with the opening of the popular International Film Festival at the Lido, which always attracted worldwide attention. Over the next days, all the front pages displayed a picture of Salvador Dalí with his wife, Gala, by his side, crashing the Lido festival at the front door, displaying two huge antique revolvers, one in each hand, to be allowed in without an invitation—another publicity stunt. All the paparazzi forgot Gina Lollobrigida and Sophia Loren, running over each other to cover Dalí. At the opera, waiting for Dalí, we were all amazed but not amused.

The Alvarys had decided to not sell tickets for the two performances but instead presented it as a "must attend and be seen" gala, by invitation only. The guest list was over the top, starting with the notorious Elsa Maxwell, the plump, famous party giver in America at the time. She loved the pizzeria next door to La Fenice, where she could be seen holding court while unashamedly trying to eat two slices of pizza together as a sort of sandwich. She brought with her the cream of American society. The audience included royalty from across Europe and several major political figures. Opening night had gone without incident, except for the lethargic nonreaction from the audience. Dalí joined us the following evening, and he noticed immediately that the audience was not the usual opera-going crowd and seemed quite bored, some even asleep. Around the middle of the performance, Dalí asked me, Bejart, and two stagehands to accompany him to the pizzeria next door. There Dalí purchased thirty or more large shiny white plates, which we all carried, incredulous, back to La Fenice. Dalí then gave himself and each of us about ten or so plates and ordered, "Let's wake up this audience," leading the way to throwing the plates at the unsuspecting, elegantly dressed audience—fortunately not hitting anyone directly, but crashing onto the floor, all while the singers onstage stopped singing and looked on at us in horror. After one or two plates, I stopped, but Dalí picked up the rest of my "weapons" and threw them at the audience as fast as he could. The public got up and ran away in a hurry while Alvary's wife stood alone in her box, as incredulous as the audience, murmuring, "Please don't leave; please stay; it's not over." She could hardly hold back her tears. It was a pathetic scene. Everyone backstage was in a terrible mood. I avoided Doráti's eyes and walked back to my hotel. The following morning, Dalí convened a press conference. This provoked another unforgettable scene. Newspaper reporters and restless paparazzi were lined up in front of the theater at the announced time, all anxiously waiting for Dalí's appearance. Surprise: he appeared on the balcony, above the theater's front entrance. Before the crowd below could react, but as soon as the photographers were camera-ready, Dalí bent down and picked up two huge cans of paint, and, before the crowd below could run, he poured all the paint on them, creating the kind of havoc and pandemonium only to be seen in period comic films—but this was happening in real time. The paparazzi quickly took pictures of the crowd and each other and the chaotic scene, which once again dominated press coverage, bypassing any mention of the opera, which was soon forgotten. Household name recognition for the wonderful artists involved would have to come another time, another way.

Four years later, while working with Stokowski and the American Symphony Orchestra, I happened to take the Carnegie Hall elevator in the office section of the building, and unexpectedly Dalí was in the elevator. I mumbled, "I don't know if you'll remember me; we were together in Venice." His reply was instantaneous: "Of course I remember—especially the fun we had throwing plates to wake up that terrible audience." Before I could think it over carefully, I mentioned that there would be a concert that same evening at Carnegie Hall, with Stokowski conducting, and I invited Dalí to my box. He seemed delighted: "What a lovely thought. Let me ask my wife, Gala, if we are free. Call me at the St. Regis Hotel in an hour." He and Gala came to the concert. Suddenly, I began to panic: What would he do to attract publicity? I could surely lose my job. Dalí and his wife arrived. He wore a tuxedo but had on white sneakers. Other than this eccentricity, he behaved all night like a gentleman, and there were no problems. He truly enjoyed the concert and asked me at the end if he could go backstage and congratulate the maestro. I took him there, and Dalí expressed his enthusiasm beautifully. Stokowski never stood up or looked at Dalí. He simply mumbled, "Thank you," coldly. Dalí and Gala left the room quietly, and I wondered for a moment if I should escort them or stay with my boss. I stayed. That was the last time I saw Dalí. Perhaps I should not tell the rest of the story? After Dalí and Gala left the dressing room, I asked the maestro if anything was wrong. "As an artist, he is magnificent, unequaled," Stokowski replied. "As a person, he is a fake." So many people had also said that about Stokowski and his intermittent mid-European accent.

In 1968 you started your amazing recording career with the London Symphony Orchestra.

George Szell had recommended me for this, my first recording, as the scheduled conductor had become unavailable at the last minute. To both the record company—Desto, at the time of vinyl—and the directors of the London Symphony Orchestra, he introduced me as capable of learning a score overnight. I didn't see the music until I arrived at the podium for the first recording session. In addition to *Sebastian*, a thirty-eight-minute ballet score that Gian Carlo Menotti had written in 1943 and that had been premiered in 1944 by Grand Ballet du Marquis de Cuevas, we recorded the ballet *Souvenirs*, composed in 1952 by Samuel Barber. George Szell had informed me of this sudden commitment in the middle of the night, and I flew to London the next day on the first-available flight. I was welcomed at the airport by Stuart Knussen, the first double bass player and president of the orchestra, who drove me straightaway to the studio in Walthamstow, situated in the suburbs of the English capital. During our journey there, he talked to me about his son, Oliver, then aged seventeen, who was a composer. André Previn had shown interest in his music and intended to have it performed. I took a quick look at the scores and offered them straightaway to the Kol Israel Orchestra in Jerusalem, and we performed it the following season. Oliver Knussen quickly became one of the most prominent musicians in Great Britain as both composer and conductor. He and I became great friends. His premature death was a shock to everyone.

The London Symphony was then at its zenith, with instrumentalists like Gervase de Peyer as first clarinet, Neville Marriner as leader of the second violins, Barry Tuckwell as first horn, Stuart Knussen first bass, and countless other stars. I took infinite care of ensuring that the orchestra did not realize that I was sight-reading the scores at the same time as they, as it might have prejudiced them. Nobody seemed to notice that the scores were new to me, and our collaboration was so fruitful that at the end of the last take, the musicians all came to invite me for my conducting debut in London, the following month, at the Royal Festival Hall. I accepted, of course. I conducted Mozart's Twenty-Fifth Symphony, the *Manfred* Symphony by Tchaikovsky, and, for the first time in England, Manuel Ponce's *Concierto del Sur* for guitar and orchestra, with the extraordinary John Williams as soloist.

You organized Festival Miami and became its artistic director for many years . . .

We started the festival in 1984 at a time when there were hardly any classical-music activities left in Miami. The symphony orchestra had disappeared. For this project, we had the help of William Hipp, then dean of the music school at the University of Miami, who had proposed the idea of a festival during a luncheon, and from composer William F. Lee, vice president of the university. We organized it in record time: two weeks. We commissioned Elliott Carter for a string quartet (his fourth) he wrote for us soon after our festival performed his three existing quartets. I invited the Pittsburgh Symphony Orchestra, London's Philharmonia Orchestra, the American Symphony Orchestra, Fort Worth Chamber Orchestra, and their conductor, John Giordano. I had the opportunity to conduct them all in various programs. We gave the American premiere of Franz Liszt's only opera, written when he was fourteen years old, *Don Sanche, or The Castle of Love*, as well as an untitled overture by Richard Wagner, which he had composed when he was about seventeen years old. The English Opera Group presented several operas under my direction. We tried our best to offer a variety of music: chamber music, choral and symphonic music, operas, jazz concerts. We hadn't forgotten the students and school children, organizing special events for them. I invited Mrs. Lina Prokofiev, widow of the composer, along with her son, Oleg, a sculptor whose artwork was exhibited on this occasion. She recited, to celebrate her ninetieth birthday, *Peter and the Wolf* (1936), which she had previously recorded with Lukas Foss.

Of all the scores played over the years at Festival Miami, I must mention a few. The highlights were jazz clarinetist Paquito D'Rivera, Otto Luening conducting his *Potawatomi Legends*, Carlos Suriñach conducting his *Sinfonía Chica*, John Giordano conducting Beethoven and Villa-Lobos, the Composers String Quartet performing William Schuman's String Quartet no. 3, and the Boehm Quintette's premiere of Francis Thorne's Divertimento No. 3. From Elliott Carter, apart from the quartets previously mentioned, we included the Triple Duo and *Riconoscenza* for solo violin, dedicated to Italian composer Goffredo Petrassi. Scores by Mario Davidovsky, Gunther Schuller, and William F. Lee (*The Masque of the Red Death*, based on Edgar Allan Poe's short story of the same name, and previously put to music by André Caplet) were played in their presence. Gideon Waldrop's *Songs of the Southwest* and Uruguayan composer Pedro Ipuche Riva's world premiere of his Timpani Concerto rubbed shoulders with Gershwin's *Rhapsody in Blue*, performed by pianist Ivan Davis, and with Ravel's Concerto in G Major, with pianist François-René Duchable and the Pittsburgh Symphony, which I also conducted. Also "Decoration Day" by Charles Ives and the *Manfred* Symphony by Tchaikovsky. I invited Ivan Davis to perform Liszt's Piano Concerto No. 2, and Rudolf Firkušný to perform Beethoven's *Choral Fantasy* with the Philharmonia Orchestra. In 1987 we had operatic bass Nicola Ghiuselev sing scenes from *Boris Godunov* by Mussorgsky, and on the same evening I conducted the US premiere of "The Gadfly," op. 97, by Shostakovich, extracted from the film *The Gadfly*. We gave the world premiere of a work by Belgian composer Paul Uy, performed by the amazing harmonica virtuosos "Toost"

Thielemans. On another program, conducted by Ettore Stratta, we included film suites by Bernstein, Korngold, and Steiner. The University of Miami orchestra participated regularly in the festival, as did the UM Concert Jazz Band. Guiding the festival brought me a lot of pleasure, as it allowed me to work with great international orchestras, to introduce dozens of composers, to bring a new life in music to the city of Miami. That was the target that Bill Hipp and I had set, and we achieved it.

Touring with the Juilliard Orchestra was your first major international tour.

The idea originated with Elias Grapa, the enterprising artists manager from Argentina who had recently opened an office in New York, at the same prestigious Broadway address as my manager, Harold Shaw. Grapa could have had a career as piano soloist and had originally come to the United States to continue his piano studies. When returning to Buenos Aires he had opted for a new career as manager, and within time his office had become the most successful in Latin America. It was at that time that he thought of expanding further by opening the New York office and adding new markets. One of his early projects was to tour the Juilliard Orchestra all over Latin America with me at the podium. I introduced Elias to Peter Mennin, then president of the Juilliard School, and it was agreed that Grapa would travel to Washington, DC, and present the project to the State Department to secure the substantial funding required for the tour. I was conducting in Perth, Australia, when the news came from Peter Mennin that the tour had been approved, that Grapa had booked seventeen concerts in as many cities, but . . . the State Department needed to have a US citizen at the podium in order to sponsor the tour. I was still on a student visa. From Perth, I contacted Leopold Stokowski. He in turn contacted Robert Kennedy, secretary of state at the time, and before I finalized the Australian tour I received the news that I would have my US passport the following week. Touring Latin America was an extraordinary experience. Years later, Grapa managed my South American tours with the National Chamber Orchestra of Toulouse, the Scottish Chamber Orchestra, the Russian National Orchestra, and others, but the Juilliard tour remains in my memories as a wonderful learning experience. We performed a varied repertoire in major and minor cities from Central and South American countries. At first, I was concerned about this ensemble made up of brilliant graduates who had the ambition to become soloists but lacked ensemble experience and did not know basic orchestral repertoire or styles. As each concert got better and better, midway through the tour it was sounding like a seasoned virtuoso orchestra. In Lima, Peru, we had to perform eight encores, as the public refused to let us end the event. In Bogota, Colombia, the young musicians were received at the airport like a rock group, with hundreds of young girls lined up begging for autographs. The mayhem was such that I missed the bus to take us to the hotel. Eventually I took a taxi, not knowing the name of the hotel, which neither Grapa nor his assistant had ever told us. The taxi driver took me around Bogota, trying to figure out which hotel might be mine. We tried calling the US Embassy, but it had an answering machine, it being late evening. Finally, after visiting two or three hotels, we saw Grapa outside a hotel door, hoping I would find them. This was long before cell phone or laptop computers made instant communication possible. Today the management is in the excellent hands of Carlos Grynfeld, long time associate of Grapa, and the name of the company has been changed to CG Management.

At Teatro Colon in Buenos Aires the success was such that the music critics ventured backstage to see with their own eyes whether these musicians were really as young as advertised. I figured out that we needed to keep the repeated performances fresh, and I discovered that one way was to slightly alter the speed of some movements, to avoid performances becoming stale repetitions. I never had to explain these unexpected changes to the young musicians, who intelligently realized what I was trying to accomplish and never questioned it. When we arrived at my home country of Uruguay, where the State Department had arranged for a longer stay—six days—the musicians asked why didn't I live there any longer, mesmerized by the interminable beaches that surrounded Montevideo, the warmth of the people, the intense musical life, the amazing resorts. I tried explaining that my life now oscillated between Europe and the United States, that I returned to Montevideo to conduct whenever my time permitted, but that it was far from the center of the musical world. As soon as we had landed in Montevideo, a United States embassy official welcomed us with the shocking and unexpected news that Peter Mennin had died. The school's dean, who until then had traveled with us as a sort of custodian, took the first flight back to New York. Mennin had become a friend since the time years before when I won the American Conductors competition, which he had started in Baltimore, sponsored by the Ford Foundation. I performed his compositions around the world, especially *Moby Dick*, and I recorded his Ninth Symphony with the Adelaide Symphony Orchestra in Australia, recently reissued. Mennin had regularly invited me to conduct the various Juilliard orchestras at Tully Hall in Lincoln Center. One time, when we were performing Mahler's First Symphony, he had rushed backstage, looking upset, to ask me, "Whose idea was it to have the entire horn section stand up at the end?" I replied, "Mahler," and smilingly showed him the score. Mennin embraced me. Another time, he had called me into his office, casually, with both feet on the desk, and he had invited venerated American composer Roger Sessions along to ask if I might be willing to conduct the Sessions Sixth Symphony. Mennin confessed that a longtime faculty member, famous cellist and conductor Alfred Wallenstein, had resigned from Juilliard and moved to California rather than conduct the Session Sixth Symphony because it was so difficult for the student orchestra. I was handed a score. My immediate reaction was, "Let me read it through with the orchestra and see what problems it presents, and then I will give you both my decision." The reading went on without a hitch, all except for a tricky section where the first violins had to perform a high and rapid sequence of notes, which would surely sound out of tune even after many rehearsals. The elderly Sessions was one of the most respected and admired composers in America, a national treasure, and one of Juilliard's best composition teachers. He was also a kindly gentleman. When I explained the minor problem and suggested that the solution be to have that long passage performed by a solo violin rather than the entire section, Sessions smiled, agreed at once, and published the score that way, along with a few of my other minor adjustments. At the Juilliard rehearsal's first reading, I asked the students how they felt about performing it, and they agreed, smilingly. The concertmaster, who has since then become a famous soloist, went even further: "We must play it!" I had no idea the concert was to be recorded for archival purposes and was surprised and delighted when told recently that it can be heard on YouTube. It deserves to be, as a historical document. Another time Mennin had requested to see me; he said, "We are being criticized for not performing any *repetitive* music. Would you consider conducting this?" I was handed a one-page score with few notes and an indication to repeat it innumerable times. My reaction: "Not this one, but let me look around for other possibilities." I then asked my friends at Broadcast Music Inc., BMI, and they suggested I look at music by the young San Francisco–based composer John Adams, since I was on my way to conduct in Auckland. Adams was at the airport when I arrived, and we went to his large residence, which had few furnishings but music manuscripts all over the place. I chose his new "Common Tones in Simple Time" and the following week we read it with the Juilliard Orchestra, again with me asking the young players for their opinions. It was unanimous: they loved it, and the premiere was a great success—apparently the first time one of Adams's pieces had received an orchestral performance. The rest is history.

We gave several concerts in Uruguay, more than in any other country. One of these was in a town I had never visited before, a five-hour car ride from Montevideo. The orchestra was provided a comfortable bus. I was given a car and driver and an unexpected escort—John Graves, who had recently been assigned by the State Department to an undisclosed new position at the US Embassy in Uruguay. Not long before, I had seen John Graves and his colleagues receiving a nationally televised ticker tape parade on Fifth Avenue in Manhattan. Graves was poster child for the famous group that had been kept hostage in Iran for 444 days until President Carter had finally managed to negotiate their freedom. And here I was on my way to conduct the Juilliard orchestra in a small, distant city, seated next to John Graves, asking him as many questions as he was willing to answer. Was he CIA? "If I were, I couldn't tell." "Why did the State Department send you off to a remote destination with no specified duties—although being escorted by you on this trip is a welcome, flattering experience." "No idea why I was sent to serve in Uruguay. Perhaps they wanted me out of the way?" We became fast friends, and on subsequent visits to Montevideo to conduct the local orchestra, John invited me and Carole to their home for dinner several times.

Some amusing anecdotes from your touring experiences?

While conducting in Caracas, I was in the hotel and saw this couple walking away from me with a strange-looking child. It looked as if it was deformed. We happened to be in the same elevator together, and I realized it was not a child but a monkey dressed as a child. They were from Los Angeles, and later we met at the pool. I saw the monkey seated, wearing a bathing suit and sharing a Coca-Cola with the two trainers, drinking from the same bottle. At one point the women befriended me, and we spoke for a while, when I noticed that the trainer was calling him Zippy—which was the name of the monkey. I gathered he was a famous monkey and found out that different generations of Zippys had been in several movies. When he wasn't obeying, they would say, "Zippy, are you listening to me?" and Zippy would make a rather strange sign, sticking out his tongue and plugging his ears with both fingers. It seemed obvious he was a professional monkey who was there to do a TV show in Caracas. This gave me a great idea. I asked what he wore, and they told me formal tails, and which point I asked if they could bring him to my rehearsal the next morning, which they did, and we plotted the practical joke. I was doing Ravel's Second Suite from *Daphnis and Chloé*, and I conducted it so quickly in that rehearsal that the orchestra was left totally out of breath. The ending is a fast race, and I took it at breakneck speed. When we'd finished, before they could think, *What is the conductor doing?* I said, "I'd like you to meet a friend of mine, a conductor from Africa named

Arturo Toscanone." They began to applaud, because I was a serious conductor introducing somebody important. They could not see the monkey at first because he was too short, and before they knew it, the monkey was standing on the podium, looking at them, dressed in concert tails, with a baton that I had given him. They thought that was the joke, so they laughed, but the real punch line was yet to come. I asked him, "Maestro, how did you like the National Symphony of Venezuela's performance of Ravel's *Daphnis et Chloé*?" His reply was to put his fingers in his ears and stick his tongue out. The laughter was unstoppable. Some of the more generous players said, "Finally, we have a conductor with a sense of humor."

· 3 ·

Serebrier on Ives

Reprinted from Bernard Jacobson's book *Conductors on Conducting* (1979).

During the last few months of Leopold Stokowski's life, I made several attempts to reach him with the idea of asking him to talk about Ives for this book. But his agent explained that Stokowski, already in his middle nineties, was determined to give no more interviews but to devote whatever time he had left to recording. Then, early in 1977, I received for review a new recording of the Ives Fourth Symphony by Seiji Ozawa and the Boston Symphony Orchestra. In the course of making critical comparisons, I became acquainted for the first time with the RCA recording made by José Serebrier in 1974. I found the Serebrier performance breathtaking in its spirit and accuracy. And recalling that Serebrier, a very gifted composer-conductor, had been Stokowski's associate conductor at the long-delayed world premiere of the work, I decided to see whether he was willing to talk about his own experience with this phenomenally difficult piece and about his participation in the Stokowski performance. Serebrier agreed, good-humoredly accepting once more the role of understudy that his own success had by now rendered inappropriate. The conversation that follows was taped in his Riverside Drive apartment in New York at the beginning of October 1977, diversified only occasionally by an appropriately Ivesian counterpoint of squeaks from a revolving chair and door-knocks from Serebrier's baby daughter.

—Bernard Jacobson

∿

I'm going to reply first about Stokowski. I think it's important to mention Stokowski because the first time I heard of Ives was from Stokowski. When I was a student at the Curtis Institute in Philadelphia, I was about seventeen, I received an urgent message from Stokowski to call him in Houston. I didn't follow up on it because I thought it was a practical joke being played on me by one of my friends. I was always playing jokes on them, leaving messages to call up Arthur Judson, the manager, and so on. But the next day, another message came, and finally a telegram. I called Stokowski—it was in November 1957—and he said, "I cannot play the Ives Fourth Symphony"; it had been announced as the world premiere, and critics from all over the United States were coming to hear the Fourth Symphony; it was going to be a big occasion. He added, "Orchestras cannot play it. May I play your symphony instead?" I happily replied, "Fine!" He said, "Good. Come tomorrow with the music. I have the conductor's score; you bring orchestral parts." Just like that! Well, the score existed, but there were no orchestral parts. Many in the student body, some of whom are now very famous artists, sat up all night helping me copy the parts so that I could take the 9 a.m. flight to Houston. There was no Internet in 1957 nor photocopying machines.

How did Stokowski know of your symphony?

It had won the BMI Student Composers award, and shortly after a new musician in his orchestra, Harvey Wolf, showed Stokowski my manuscript. After a quick glance, Stokowski chose my symphony to replace the Ives Fourth. I went to Houston. I didn't have enough money for the trip, and Mrs. Curtis Bok purchased my airline ticket. That's when I became curious about Ives. The critics were curious, too, about what had replaced the Ives, and as they were all there, they stayed for the performance. *Time* and *Newsweek* were there. Stokowski only had two rehearsals, and he did a fantastic performance of my First Symphony. But practically nothing came out in the press: the concert coincided with the space launch of the first Sputnik, so there were no music reviews! I then looked at the score for the Ives Fourth, and I couldn't make heads or tails of it, so I just put it aside. My next encounter with the score was when I was already working with Stokowski as his associate conductor with the American Symphony Orchestra in New York City.

Which started about 1962?

Yes, the fall of 1962. And in the fall of 1963 Stokowski said, "Now I'm going to try for the third time"—the episode in Houston had already been the second aborted premiere of the Ives Fourth. Frankly, what had happened was that the Houston orchestra couldn't get past the fourth or fifth bar; they just couldn't play it, partially because the music was extremely hard to read in manuscript. Stokowski sent all the material back to the Fleisher Collection in Philadelphia with the request that they make it clear—not simplify it but clarify it. The score was very confused. This had been in 1957. Anyway, in my first year with Stokowski at the American Symphony Orchestra he never mentioned the Ives Fourth. He conducted my *Elegy for Strings*, and he did two other works of mine. Then, in 1964, he received a big grant to rehearse only the Ives Fourth for a month and a half or two months.

You had not been working on Ives in any way in the intervening time?

No. Then I said to Stokowski, "I hear that the work requires more than one conductor. Do you need me? Do you want me to begin studying the score?" "No, not necessary. I don't believe in these gimmicks. I think we'll do it with just the one conductor." In fact, I remember, when I saw the score in Houston, what had struck me was that the score very clearly indicated "four conductors," and Ives wrote it with four conductors in mind. That's in the manuscript: conductor I, conductor II, conductor III, and conductor IV, all over the score.

Those things one sees in the big, blue-bound AMP printed edition, about conductor I, conductor II, and so on, they are Ives's own markings?

Yes. Originally it was for four conductors, which added to the confusion. Stokowski said, "It's too many conductors; it's too complicated." When he asked the Fleisher Collection to clarify the material, they helped by taking out conductor IV and splitting his contribution among conductors I, II, and III. But Stokowski still didn't believe it should be done with more than one conductor. Now it's so common with this symphony, but at that time it was still sort of strange, even for him. He told me, "No, don't bother; I'll do it myself," so I never had a chance to look at the new Fleisher score. In fact, the first time I saw the score for this performance was the historic day of the first rehearsal of the Ives Fourth in Carnegie Hall. In typical Stokowski fashion, he invited the press. Harold Schonberg of the *New York Times* and about eight or ten other critics were there. Virgil Thomson was no longer a critic, but he was there. Leonard Bernstein had been invited, but he couldn't come. And there were about a dozen musicologists and Ives experts. For the first few minutes, Stokowski stood on the podium, staring at the score. Nothing was happening. He looked at the orchestra; he looked at the score.

Then he saw me walking by, in the wings. "Ah, maestro," he said—he always called his associate conductors "maestro," perhaps as a way of not having to remember our names—"please come over." I walked over to the podium. "Please conduct this last movement"; he was starting the rehearsal with the last movement. "I want to hear it." At which point my heart fell; I had never even read it! So that was really my first look at the score; my first exposure to the score was conducting that last movement before an audience of critics and musicologists! It is incredible, even today, that last movement. You always have to open the music up sideways because it's so large. It was a huge thing. Stokowski had two music stands fixed together to hold the version he used. I could hardly see the entire score, much less take in the tempo changes and so on. Miraculously, we got through it from beginning to end. I don't know how, but we got through it. To this day, it was the most difficult moment of my life. Afterward I told him, "You know, I was sight-reading!" And he said, "Oh, so was the orchestra." He got to hear it, and it broke the ice, so to speak. And then he said, "All right, now we start work," and he went back to the first movement. He didn't touch the last movement for about two weeks. The way he proceeded in rehearsals—and this is why it didn't work and why it took so long—was to take one bar at a time. He said, "Let's play the first bar." Stop and think. "I will think." "Let's play it again." "And again." And then on to the second bar; play it, play it again; play two bars together. Maybe you would do it that way if you were practicing piano and you came across a difficult piece, but with the Ives Fourth, that way of working took forever—in fact, over a month of daily rehearsals.

This was not his common method of working?

No, never. In fact, Stokowski had the most fantastic rehearsal technique. This has nothing to do with music making, but Stokowski's rehearsal technique was the most businesslike and practical and made the best use of time. But he had such an awful experience with the Ives Fourth; he was terrified. And it's incredible; I don't know how old he was then, around late eighties, but he still wanted to do it! Nobody else did it, and at his age he took the trouble to learn this work. However, I feel he let a lot of things slide, and I think my performance is superior to his. I think one must credit the maestro with having done this first performance and really with having discovered quite a bit of the work's character. Not the second movement, perhaps, but the fourth movement and the first are beautiful in Stokowski's version. With his second movement, well, I totally disagree. By doing it the way he did, he didn't really go deeply into the piece or find the problems. It did get better as the orchestra played each bar over and over. But it frustrated the musicians. At the end of the first week, the musicians were fed up; they were very, very tired of rehearsing with this system. I didn't get involved with the score, because all through the first weeks of rehearsal Stokowski still felt that it should be done by one conductor. In fact, I just attended the rehearsals, but I didn't understand anything that was happening on the stage. Stokowski eventually realized that the score, the way it had been prepared by the Fleisher Collection, required three conductors. Eventually, he asked me to look at the score and decide how much I wanted to do of conductor II and how much of it could be done by the first conductor. From then onward, he began to rely more and more on my help and advice in preparing this thing. I could see why it had not been possible in Houston. They had been working a bar at a time until they knew it sideways, but they would go back to it a week later and it would feel new all over again. The main problem, which I found out later when I did the symphony on my own, was that he could have rehearsed it for three years that way and it wouldn't have helped, because of the complicated rhythms, with so many parts doing something different from everybody else. Unless the musicians can hear the others playing something entirely different, they simply cannot coordinate. But I didn't know this yet. I just simply began helping him, correcting what seemed like wrong notes and discovering problems in the score. It became a two-conductor piece, because the third conductor was relegated to doing only the percussion ostinato in the final movement, and to this day the Ives Fourth is done this way. The changes I made were necessary because the Fleisher Collection had left the symphony in a format that was still almost impossible to conduct. If conductors II and III did what is in the score, it would be impossible unless they had computer minds to synchronize 3/8 against 2/8 against 4/8 and then 6/4. In the second movement, the musicians are asked to play two bars following one conductor, three bars following another, and the conductors need to do the same thing, conduct the violins for two bars, then switch to the oboes, then switch to the flutes—utterly impractical.

You say if it's done the Fleisher Collection way it's impossible, and you say you divided it the way it's now done. Which of those ways is the one in the AMP printed score?

The printed score is a combination of the Fleisher Collection version and my simplification. The orchestral material that most people use has my markings. In other words, the printed score is a sort of halfway house between what you originally got from Fleisher and what is written in the orchestral parts.

The parts that are used now are a third form, which is the one I edited. The score was already printed by then, so it couldn't be put into that. There is yet another version, the Gunther Schuller version, which we'll talk about later. In any case, if you look at the printed score, you'll see that it's quite impractical. For the premiere, what happened in the end was that I gave myself very little of the actual conducting. Stokowski wanted to conduct most of it, and he was right in thinking, from the beginning, that the fewer the conductors and the less the division of conducting duties in the work, the better the performance would be. Following that principle, he did most of the task, and I conducted only when there was absolutely no choice but to have a second conductor. Really, then, it's a two-conductor piece. The third conductor came in because I felt it was necessary for the orchestra's other associate conductor to do something too. We decided that he could conduct the percussion in the last movement, an ostinato almost completely separate from what the rest of the orchestra is doing; but conductor II, who has nothing to do in the last movement, could have done it simply by walking offstage. Some of the places where it is utterly impossible to do it with less than two conductors are in the second movement. One is the so-called "collapse" section. Stokowski used to joke and call it the "calypso." When we performed it together, he said, "You're a wonderful *collapser*—or should I say *calypser*?" This section is in the middle of the second movement, one of the most imaginative passages in the work, where the strings and some percussion remain soft and slow and almost static, and then are suddenly interrupted by the second orchestra. Ideally, in Ives's vision, there should have been an entirely separate second orchestra in a different part of the hall. It has never been played that way, as it's so expensive to have a second orchestra, but the effect was achieved in the original quadraphonic version of my recording. In actual performance, it's only practical to have everyone on the stage. Ives was very impractical, but not completely so. He didn't score it for a full second orchestra. What he did was divide the orchestra into two separate halves. Half the orchestra continues in this monotone while it's interrupted by the other half. The orchestra that has the monotone must be conducted at a slow three or subdivided six. The other orchestra comes in at a completely different speed, different meter, and in fact goes *accelerando*: it goes faster and faster. And then when the second orchestra stops, the first orchestra is still playing in the old slow monotone. You cannot do it without two conductors here. Even Boulez, who prided himself on conducting some Ives—he did *Central Park in the Dark* with one conductor by beating different rhythms with each hand, and successfully—even he could not do the Ives Fourth by himself, and he had to have an assistant conductor in the second movement.

Presumably because it's one thing to conduct two steady rhythms with two hands, but to conduct one steady rhythm and one *accelerando* rhythm with two hands is beyond anyone.

Yes. Now, in the world premiere performance, I conducted a few bars in the first movement, but I have since clarified them, and it's not necessary to have a second conductor for this movement. The second conductor is needed mostly in the second movement. Sometimes the violas, sometimes the second violins, sometimes the brass have a rhythm so different from the rest of the orchestra that it requires a second conductor, especially in the "collapse" section I referred to, and in two other sections in the second movement where once again the rhythms are quite different. But the "collapse" is the only section where there really is no coordination between the two parts; one just hopes they will somehow end where they're supposed to. Eventually, after two months of rehearsing, the Ives Fourth had a brilliant performance; the world premiere in Carnegie Hall was a tremendous success. But then, nothing had ever been rehearsed for so long. Even *The Rite of Spring* didn't get so many rehearsals for its premiere. In fact, Monteux told me he only had nine rehearsals. That was part of the reason the first performance was such a fiasco: it hadn't been well done; nine rehearsals had not proven sufficient, and the dancers had had little time to coordinate with the music. But something happens with these difficult works. As they go from one city to another, each new performance becomes easier.

I was going to ask you precisely this. It's a curious metaphysical experience that I've had. I've had it with a work that's not actually all that difficult: Wilfred Josephs's *Requiem* has been performed perhaps a dozen times in different places, and each time it has been much easier to do. How do you explain this?

There are some practical reasons why it becomes easier. The parts, after each performance, become more marked up, and hopefully they have fingerings and bowings, and mistakes have been corrected each time. Perhaps there's a tape of the first performance that may help the conductor. If a work has been heard, you know what it's supposed to sound like. *The Rite of Spring*, for example, is no longer a mystery. Even an orchestra that has never played it knows how it sounds; they hear it in their minds. But there is also an element of mystery in the way it becomes easier. The best example is the American Symphony Orchestra itself. When we repeated the Ives Fourth the following season, it wasn't the same orchestra—Stokowski changed many of the play-ers every year; there was a turnover of about 40 percent—yet the next time around, the work was prepared in the usual four rehearsals, and it was as good a performance as the year before.

Over those two years, I learned a great deal about Ives, and frankly I wasn't that impressed at first. I was impressed with the imagination, but not nearly as much as I would be later on, when I learned more of his music. I know Stokowski admired Ives enormously, both because of the great imagi-nation of the man and for his principles and ideas, and he really wanted to do justice to the work. He understood the universality of Ives, he understood the drama, he understood the technical aspects up to a point. But he missed the humor, which is one of Ives's most important elements. Few composers in history have had the sense of humor of Charles Ives, and I am sorry to say that that has been lost. Stokowski personally had a great sense of humor—quite a bit of dry British humor—but he did not have it when making music. Making music was a solemn experience.

It was still the nineteenth-century divine experience.

Yes, absolutely, so he never quite understood Ives's humor, which is so ir-reverent. But he understood very well the so-called religious experience of the fourth movement and especially the organ-like quality of the third move-ment. In fact, Stokowski established a pattern of how to perform the third movement that I followed in my own way, in my own version. This is perhaps the only respect in which I was influenced by Stokowski's performance. The Ives experts, by the way, do not entirely agree with us regarding the third movement, because they feel both Stokowski and I do it too slowly and too solemnly, and they feel that the ending especially, with the quotations from hymns and so on, should be humorous and not pompous. They have a point, yet we have a point too, because Ives didn't indicate anything. Incidentally, I do it even more slowly than Stokowski. I don't think the third movement is so very humorous; at least, it doesn't sound humorous.

At that time, as I said, I was not yet in love yet with Ives's music. I didn't even own a score of the Fourth Symphony; after the Carnegie Hall performances, my score went back to the Fleisher Collection. But I became interested in other Ives works. I began to do *The Unanswered Question*, which is an incredible piece, and I did it all over the world. And I specialized mostly in "Decoration Day," from the *Holidays Symphony*, which I still think is Ives's best piece. "Decoration Day" is the most concise, the whole Ivesian world in nine minutes, and it's the best-written piece. And I'm proven sort of right by the fact that it's the most performed of his works. The Chicago Symphony took it on a European tour and to Japan, and the Cleveland Orchestra took it to South America; it's a practical piece—that's part of it—and a very successful one. Then I did the complete *Holidays Symphony* once or twice, and I've accompanied some of his songs. I think the songs are fantastic, among the greatest Ives works: each song is a complete world, so imaginative, and their humor is just marvelous. But my appreciation for the Fourth Symphony came slowly. It had escaped me for years. I hadn't understood it at the time of the premiere. After the premiere, as you know, we made a film for National Educational Television—NET, predecessor of PBS—and we made a recording for Columbia. And then, over the following two years, we repeated the Ives Fourth in concert at Carnegie Hall. Many years later I conducted it by myself at Carnegie Hall with the American Symphony Orchestra, and took it on tour to my Festival Miami, including the choir.

But it still hadn't really gotten to you.

No. Speaking as a young composer myself, I had no doubts about Ives's imagination and his formidable ideas, but I was disgusted by the complete lack of neatness—as opposed to Ravel, let's say—and by the impracticality of the writing, which made it so difficult and unplayable at times, and by the complete lack of stylistic unity, especially in the Fourth Symphony.

Between, say, the second and third movements most extremely.

Extremely, indeed, feeling as if they're two works that really don't go together. I in fact suspected that the work was never meant as a symphony; at the time I suspected that he just pasted four movements together because they represented such different worlds. The prelude is so short—it's three minutes—and it is almost as an introduction; and I really saw the second movement as a work that could stand by itself, as is the third movement.

**Which of course it does in part as
"The Celestial Railroad," in the form of a piano piece.**

Yes, but it could never really be played by itself, the second movement of that symphony. In the *Holidays Symphony* you can play the movements separately, but not in the Fourth Symphony. Only the third movement of the Fourth is in fact published separately, as a piece that could be played by itself, but not the second, which I think is the most exciting for me. And I felt the third movement didn't belong, and with the fourth I was intrigued, but I didn't quite figure it out as, again, it was in a different style, and I felt the whole thing didn't add up. I wasn't interested in it, and I didn't see any practical way of playing it anywhere, so that was that.

Years later, as it happened, when I was planning to do my own solo recording, I was in London, and I heard about a performance of the Fourth Symphony that John Pritchard was conducting in Manchester with the Hallé Orchestra. I went there, and I was extremely impressed, because he was the first conductor—I thought—that followed the tempo changes Ives had indicated, and by doing so he suddenly revealed the work much better to me than before. He had done the Ives Fourth quite a few times. He also used a second conductor. In fact, he gave the second conductor the main podium: Pritchard, in a great show of modesty, stood at the side on a smaller podium, and the second conductor only conducted a few times, but he had the main podium. I didn't understand why he had done it like that. But Pritchard said to me, "I understand you're going to record this work; you're going to have lots of trouble." He asked me, "What do you think of this piece?" and I said, "I'm still considering it." Then he must have read my mind, because he said, "I wonder if one could ever do it skipping the third movement." We were of one accord regarding the third movement. We liked it as a separate piece but not necessarily as part of the whole symphony. This happens with other works of Ives; in the string quartets and the piano sonatas you have this problem. But eventually I realized that the third movement has to be in there, that you can't do without it, and that you need the calm of the third movement. And it happens in performance. You do the second movement; the audience, if they are a bit sophisticated, laughs, always, at the end of the second movement. It's so funny, this ending, the "collapse" section, and then the ending with the violas left hanging out. They always think, "Oh, it's one big joke." And the third movement has a strange tonic effect of calming everybody's nerves down. I can't think of anything but this third movement now that would work as well as it does, after that second movement ending, as a complete tonal wash of one's ears.

Is it true to say that, if one thought of it as a three-movement piece, one-two-four, it would be on too intense a level of intellectual concentration?

Yes, it might not work. And you need to have a moment of respite. Now, why not do it in the same style becomes the question. Stravinsky would never have done anything like that. But this is Ives, and that's the way he solved his problem, and it works. In fact, he borrowed from the Concord Piano Sonata for the second movement, and the third movement comes from the First String Quartet. As far as I know, the fourth movement—most of it—is original for the symphony. But he was constantly doing this pasting together.

The first movement is a song, isn't it?

That's right. But somehow it all works together, and it does fit as a symphony, and by now it's almost considered a classic. I learned to accept the stylistic anomalies and to make the best of them. I realized that Ives couldn't care less about stylistic unity, just as he couldn't care less about harmonic continuity and all the stipulations about form and orchestration, the notions of which he completely revised. He was not tied up by performance problems because he did not expect performances. He was in the unique situation of not being a professional composer writing for a public. He could write as he pleased, for himself, in an abstract world. So he cannot be analyzed with the same strictness with which we would analyze Beethoven or Stravinsky, who wrote for a public, or even Schoenberg. This is the first consideration in Ives: that he wrote in a sort of vacuum and could thus permit himself flights of the imagination that remain amazing to this day. He could permit himself to write rhythms so difficult they are almost impossible to play, though by now we have learned to live with them, almost to master them. One simply has to understand that this is the way Ives worked. In other words, I didn't learn to live with it other than to accept it, because it's Ives. America has made a hero of Ives, and everything he wrote is considered great. The stylistic differences found especially in the Fourth Symphony are, incidentally, not encountered so much in Ives's earlier works. You have to look at them to know how well-schooled he was.

The First Symphony?

The First Symphony—and even a work like *The Celestial Country*, a big cantata that was his last student piece—it isn't a great work, but it's a beautifully written work, with perfect modulations, and in fact already some touches of Ivesian imagination in it. You can see that this composer might come through. But it's very classical. In a way, you can almost say the same thing of Cage. Have you ever seen any of Cage's earlier, student works? Perfectly tonal; it's quite extraordinary. You know that Cage studied with Arnold

Schoenberg. I'm not speaking in defense of Cage, but it's interesting, because some modern composers that I know, and in fact some young composers today who are quite successful, have never bothered to study harmony, fugue, and counterpoint. What for? If you intend to do aleatoric music, and music that doesn't even use notes, they feel it's nonsense to go through the years of tying oneself down to the tradition of classical writing.

> **Whereas, as Stravinsky knew, you can
> only break the rules when you know them.**

Exactly. I feel that that's absolutely necessary. Anyway, we know Ives knew the rules. But as he knew the rules, he learned to break them, one by one. What challenges me most, as a composer and a conductor, is the use of form; and the most fantastic thing stylistically about Ives is that no two Ives works that I know use the same form. Ives's form is so elusive, it's incredible.

> **It's very interesting you say that, because it's possible to have a
> superficial impression from, say, the movements of the *Holidays
> Symphony* that there is a formal similarity—the slow buildup,
> the big climax, then the breaking-off for a brief conclusion.**

Yes, you can say that is in principle an A-B-A idea: it's soft and slow, fast and loud, soft and slow—but really not at all. It doesn't add up to a form, because harmonically and thematically there is no relation between the first and the final sections. Now, I dare anyone to try to describe the form of any of the movements of the Fourth Symphony. The only way you can describe it is as improvisatory form. It all hangs together but in a concept that is unique to Ives. The second movement, for example, is based on the idea of interruptions: he presents a theme and interrupts it, and that's the central concept. He tries to surprise all the time. As for the rhythms, unlike *Pacific 231*—where Honegger has worked out the idea of a train getting faster and faster and then slowing down and coming to a stop—Ives, in the similar portions of the second movement, has worked out his rhythms mathematically. If one follows the direction, which is so cleverly done and so clear in the score, the effect is marvelous, of speeding up like a train, though he may not have thought of a train. It's a wonderful effect. Ives worked many other things out very cleverly, and if one accepts the idea that he didn't care about consistency of style, then obviously one can live with the different styles that go into the piece.

It's not actually that much more extreme than, say, the stylistic disunity between the first and second movements of Mahler's Second Symphony. When you go into that minuet after the incredibly wide-ranging first movement, it's like jumping into a different world.

Absolutely. I'm glad you mention that, because there are some parallels between Mahler and Ives, strange as it seems. You know that it's presumed that they met, at Ives's copyist's, and it's further presumed that Mahler was impressed with the score of the Ives Second Symphony and the *Holidays Symphony*, and it is presumed that Mahler took one of these two works with him to Vienna, and further that he may have played one of these two works at one of the Sunday afternoon concerts for which programs were not kept, unfortunately, at that time. This is a bit imaginative, but if you talk to some of the Ives scholars, they'll tell you about this. And Ives may well have had some influence on Mahler.

There is also the same phenomenon quite early in Mahler of tempos that don't entirely coalesce, one group starting in a new tempo before the other has finished.

Yes—you have it in the First Symphony, the Jewish dance band mixing with the other music.

Also in the Mahler Third Symphony, that passage with the birdsong coming in at a different tempo than the rest of the orchestra, and the Fourth Symphony again—though these are all presumably too early to have been influenced that way.

Yes. This is just a conjecture, because it is known that Mahler visited the copyist who was working for Ives; that is a known fact, so it is quite possible that he may have seen the scores. We know that Schoenberg was acquainted with Ives's music; you know the famous quotation: "There is a great man living in this country—the United States—a composer. He has solved the problem of how to preserve one's self and to learn. He responds to negligence with contempt. He is forced to neither accept praise nor blame. His name is Ives." Ives was not unknown to some of the major composers of his time. They probably thought of him as some strange phenomenon. But it took forever for his music to become known, and, in fact, no publisher wanted his music. It was only Peermusic that accepted his music at first, and it proved a visionary wisdom on their part.

Speaking of accepting his music, how did you come to record the Ives Fourth Symphony eventually?

In fact, it was not my idea to come back to the Fourth Symphony. It was RCA's idea. RCA knew the Ives centenary was coming up, and Peter Munvies, then the head of the Artists and Repertoire department, thought they should do something. He had been at Columbia when they'd done the world-premiere recording, so he remembered the success. It was a best seller. Ives was already beginning to acquire a name in the American musical world when Stokowski made the record, but that's what did it, the Fourth Symphony, and the recording was selling in supermarkets! And it sold thirty-eight thousand copies, which in America for a record of serious music was incredible, and modern music especially. In fact, Columbia had been so afraid to record the Ives Fourth that they wouldn't do it. Stokowski had to find funding for it; the Samuel Rubin Foundation paid for the recording. Peter Munvies remembered that experience, and he thought the Ives Fourth needed a new recording.

This was about the early 1970s, presumably.

The actual centenary year was 1974. It was in 1973 that I got the call from Peter Munvies's secretary.

You hadn't made any records for RCA at that point?

No—my only recording experience had been for labels like Desto and CRI, and the only work of my own on records at that time was my Second Symphony, *Partita*, on the Louisville label. The RCA Ives Fourth was my first important record. Peter Munvies called, saying he wanted to make a new recording because the Stokowski version was already eight years old. I didn't think I liked the idea, at the time. I wanted to meet him because I was hoping to convince him to record something else in its place. I proposed Tchaikovsky's *Manfred Symphony*, which I was still anxious to record. And he said, "Fine, we might do *Manfred* if you record the Ives Fourth." I said, "But I don't think I can do it, because the Stokowski record was so great; how am I going to do it?" He said, "Listen to the record; we'll send you a record and a score, and then let us know what you think." And that's what I did. I listened to the Stokowski record in which I had been the second conductor. I had never heard it before. I listened to the record with the score over and over, a whole day, twenty times, and I couldn't believe it. In the second movement, all the tempo changes, which are the key to the movement, and which are so well worked out by Ives for the effect he'd wanted, but Stokowski just went through them, missed them altogether.

Not to the degree that Ozawa does.

Oh, yes, that's something else. In Stokowski's recording, there were some things that I felt would be difficult to emulate—the first movement, which he did so beautifully, and the third movement, which impressed me so much, and the understanding of the fourth. But because of the second movement, I immediately called Peter and said, "Absolutely, I feel I can do some of it at least as well." I wanted to choose the orchestra. He said, "Only if it's a European orchestra"; they couldn't afford to do it in America. And he also said no when I asked for a month of rehearsals. So I said, "Right, but I don't want to sign a contract until I go to London and identify the right orchestra." I was actually in London a month later, conducting the Philharmonia Orchestra in the British premiere of Bloch's opera *Macbeth*, in a concert version. I met with Eric Bravington, managing director of the London Philharmonic Orchestra. I told him about the RCA project and that my first choice would be the London Philharmonic because it was already becoming one of the best orchestras in London. I was also considering the Royal Philharmonic Orchestra, who wanted to do it very badly. I had worked with the other London orchestras but not the Royal Philharmonic. At that point, most of the London orchestras were lobbying to do it because they knew that it would be an important record—for the American market, anyway. But what clinched it for the London Philharmonic was Bravington's artistic involvement. He sensed that it was a very important project. I told him that all RCA could afford was five recording sessions. There was no time to have a performance beforehand, which would have helped the recording, because the season was all mapped out, and once RCA decided to do it, it was a matter of a month or six weeks hence. Peter Munvies worked that way. He needed to release it in time for the Ives centenary. So Bravington had this idea—and it was his idea—that he could not provide a performance to make the recording more efficient, but he could give RCA a gift of one rehearsal. One more rehearsal, I felt, would do nothing, because this work needed a month. What would help would be to use that single "free" session to rehearse separate sections of the orchestra individually, and this is what we did. It was a very eccentric request, and very few managers, unless they have Bravington's vision, would ever agree to such a thing—to give a free rehearsal in order to ensure a recording's done correctly but then to have that rehearsal broken up into thirty groups! It means that the orchestra lost a week of work, practically, because there was always a group missing. But for the LPO Ltd. it only cost one rehearsal, because each group was only working three hours, though they also paid for the rehearsal hall. And so that they wouldn't lose a whole month, I rehearsed every day from nine in the morning until midnight. I can't remember the exact order, but I divided them in this fashion: first violins, three hours; second violins, three hours; violas, three hours; cellos alone, three hours; basses alone, three hours; flutes alone, three hours; the solo violins that play in the first and last movements, three hours; harps, the three pianists—who have impossible parts— three hours; the solo pianist—that was cheaper; I met with him several times for an hour at a time, and it did wonders; organ, three hours, by himself; celesta—such a difficult part—three hours; brass, divided into groups, three hours; percussion, divided into groups, three hours; and so on and on. I had never worked so hard. Since that crazy week I've done similar things, but it was my first such experience working from nine to midnight. We got it all done, and it involved quite a few logistics, with letters going back and forth, telling people where the rehearsals were to be held, because they could not all be in the same place. Sometimes I had half an hour in between to get from one rehearsal venue to another across London.

> **The idea of this presumably being to get the sound of the whole part into the players' ears so that they could then concentrate on hearing the other people.**

Exactly. I felt that the system of rehearsing one bar at a time didn't work, because the orchestra couldn't hear anything of what was happening. My idea was that they should at least be able to hear themselves and thus get each part clear.

> **Parenthetically, is the sectional-rehearsal technique something you only do in Ives?**

Let's see—I use sectional rehearsals when I do some very difficult works, like the *Manfred Symphony*, not to that extent, but I ask for a wind rehearsal and a string rehearsal, which helps enormously, because it's rhythmically very difficult too; and for *The Rite of Spring*, and even for the Second Suite of *Daphnis*. But Ives, I think, cannot be played any other way. All this, though, was only the finishing touches to the preparation. Before that, there was the incredible problem of the orchestral parts. I had Schirmer send me two sets of parts: I was inundated with parts. There were about five sets, and I wanted to see two of them: the parts Stokowski had used and the Gunther Schuller set—he called it the Gunther Schuller version)—which he had arranged for one conductor. For the past few years, Schuller had been doing it without the aid of other conductors, and he had fixed a set of parts. I looked at this set first, because I thought it might be fun to do it on my own. Then I realized what he had done: He had rearranged the rhythms Ives wrote that require two conductors in such a way that the players would only have to follow one. But in doing so, for the privilege of having only one conductor, he had made it a hundred times more difficult for the players. So what was the point? For example, there are parts where the players have a triplet over two bars; three bars have to sound as long as two, and with two conductors it works, because the conductor concerned bothers to beat it faster than regular bars in order to fit it within the framework. Schuller rewrote it so that it will fit in two bars and wrote it beautifully . . . but it made it even more difficult than the original.

By changing the note values . . .

. . . To a point where the player will have to have a computer next to him as he plays it.

**In a sense, it's the reverse process of Stravinsky's
later simplification of the rhythms in *The Rite of Spring*.**

Exactly. So, I felt, this is absolutely not doing justice to the work; it's making it more difficult. And I think part of the problem with the Ozawa recording, I'm almost sure that he used the Schuller version. And in spite of the fact that the Boston Symphony Orchestra has played it any number of times—they toured Europe with it; he's done it in New York and all over—part of the problem is that they haven't done the extensive sectional rehearsals that help to clarify the score.

I discarded the Schuller version and began to look into the Stokowski parts. They're not Stokowski's personal set of parts; they're the parts that he used. I couldn't believe my eyes. The players had been so bored, they'd scribbled things all over the parts. I found that there were pages upon pages without any dynamic markings in the parts, in the brass, in the winds. I think the Fleisher Collection had done a marvelous job, but many, many mistakes had been let slide, with an enormous number of mistakes, wrong notes, missing dynamics. Sometimes Ives wrote "wrong notes," I know, on purpose.

Some people who know that I've corrected so many mistakes in the Fourth Symphony, and also in "Decoration Day," have asked me, "How do you know which are wrong notes and which are meant to be wrong notes?" It's important to try to clarify this. When I revised the parts, some were obviously wrong notes. Sometimes I found a whole page in the cellos where the notes were correct but the clef was wrong: They had left a bass clef, and it was supposed to be tenor clef—a slight mistake! When a whole page is in the wrong clef, there's no question about it. Other times, we know there are wrong notes when a whole section is playing in unison, all the violas, cellos, and basses, for example, with one note different in the violas. It's quite simple; it's no mystery. And, in fact, someone on the West Coast is writing a whole errata book on the Ives Fourth Symphony—a musicologist working at UCLA. I sent him my list of errors, and he found a few others from that edition.

**But then there are the other sorts of wrong notes,
the ones that have a humorous effect or the ones that—**

Oh, that's something else, because they're obvious. It was quite simple for me to figure out which were mistakes.

One wouldn't correct the last chord of the Second Symphony, for example.

No! That's a good example of it. But then there are cases that were obviously copyists' mistakes. I couldn't believe that so many things were wrong, so I called Peter Munvies and said, "Look, this is going to take me months of work; we cannot possibly do the recording next month." We postponed the recording for six months. I worked hours and hours every day to fix the musician's parts. I cleaned them up and put bowings in the strings, as there were no bowings in the parts, which was one of Stokowski's approaches: he always demanded strings perform with separate bowings, and that worked like magic in Romantic works, to get that lush sound he envisioned. I edited the parts. I felt that part of the problem in playing Ives is the tendency to play him literally, as written, the way one might play, for example, Handel, where there are no dynamic markings most of the time, and there are no *crescendos* or *diminuendos*, and there are no expression marks. Does that mean we should play Bach and Handel without any expression and only with the Baroque *forte-piano* type of balance and no *mezzo fortes,* no echo effects, because they didn't bother to indicate them most of the time? I won't go into the question of how you play Bach and Handel, but I *will* go into the question of how to play Ives. I don't think he intended his music to be played without expression. I did not edit it to the extent that Beecham would have edited it had he gotten hold of the score, but I did use some of the Beecham-type ideas, which I admired, feeling that the music could come more to life if the conductor or the performer would read into it to find the contour to the melodies, to the lines, and bring them forth. Much of my work with the Fourth Symphony, then—and I've since done the same thing with "Decoration Day" and some of the chamber music—was doing what Ives had never bothered to do, which was to add these editorial performance effects such as crescendos, diminuendos, some balances. I think the reason he didn't bother with this was that he didn't expect performances. Getting his music down on paper was enough for him. If he'd had performances, quite possibly he would have bothered, for example, to consider how many notes a violin can play in one bow before it has to change direction. But as it was, when he did write slurs for the strings, he just wrote them as expression marks, which run over for about eight bars. Now Mahler, in his symphonies, also wrote slurs that go for twelve bars at times for the violin, but then below that he very clearly indicated, sometimes, where the bow should change. Mahler scores are inundated with expression marks from bar to bar, sometimes three different expression marks for one note. He did it because he was a conductor. He knew how much this editing helped a performance. Much of it must have come out of performances, and it helps. But Ives didn't have the experience of performances, and this is part of the problem. And if his music is played literally, without expression marks because he didn't put them in, and without the sectional rehearsals that would clarify each part, then the result is an undifferentiated mass of sound, and people may think this is the way Ives is supposed to sound.

The reason my recorded performance sounds so clear is that I took the trouble to put bowings in and to clarify it. I did not simplify it. I did help the players to this extent—that whenever they had complicated rhythms, I put lines on top, showing where the beat falls. And I put dynamics in, many of which were missing from the parts, and added dynamics of my own to balance the piece. In parts of the second and fourth movements, for example, Ives has everyone playing every note in the scale, and in all kinds of rhythms, and the result is, you don't understand a thing. I don't think Ives meant that; I think he would have wanted at least half of it to come out in the foreground. So I helped a little bit with the dynamics, the way one does with a Beethoven symphony, or even a Brahms or Bruckner symphony, where everything is marked *forte* in the score, or everything is marked *piano,* but if you do it that way, it will never come out right; a brass instrument is louder than a flute.

Piano means a different thing when it's written for a trumpet . . .

That's right. Now, I had never conducted the piece on my own—as opposed to being second conductor—before the recording. A week before the recording, I was engaged to conduct a concert in Poland, with the best Polish orchestra, the Katowice Radio-Television Philharmonic, and I had this sudden idea that I might suggest replacing *The Rite of Spring* on the program with the Ives Fourth. And they agreed.

They presumably didn't know what they were getting themselves in for.

They didn't. I was in Germany when I cabled them; I was conducting, of all things, *Traviata*, at the Cologne Opera, and I was spending every free minute on the Ives parts. I remember I had a deadline for sending them by air to London, as I wanted the London Philharmonic to have them a week before rehearsals started so the musicians could study them. My whole room in the apartment in Cologne was filled with parts. I was working on the harp parts up to the very last minute. I barely made the flight.

It meant that I couldn't use the LPO set of parts in Poland. In Poland I had to use an uncorrected set of parts, and the set arrived without the piano parts, which are extremely difficult, so I telephoned New York to get the piano parts, but some orchestra that had played it before hadn't returned them. The publisher didn't have the crucial piano parts, so the librarians in Poland stayed up all night and, from the score, copied these piano parts, which are like large books—they're as thick as three Beethoven piano sonatas. I had three days of rehearsals for the Ives Fourth, and my program was the Ives Fourth, Brahms Violin Concerto, and *Daphnis* Second Suite. But it's a wonderful orchestra, and of those three days my first day was devoted to sectional rehearsals. They weren't as extensive as in London. I had to do it all in one day with the Katowice orchestra, but it worked. And even with an uncorrected set of parts—we fixed as many mistakes as we could—they did wonderfully. I was grateful for the opportunity to have done the Ives Fourth once myself before I recorded it in London.

In Poland I used the assistant concertmaster to lead the "collapse" section in the second movement, and I used a local composer to conduct the percussion in the last movement; those two cannot be done without in a concert performance. But for the London sessions, I simply recorded it twice myself. I had a second conductor stand by, an English composer, because I didn't know until the recording session how we were going to do it, and it all worked out as we were doing it. We decided that the most important thing was to do a quadraphonic version, because at that time quadraphonic records were coming into their own; so for the quadraphonic version especially we recorded the brass interruption orchestra separately, and then it was super-imposed. And if you hear the quad version, it's ten times more exciting than the stereo version. Another thing we superimposed was the percussion in the last movement. I decided to record the percussion separately and then add it, and to this day we can't understand how it worked. We only did one take, and it worked, to the second. That's how it was done with a sole conductor. And over the whole piece, we worked so quickly, as a result of the sectional rehearsals, that we finished the recording in four sessions instead of the five RCA had allocated.

You spoke earlier of learning "to make the best" of the work's shifts of style. As a conductor, preparing a performance, considering your conception of the work, considering your interpretation of it, do you do anything special, anything specific, in response to this particular stylistic characteristic? You accept a composer's disunity of style; therefore, do you enhance disunity of style? You don't play it down, but do you perhaps play it up in performance?

That's an interesting question. I have not done so. I have played it as is. Well, I play it up—you're perhaps right, after all. In other words, I don't try to make the third movement "fit" by trying to make it sound more modern than it is. In fact, I play it as Romantic music, as it is written, with full emphasis on the Baroque turns. I make my strings vibrate for all they're worth.

One other thing we did in the recording may be relevant here. In the third movement we used a real organ—in the Stokowski recording he'd had to use a little Hammond electric organ—and the entrance of the organ, in the quadraphonic version, is spellbinding, because it was like a church organ. Suddenly, from one speaker, you hear the sound of the organ—it's another interruption. And in the second movement, it's the only recording that has a quartertone piano. Neither the Stokowski nor the Ozawa used a quartertone piano. Ives wrote very clearly that, if no quartertone piano is available, the part should not be played at all, which makes sense. If you play it on a standard piano, the notes are different: it just makes no sense whatsoever; it's a different effect. If you listen to this section of the second movement with Stokowski, it's a regular piano tinkling away. I insisted on a quartertone piano, which doesn't exist in London, so we had a tuner pick up a small upright Steinway and retune it, and I had to write a special part for the pianist. And if you listen to it now, it's a section where the solo violin plays, and the quartertone piano is behind it, and it's fantastic. It's a section Ives wrote about: He pictured someone in a very crowded street and walking suddenly into a church, where the organ has been playing forever, for ages, and it's musty and dark; and you feel that in the music. It's really a wonderful tonal picture. And the quartertone piano pro-duces an effect that perhaps only one or two people may notice, but it's what Ives wanted. Yet this raises the whole question of literalness.

Conductors generally pride themselves on being literal: The more liter-ally you follow the score, within an artistic frame, the better you are. Now, I feel that Ives couldn't have cared less about artists who try to be literal; in fact, he poked fun at them. He felt that the artist should interpret music freely within the dictates of the score. And being a composer myself, I know how important it is to take the composer's words with a grain of salt and to inter-pret. On the opening page of the Fourth Symphony, Ives makes what could be construed as a joke: For the choral part, he writes, "Preferably without voices." Well, if you have a conductor who wants to do it exactly the way the composer wanted, what to do there?

In some pieces, Ives gives the conductor a choice of instruments: in one case, saxophone or bells or piano! Can you think of three more different in-struments? How are you going to be literal? This is in *From the Steeples and the Mountains*, one of his best pieces. He has a choice of instruments to use for bells—a carillon or a piano. Can you imagine a piano playing in place of bells? In *The Unanswered Question* you can use either four flutes or a variety of other instruments. So, in a way, much of the time he's writing in the abstract, al-most—and this should not be a sacrilegious comparison—but almost as Bach wrote *The Art of Fugue*, which is really in the abstract. In the second movement of the Ives Fourth Symphony, again, the conductor has the option of either a bassoon or a saxophone. Stokowski used both playing together—he couldn't make up his mind—and that adds to the muddiness of the movement. Since Ives gave the option, I decided that sometimes the saxophone gives a more interesting sound for a particular passage, sometimes the bassoon. I used both, but separately. I helped what Ives had in mind, because he really couldn't make up his mind, except in one passage where it's specifically saxophone.

I think it's important to be conscious of how recent the idea of
literal adherence to scores is—the result of one or two artists' work
in the twentieth century rather than a sort of law that goes back through
the nineteenth century. There is, in fact, a paradox involved in this,
because if you are faithful to the letter of a nineteenth-century score,
you can for that very reason be unfaithful to the spirit,
since the composer expected you to use your imagination.

Yes, exactly—you're right. Ives was still in many ways a nineteenth-century composer, a nineteenth-century composer gone wild. Don't forget that when

Ives was beginning to compose his imaginative modern works—so called—the latest composers known to him were Brahms, Tchaikovsky, and Wagner was beginning to be popular in America; this was in the 1880s. And so, it's even incredible that he could come up with these fantastic, wild ideas. He was still, though, at heart, in many ways a nineteenth-century composer. He was fighting Romanticism by breaking with everything. In the structural sphere, this made his forms very free, and this in turn makes his music very difficult to interpret, because one of the ways a performer makes up his interpretation of a work is by shaping the form.

This is the way I do it: I study the form of a work, after studying the harmony, the orchestration, and it gives me the speed of it; it gives me the breadth of it and the way I want to make an impact with it. It gives me the way to present it. The only other composer with whom I've had a similarly difficult experience with form was Delius, when I conducted his Violin Concerto in Liverpool on a few hours' notice without ever having conducted a note of his before. The quickest way to learn a score is to find the form: identify the main entrances, and develop an idea of the piece. I couldn't figure out the form of the Delius Violin Concerto on just a few minutes' notice.

There isn't one.

Now, with Ives, I've tried unsuccessfully to come up with the form in many of the works. What I've come up with is some idea of what went through his mind, and in many instances I think it's like a written-out, carefully thought-out improvisation, in which ideas sometimes recur—A, B, C *do* come back once in a while, but not as part of a consciously determined, *a priori* form. In this context, the first movement of the Fourth Symphony is the closest to a simple A-B-A form, but only because, as you mentioned before, it starts off softly and slowly, and it ends softly and slowly. The third movement is more classical and can be pinned down to some sort of form. He calls it a fugue, but it is not actually a fugue, though it has fugal entrances. It's no more a fugue than the last section of Verdi's *Falstaff* is a fugue. And the last movement is a fantasy, a very free form, like the second movement. The string quartets and the piano sonatas are in very free forms. Some of the songs have simpler A-B-A-C-A form. But, in general, the freedom of form is something that makes Ives particularly difficult to conduct. What helps sometimes is following the speed changes, which are so clearly indicated and thus contribute to bringing whatever form exists to the fore. I'd like to emphasize, finally, that I don't consider myself more of an Ives expert than a Schubert expert and, if anything, I consider myself perhaps a Tchaikovsky expert. I do more Tchaikovsky than anything else.

Well, everybody's entitled to some eccentricity.

No, what I'm trying to say applies, with all respect, to my eminent colleagues too. Haitink, for example, is a great Mahlerian, but he also does many other composers very well. I would say that I conduct Ives the way I conduct any other composer. There is no question that when I do, let's say, Schubert, I can't help it, I have a different frame of mind from when I conduct Mozart. Then again, recently I conducted a concert of nothing but Mozart and Schubert, and the next concert was nothing but Tchaikovsky and Stravinsky, and it was so different, it was like a different world; it was almost like changing professions. When I conduct Ives, I don't apply any specific secret ideas, but there are specific things about Ives that come through: one can't help it. When I do Prokofiev, there is a percussive quality that comes through, and an edge, an angular quality, which also comes through in Stravinsky, and in many works it comes through in Ives. And when performing Ives I try to bring out the humor.

The José Serebrier Ives discography is regrettably brief but precisely pertinent to our chapter. It consists of the two recordings of the Fourth Symphony discussed at length above: The 1965 Stokowski version on Columbia/CBS, in which Serebrier served as second conductor, and Serebrier's own "solo" version on RCA, released for the Ives centenary celebration in 1974, and currently available on several labels, and his first GRAMMY nomination for "Best Classical Recording of the Year."

Columbia Publishing Company (reprinted with permission).

• 4 •

Composer's Notes

SONATA FOR VIOLIN SOLO, OP. 1 (1948)

I had only taken a few violin lessons when I began writing the first segments of the sonata. At the time, I had no idea what a sonata was nor any other musical form—or key relationships or anything else about music theory. The piece evolved purely out of intuition. Many years later, after it was published, I was surprised to hear that a class at a university in Texas had made a special analysis of it, which went on for many pages, discussing the formal structure and the key relationships. This essay was published in 1965. There are indeed some things that can be analyzed, as an afterthought. The opening melodic line, which recurs from time to time, has a modal quality. The piece seems to evolve naturally, developing a form of its own, like a well-planned improvisation. The appoggiatura over a major seventh chord, which becomes a recurring element, would later become almost obsessive in many of my early works. The piece is quite difficult to perform, making virtuosic demands at every stage. I quoted extensively from this sonata in my *Winter* Violin Concerto, more than forty years later, to tie a full circle between my earliest and a more recent work for the violin.

ELEGY FOR STRINGS (1952)

This piece was premiered in Belho Horizonte, Brazil, conducted by my composition teacher, Guido Santórsola. I did not hear that performance, but I was present when he conducted it in Montevideo a few weeks later.

To this day, I recall a local critic writing that he enjoyed this dark, brooding piece but that it had to be impersonal, because it seemed inconceivable to him that a fourteen-year-old boy living in Montevideo could write such sad, dark music. I do not recall if this critic had further opportunities to hear music that I wrote years later so he could reevaluate his first impression. The Elegy was my first orchestral essay, the second being a rather ambitious large-scale fantasy overture, *The Legend of Faust*, premiered two years later by Eleazar de Carvalho and the SODRE National Orchestra in Montevideo, after the work had won the local composition contest. The Elegy was a first in many ways for my beginnings as a composer. It was my first published composition—by the Pan American Union in Washington, DC, which in turn led to my lifelong relationship with Peermusic publishers. It was my first work to be heard abroad, with performances at Radio France in Paris, conducted by Juan Protasi, and a New York premiere at Carnegie Hall, conducted by Leopold Stokowski.

MOMENTO PSICOLÓGICO (1957)

Shortly after my arrival to the United States, I started my studies with Aaron Copland, and it was he who suggested the title for this enigmatic work. I had mentioned to Copland the motive behind this work: "There is that crucial moment in life when you must decide whether to make a left or a right turn, and that choice can shape your destiny." Copland replied, "It's a fateful, psychological moment." Scored for string orchestra, there is also a distant trumpet sound—just one note, always present, sometimes whispering, sometimes screaming.

PIANO SONATA (1957)

Composed while still studying at the Curtis Institute of Music in Philadelphia, the Sonata is conceived in the classic three-movement form—*allegro, andante, presto*—but it is anything but traditional. It was my first work to reflect veiled influences of Latin American rhythms, perhaps because of subconscious nostalgia. The driving third movement, Presto, has a distinctly Latin flavor. My only other work featuring piano was written in 2017 and 2018, *Symphonic B A C H Variations for Piano and Orchestra*, premiered in Dublin in 2018. This work reflects instead my Slavic background.

FANTASIA (1960)

After graduation from the University of Minnesota and Doráti's departure from Minneapolis, with my Guggenheim grants used up, life became a big question mark. While driving back to New York, I stopped for gas in a small city in upstate New York and saw a newspaper announcement that on that same evening the local orchestra was auditioning conductors. With a spirit of adventure, I called to ask if it was still possible to apply. The audition was successful, and I became music director of the Utica Symphony, a semipro-fessional orchestra. The position in Utica was so underpaid that the only housing I could afford was a little room at the YMCA. I think my salary was two thousand dollars per year. The position came as a package with a part-time assistant professor position at the local college to teach violin and composition, which paid some additional sum. This school, part of Syracuse University, used makeshift classrooms and was new and poor, but at least I had my own office and a school library room where I could compose. It was in this school library/cafeteria that I wrote every note of my *Fantasia* for String Quartet. The noise and the constant chatter failed to distract me. I enjoyed writing this piece, which I did on commission for the Harvard Musical As-sociation in Massachusetts. During my last months in Minneapolis, Mr. Doráti told me that he had noticed an announcement that this association had announced a competition to commission a string quartet. I applied for it and won the contest. The prize money was quite minimal, but it included a premiere by members of the Boston Symphony at the Harvard Musical As-sociation's beautiful salons at Harvard. The premiere, in the spring of 1961, was a wonderful event. The next time it was played was in Washington, DC, at the Inter-American Music Festival. I was unable to attend but was amused by the *Washington Post*'s review, which declared it an instant "hit," "a veritable *1812* of string quartets." That was not what I'd had in mind at all, but I was delighted that it had communicated so well. Later, Vladimir Lakond, editor at Peermusic, suggested a string orchestra version of it with double basses added, and he published both versions. As time passes, I still feel quite close to this piece, which poured out of my pen in less than a week.

After a short introduction that sets the mood, a folk-like melody of a melancholy nature is followed by a persistent solo violin that uses unexpected melodic and harmonic structures. This recurrent solo, a sort of devil's trill, is purposely out of place. Its closest "cousin" would be the solo violin in Mahler's Fourth Symphony—however, I did know this work at the time. The music goes back and forth in a truly improvisatory manner that justifies the title. The closest it comes to a set form is the recapitulation of the solo violin section, which leads to an unexpected, driven coda. This ending may come as a surprise, since the bulk of the piece is so lyrical. The title has to do with the free form of the piece, but it was also a kind of homage to Stokowski and Disney's wonderful film. When I wrote *Fantasia*, I had not yet started to work with Stokowski in New York—that would come eighteen months later—but he had already premiered two of my works, my first symphony and the *Elegy for Strings*.

VARIATIONS ON A THEME FROM CHILDHOOD,
for trombone and strings (1963)

During my first years with Stokowski's American Symphony Orchestra in New York, I was still writing music regularly, mostly encouraged by him and some of his best musicians. Stokowski had assembled an orchestra with some of the best freelance virtuoso musicians in the New York area. Two of the star performers were Paul Price, who commissioned my *Symphony for Percussion* for his Manhattan Percussion Ensemble, and Davis Shulman, who commissioned a work for trombone and strings. The *Variations on a Theme from Childhood* can be performed on trombone or bassoon. It requires a virtuoso of great technique. The strings are also stretched to the limits, with extremely high writing.

VOCALISE (ADAGIO) (1963)

The original version is *Vocalise* for choir a cappella, written when I was fifteen, as a follow-up to my only other choral piece, *Canción del Destino* (*Song of Destiny*). While planning a new recording project, the orchestra asked me to consider including a work of my own. They had given the premiere of my new Flute Concerto with Tango a few years ago. I decided to orchestrate for string ensemble my old *Vocalise* and renamed it *Adagio* to avoid confusion. Interestingly, I had not heard a single note of Rachmaninoff's music when I wrote my *Vocalise*, and indeed they are quite different. Yet there is some similarity of mood and spirit. A further coincidence is that year I was asked by the Russian National Orchestra to make a new orchestration of the Vocalise by Rachmaninoff for our concert and a live CD recording of the final event in Moscow of the First International Rostropovich Festival. My version has been published and the recording released. But this is the first recording of my own *Vocalise* (*Adagio*)—in any version. In its minimal duration, it paints a portrait of desolation, perhaps unexpected for a boy of fifteen, and the tempo indication at the start, which surprises me now just as much, indicates, "Slowly, and as sad as possible." I do not recall any particular reason why I wrote in that frame of mind, since I was a happy and contented teenager, but most if not all of my early works have that Slavic dark touch and an elegiac and nostalgic mood.

PASSACAGLIA AND PERPETUUM MOBILE,
for accordion and chamber orchestra (1966)

At about the same time as writing the *Variations on a Theme from Childhood* and the *Symphony for Percussion,* I received a commission from the American Accordionists Association, to write a work for accordion and chamber orchestra. The instrument was entirely foreign to me, but Elsie Bennett, longtime president of the organization and the brains behind their massive commissioning series, lent me an accordion, which I studied for weeks. It was a great challenge, because the chords provided by the buttons on the left side of the instrument were ready-set, giving the composer very little freedom for tonal imagination and variety. The instrument has since then been improved, and composers today do not have that problem. I gave the commissioning organization a bonus, a piece for solo accordion, which I wrote at the same time. Less than a week after I sent all the music to the AAA, after a rehearsal at Carnegie Hall, I went across the street from the stage door, on Fifty-Sixth Street, to Patelson's Music House. There in the window, displayed for all to see, was a published copy of my new work for solo accordion! I was stunned! The ink was still wet on the manuscript. I went inside and bought a couple of copies. Wladimir Lakond at Peermusic called the accordion publisher, Pagani, who simply said they just hadn't gotten around to sending the contract. That publishing firm has since ceased to exist.

NUEVE (1970), Concerto for double bass and orchestra

I wrote it for Gary Karr during my two seasons as composer-in-residence for the Cleveland Orchestra as a companion piece to my harp concerto *Colores Mágicos.* Both concertos have much in common: aleatoric writing, distance between the musicians, and, most disturbing for conductors, no bar lines at all. Conductors can't do what they do basically—beat time. The harp piece became a ballet with the Joffrey Ballet and toured the United States and Canada. In it, the only musician on the stage was the harp soloist, with the orchestra in the pit, like in an opera. In *Nueve*, the solo bass is surrounded by the string orchestra, while the only woodwinds, two clarinets, are "incognito" in the audience. During one of the variations, a jazz segment, the two clarinetists stand up and play along, surprising the unsuspecting audience. At the climax of the jazz variation, the brass erupts in the balcony. All along, the soloist also reads poetry, a poem by Shelley. While in the concerts the poetry reading was done beautifully by Gary Karr, for the recording he suggested it be done by an actor, and we had the great fortune to have the incomparable Simon Callow. At the end of *Nueve*, while the orchestra reaches a tremendous climax on one note in unison, a choir emerges in the distance and can be heard in an ethereal chant, adding an element of timelessness and perhaps eeriness. This is in direct contrast to the noisy jazz variation in which two opposite jazz drummers have a sort of "combat," alternating and finally joining in the game. The work has nine variations and uses mostly nine notes. The reason for the title and the concept was that my New York apartment was, and remains, on Ninety-Ninth Street, on the ninth floor. *Nueve*, of course, is Spanish for the number nine. While it may be a "period piece," unsurprising at the time it was conceived, something about its concept remains close to me and is not different in its ultimate message from previous or later works, regardless of the different musical language used.

COLORES MÁGICOS (1971), Concerto for harp and orchestra

It was during my years as composer-in-residence for the Cleveland Orchestra, when George Szell was conductor, that a member of the orchestra told me I should meet an inventor in Cleveland—Stanley Elliott—who had produced a magical machine that transformed musical sounds into the most colorful images. Having read so much about Scriabin and his interest in the combination of colors and music, I visited Mr. Elliott and was fascinated by his invention. At the same time I had a commission from Colonel Samuel Rosenbaum to write a concerto for his wife, Edna Phillips, the famous harpist of the Philadelphia Orchestra. He had already commissioned Ginastera, and mine was the second. This was a perfect opportunity, since the sound of the harp seemed to produce the most wonderful images on the Synchroma. *Colores Mágicos* was premiered in Washington, DC, by Heidi Lehwalder, using the Synchroma to project images on her and onto a screen on the stage. The orchestra was in the pit, while the soloist was the only person on stage. Mr. Elliott asked Ms. Lehwalder to wear a white suit so he could project images onto her, from a second machine he'd invented—a slide projector that came alive when the music started. The short concerto, about twelve minutes long, is a set of variations. It has been done often as a ballet. Nancy Allen, currently the celebrated solo harpist of the New York Philharmonic, performed it extensively with the Joffrey Ballet, at the New York City premiere, which I conducted, and all over the United States, conducted by Seymour Lipkin.

DOROTHY AND CARMINE! for flute and strings (1991)

When I first met this wonderful, colorful couple, Dorothy and Carmine, I was organizing Festival Miami. My composing time had by then been reduced to the wishful thinking of ideas, with no time left for writing them down. Every moment was taken up by organizational work for the new festival and guest conducting all over the world. This little essay, written to celebrate the marriage of longtime Miami friends Dorothy Traficante and Carmine Vlachos, is meant as a wedding gift rather than a musical picture. I experimented with sonorities by pairing strings with two wandering flutes, one of which appears out of nowhere in the audience, almost like a dancer who is sometimes invited to join the stage proceedings. The flutist is sitting in the audience, unbeknown to the public, and sometime toward the end of this puzzling—to me as well—piece, the flutist seems to get excited or inspired by the happenings onstage and starts playing. By the time the public becomes aware that an "intruder" is daring to interrupt the concert, the flutist stands and starts to walk toward the stage, all the while playing faster and faster until reaching the usual soloist's spot on the stage next to the conductor. After a brief climax, the flutist exits slowly to the backstage area and can still be heard repeating a haunting drone as the orchestra comments with background sounds. Finally, the sound of the flute can still be heard, but, magically, this time the sound comes from the back of the auditorium—or the balcony—as a second flutist echoes the dying notes of the first flute. Do not try to read any meaning behind the notes here—or in the other essay of this series. Listeners can make up their own storyline if it helps them enjoy the music.

VIOLIN CONCERTO, *WINTER* (1991)

Around Christmas in 1991, Michael Guttman approached me with an idea to record *The Four Seasons*, but not by Vivaldi. He knew only of two works:

the Milhaud and the Rodrigo. I was asked to locate an autumn and a winter concerto, but the search proved very frustrating. There are a number of works inspired by the seasons, but they are symphonies, ballets, oratorios, not violin concertos. Robert Matthew-Walker pointed out Chaminade's "Automne," but there was no winter. None of the prominent composers we approached would agree to compose a concerto in less than two or three years, so I had no choice but to write it myself. The concept and form of the work evolved, ironically, walking the beautiful white-sand beaches of Key Biscayne, Florida, at Christmas 1991. I had never meant to literally portray the season of winter. My winter concerto would have to be a poetic vision of winter, not so much the actual season as the winter of life, the time approaching death, when presumably all memories come back in a flash; when reality, futility, purpose, memories all mix in a mocking parade, a never-ending dream. The work starts with the solo violin cadenza, joined by the orchestral violins, barely audible. Toward the end of the cadenza, we hear a duo between the solo violin and the concertmaster, leading to the main portion of the work: a virtuoso, relentless *allegro*. At the climax, three great composers' visions of winter are quoted: first the introduction of Haydn's winter from the oratorio *The Seasons*, which harmonically fits the concerto like a glove. Next, that wonderful first page from Glazunov's "Winter," from the ballet *The Seasons*, which finally transforms itself into a heroic quote from Tchaikovsky's First Symphony, *Winter Reveries*. Throughout the concerto I have quoted my own first composition, the solo violin sonata, written at the age of nine. That quotation became the main element of the work, from which everything else evolved. Since the concept of "movements," as in classical/Romantic works, no longer applies, the work was composed in one movement. The concerto ends triumphantly, with a flourish.

NIGHT CRY (1994)

In a note in his diary, painter Edvard Munch wrote, "I was walking along a path with friends; the sun was setting; suddenly the sky turned blood red; I paused and leaned on the fence; there was blood and tongues of fire above the blue-black fjord and the city; my friends walked on, and I stood there trembling with anxiety, and I sensed an infinite scream passing through nature." This impression inspired the creation of one of the most recognizable paintings in the world. The original German title given to the work by Munch was *Der Schrei der Natur—The Scream of Nature*—although it is best known as *The Scream* or *The Cry*. During a trip to Norway, I was captivated by Munch's painting and inspired to compose a short "musical essay" on the experience. *Night Cry* is not a description of the work so much as a fleeting musical thought on the powerful impression created by the painting. *Night Cry* is written for the typical forces of the brass section in a symphony orchestra that have been divided into three groups. The only musicians on stage are two trumpets, one horn, and one tuba. Another horn and trombone perform offstage, and two trumpets, one horn, and one trombone play from the balcony behind the audience. The antiphonal nature of the music pays homage to the brass choir works of Italian renaissance composer Giovanni Gabrieli (1554–1612). Similar to the call-and-response choral style of much of Gabrieli's music, the balcony group in *Night Cry* answers the other two ensembles. While each of the three groups speaks in a different musical language, they sometimes interact and imitate each other. Throughout this interplay, even within moments of respite, a thread of quiet angst is palpable. It is the unshakeable feeling that is also at the very core of the suppressed scream in Munch's masterpiece.

WINTERREISE (1999)

The genesis of this piece goes back to 1991, when I was commissioned to write a violin concerto. The concerto had to be the last piece of a puzzle. Violinist Michael Guttman's idea was to record music reflecting the four seasons—not Vivaldi's, but by twentieth-century composers. We had Rodrigo's *Summer Concerto*, Milhaud's *Spring Concerto*, and eventually we found an Autumn, a salon piece for violin by Chaminade. I was asked to write a winter concerto to complete the cycle. The concept and form of the work evolved, rather ironically, while walking on the beautiful white-sand beaches of Key Biscayne, Florida, at Christmas that year. I had never meant to literally portray the season of winter. My winter concerto would have to be a poetic vision of winter—not so much the actual season, but the winter of life, the time approaching death, when presumably all memories come back in a flash; when reality, futility, purpose, memories all mix in a mocking parade, a never-ending dream. I could not write it fast enough. It was my first large-scale orchestral work in several decades, but I seemed to take off where I had left before. There was a major change in approach. Thanks to the more open times, I now felt free to write as I felt. The Violin Concerto was played in New York, Miami, London, and Madrid within a short time and published both by Peermusic, which printed score and parts, and by Kalmus, which printed a violin and piano reduction. Since that time, Kalmus has ceased operations. The Violin Concerto was recorded with the Royal Philharmonic Orchestra and Michael Guttman. From the start I felt that the concerto contained the roots of a purely symphonic piece, a short, impulsive utterance based on the same idea. When Reference Recordings approached me about recording my music, I went back to that initiative and produced *Winter's Journey*, the title I gave it originally. To give it Schubert's title was daring, but in time the piece became *Winterriese*, like some people's names become them. The piece quotes almost every composer but Schubert. Toward the climax of the piece, the first quote is from Haydn—"Winter" from *The Seasons*—which has a mysterious ambience. Then there is a heroic quote from Glazunov—"Winter" from *The Seasons*—in counterpoint with Tchaikovsky's first symphony, *Winter Dreams*. Eventually, all three tunes appear together. If one listens carefully, the "Dies Irae" can also be heard toward the end, evolving naturally from the Haydn quotation. The piece is like a train ride, when one rides backward and all images fly by slightly distorted, never to return. All the trees are covered with snow, and the lakes are frozen. Icicles cling to the train's windows. There is no sky; everything seems blinding white.

TANGO IN BLUE (2001) AND *CASI UN TANGO* (2002)

While on tour in Germany with the Bamberger Symphony Orchestra, I was asked to do an unusual program with the Tchaikovsky Fourth Symphony, preceded by tangos by Kurt Weill, Stravinsky, and Piazzola. Rob Suff, who had just produced my Tchaikovsky recordings for BIS, witnessing the enthusiastic audience reaction, proposed that we make a recording of tangos by these and other composers. We proceeded to put together a mixed bag, from the German and French periods, of Kurt Weill to Stravinsky's peculiar take on the form, Satie's minimalist "perpetual" tango, which I orchestrated, and Gade's flamboyant, popular "Tango Tzigane." Piazzola could not be left out. My own contributions to the genre were conceived before this recording was planned. *Tango in Blue* was written during the long overnight flight from New York to Montevideo as an impromptu gift for the SODRE—the National Orchestra—of Uruguay, who had invited me to conduct their anniversary concert. It didn't have a title, and we performed it as an encore. I asked the public for title suggestions and was soon inundated with names, none of which seemed right. For a while it was called *Last Tango before Sunrise*, which seemed to capture the character of the piece, but I decided to save that title for a future tango. My favorite was *Blue Tango*, until I was reminded that there are at least two pieces with that name. Then a friend suggested a compromise, which I liked best, and *Tango in Blue* was born. The first four notes are a direct quote from the final four notes of my *Partita*,

Symphony No. 2, as if I were saying that that's where I'd left off, and I am back. *Partita* was one of the few compositions—written soon after my arrival in the United States—that used Latin American rhythms and melodic turns. After writing experimental works during the sixties and seventies, it was a challenge to go back to basics and write a simple tonal tune, a sort of popular piece for concert use. I had great fun composing *Tango in Blue* and was thrilled to find it so successful. After Montevideo, we played it in Lima, Buenos Aires, São Paulo, and many other cities, on tour with the National Chamber Orchestra of Toulouse. At my publishers' request, I wrote several versions of it, for violin and piano, string quartet, saxophone quartet, string orchestra, and other formations. *Casi un Tango (Almost a Tango)*, written shortly after, follows an entirely different concept, nostalgic and more "classical," for English horn solo and strings. The publishers have also printed versions for several other solo instruments—saxophone, French horn, bassoon, flute, violin, solo piano, and so on.

CARMEN SYMPHONY (2004) Georges Bizet—José Serebrier
Latin GRAMMY for Best Recording of the Year, 2004

Georges Bizet was thirty-six years old when *Carmen* opened in Paris. He died three months later, believing that his last opera had failed completely. His early compositions showed originality and a great ability in orchestration, an example being the beautiful Symphony in C written at age seventeen, but it was at the end of his short life that he truly found his innovative voice. The most successful opera composers in France at the time were Daniel-François Auber, Jacques Offenbach, and Giacomo Meyerbeer, and some of their influence can be observed in Bizet's early works. He was twenty-two when he received his first opera commission for *Les Pêcheurs de Perles*. It came after spending three years in Italy, the result of winning the coveted Grand Prix de Rome.

Five years after marrying Geneviève Halévy, daughter of his former teacher, Bizet received the *Carmen* libretto, prepared by Ludovic Halévy—his cousin by marriage—and Henri Meilhac and based on the book by Prosper Mérimée. Bizet seemed extremely happy with the libretto submitted to him by the Opéra-Comique but totally unprepared for the negative public reaction to his opera. Even though some of the most unsavory characters in Mérimée's story—such as Carmen's husband, García le Borgne—had been removed by the librettists, the subject and goings-on were still offensive to the bourgeois Parisians of the day. On the night of the premiere, the final curtain was greeted with complete silence. Bizet was devastated. A few months later, he had a heart attack, followed by a second one the next day. He died at midnight, just as *Carmen* was ending its thirty-first performance at the Opéra Comique. Upon hearing it in Paris, Piotr Ilyich Tchaikovsky announced that "in a few years *Carmen* will be the most popular opera in the world." Franz Liszt and Richard Wagner heard the Vienna production, which had removed the original spoken dialogues between scenes and incorporated in their place the new recitatives composed by Ernest Guiraud. The spoken conversations of the original version were the practice of the Opéra-Comique, but grand opera required musical continuity with sung *recitativi*. With the 1875 Vienna production, just months after the disastrous Paris premiere, *Carmen* was on its way to fulfilling Tchaikovsky's prediction. By 1878 *Carmen* was already being heard in London and New York—in Italian! It was produced in several German opera houses before it was revived in Paris in 1883. The new Paris version was watered down by the head of the Opéra-Comique, making it less provocative and controversial to avoid offending his public. Meanwhile, in the rest of Europe, Friedrich Nietzsche and Otto von Bismarck were attending the opera dozens of times and writing about its wonders. As was the custom of the times, the opera was translated into many languages, including Japanese, Chinese, and Hebrew. Although Paris eventually warmed up to it, rather slowly, *Carmen* in time became a national symbol, and by the time of Bizet's centenary, in 1938, Paris could boast having done over two thousand performances of the opera.

It is assumed that William Shakespeare never went to Italy, and yet reading *Romeo and Juliet* makes you wonder. Wolfgang Amadeus Mozart never visited Turkey, but *Abduction from the Seraglio* takes you right into the Topkapi Palace. Bizet never went to Spain. In fact, it seems he was never south of Bordeaux, but his portrayal of Spanish life and music, and his understanding of the gypsies there, is instinctive and real. For many years several record companies had been suggesting that I record the orchestral music from *Carmen* in my own version. I never paid much attention to this idea, simply because I did not see a need for it. In fact, I had recorded the well-known orchestral suites years ago in Australia for an American label that was trying to foster the Soundstream digital system, which at the time was considered a pioneer in digital recording. Recently, when BIS suggested I conduct a Bizet recording with the Barcelona Symphony Orchestra, the orchestral music from *Carmen* was proposed again with the understanding that I would produce a "new" version. At this point I decided to look once again at the existing suites and see what, if anything, was wrong with them. The answer was obvious: One of the suites was anonymous, and both in the wrong order, lacking the masterful continuity of the original and thus having little to do with the story line of the opera. The orchestration of the vocal numbers in the two existing suites reveals many problems. For example, the "Toreador Song," performed by a baritone, had been given to a trumpet, which is in the wrong register and has the wrong character for that song. The "Habanera," which must retain the vocal freedom and subtlety of the mezzo-soprano voice, is given to an entire violin section, which is not quite as free as a single instrument. However, I postponed the project for some time. While I had visualized the entire production and chosen the orchestral fragments, I could not see a way to make a purely symphonic version of the final scene; it made no sense without the voices. Thus, my thesis of making a suite in the actual order of the drama would not work. Without an ending I could not see myself even starting the project, and it was abandoned for a while. With time, however, I began to accept the fact that I would have to compromise and make a suite that followed the order of the opera except for the final number, for which I chose the fiery gypsy dance that opens act 2. This was a different experience from making a symphonic synthesis of Leoš Janáček's *Makropulos Case*, the most difficult of such assignments. This extraordinary opera has no orchestral segments, and, as my friend Oliver Knussen quipped when he saw me struggling with it, "it is the most unsuitable of operas." I was quite apprehensive when recording and releasing this orchestral version of the opera, and no one was more surprised than I when the orchestra in Brno, which knew the opera intimately, loved my new symphonic synthesis and quickly incorporated it into their permanent repertoire.

Similar to my orchestrations of Edvard Grieg's songs or George Gershwin's preludes, I decided to keep the *Carmen* pieces sounding as if Bizet had done them, staying as close as possible to the original. Thus, the orchestral interludes are left intact, except for crucial editorial markings to facilitate performance, such as phrasings, balance indications for the brass, string bowings, and so on. While adding several sections that didn't appear in the existing two suites, I felt it necessary to drop others, such as Micaëla's aria, which I felt really needed the human voice. Before recording the piece in Barcelona, I performed it in concert with the Royal Philharmonic Orchestra in London, which gave me an opportunity to find out how it worked and if it required further changes. Before the recording, last-minute adjustments were still being made with the faithful assistance of the tireless former librarian of the RPO, my dear friend Terence Leahy. At the same time, I happened to read an editorial article in the magazine *Opera*, questioning why no one had ever done a proper orchestral suite of *Carmen*, giving all the same reasons I have mentioned above, and many others. I was surprised and delighted; the article appeared as the recording was taking place. Some time earlier I had come across another article that had derided the "*Carmen* industry" and all the arrangers who had made rhapsodies for solo instruments, various ballets, opera derivations, and so on. Obviously, the universal fascination with the opera was very much alive. I decided to call my transcription a symphony. "What is a symphony?" asks American composer Ned Rorem. "Symphony is whatever you call it," he says. "A symphony of Mahler is not the same as a symphony of Bach or Haydn." Early on I decided not to call this version a suite so as not to confuse it with the existing two suites. The work is constructed in twelve "scenes" rather than twelve movements, which made more sense for segments taken from an opera.

THEY RODE INTO THE SUNSET: MUSIC FOR AN IMAGINARY FILM (2008)

Just before Christmas 2008 I had a call from Mumbai, asking if I would be willing to compose the music for a film that required Western music, a most unusual case, since Indian movies traditionally use their own music. The director of the film, Vivek Agnihotri, who was also its scriptwriter, sent me the script and asked to come and see me. We met in New York a few days later, and he explained that for three or four of the scenes they would need the music right away, before the film was even made, and those scenes would be choreographed to the music.

We read the script and mapped the sections and decided on timings. It all sounded exciting, as writing for the movies has been a secret ambition of mine since I'd started to compose, and this project seemed made in heaven. The film was to end with what the director called "a symphony," a twelve-minute orchestral work, which I would conduct, playing myself. The script depicted a young Indian composer who had studied in London, but, suffering from a syndrome that eventually paralyzed his entire body, he dictated this "symphony" from his hospital bed. The piece would include elements from several key scenes of his life. The music was needed within weeks, so I worked furiously to meet the deadline. However, just as it was to be recorded in London, the workers in Bollywood went on a long strike, and most films had to be canceled, including this one. The film was never made.

LAMENTS AND HALLELUJAHS (2018)

I have avoided using opus numbers to list my works. Instead, I indicate the year of composition. I have done this after the publication of my first work,

Sonata for Solo Violin, which I wrote at age nine. *Laments and Hallelujahs* was commissioned by Saint Martha Concerts as part of its Martha and Mary Meditations series. My original working title was simply "Meditation," but as the work took shape it evolved into an expression of sadness, lamentations, and eventually redemption, like the morning after, the sun rising, new life, and hope. Music, while able to create emotions and feelings, is essentially an abstract art, much more so than visual arts. In a simplistic way, one could argue that minor keys denote sadness or melancholy, while major tonalities can reflect good humor; but in actuality, it's much more complicated. When music accompanies a film, it seldom tells the story, because it would in effect conflict with the visual. The best film music only enhances the scenes, and at its best it stays out of the way, just adding that crucial mood element. A great exception is Prokofiev's *Alexander Nevsky*, because the music and the film were constructed simultaneously, frame by frame. And yet the score has a concert life of it's own, a true masterpiece. A unique case.

In the Baroque era, there are a few examples of works reflecting specific themes—Vivaldi's *Four Seasons* being a prime example. But it doesn't tell a story. It reflects moods. Similarly, Bach's deeply religious works are perfect examples of abstract works inspired by religious themes. In the Romantic era, one finds more descriptive works. In *Francesca da Rimini* Tchaikovsky intends to describe with sounds the short paragraph in Dante's novel that fascinated so many Romantic era artists. But even in this electrifying work, what one hears is a picture in sounds, not a specific story. Tchaikovsky's *Manfred Symphony* is another great example. It's a symphonic work inspired by Byron's story, not retelling the story in sounds. That is the case with my *Laments and Hallelujahs*. Like with Tchaikovsky's Sixth Symphony, each listener is left to create his or her own images. The music is highly evocative, but it does not follow a "story line." It was inspired by that short paragraph in the Bible when Jesus visits Martha and Mary, Lazarus's sisters, and the mystery of what happens afterward. The mystery stays in the music, with those ethereal sounds at the end that echo in the distance as the work seems to end but it dissipates into space . . .

SYMPHONIC *B A C H VARIATIONS* FOR PIANO AND ORCHESTRA (2017–2018)

This is a piano concerto comprised of four variations performed without pause, based on the four notes B (B-flat)–A–C–H (B natural). Although the note names are not specifically a reference to Bach, there is of course a symbolic relation, and this four-note sequence has been used by countless composers before. I purposely stayed away from such pieces while composing this work, trying to have a fresh perspective. Each of the four variations is somewhat similar in approach and in the relentless use of the four-note sequence. *Symphonic B A C H Variations* was co-commissioned by the American Composers Orchestra in New York, with which I have a long relationship, and the BIS record label of Sweden. The recording continues a history of many collaborations with BIS, including a Tchaikovsky series, a Latin GRAMMY–winning CD of the Bizet-Serebrier *Carmen Symphony*. The concerto was composed for French pianist Alexandre Kantarow.

CANDOMBE, for flute and orchestra (2019)

In the seventeenth and eighteenth centuries, Africans sold as slaves took the candombe percussion patterns to Uruguay, Argentina, Brazil, and even Cuba, where it developed different rhythms. It became adopted especially in Uruguay, later modifying into milonga, itself a predecessor of the tango. Candombe, milonga, and tango originated from the same African roots, but tango adopted its name and pulsation from Spain. Candombe still exists in Uruguay, especially during Carnival, when amazing drummers parade with their collection of drums played with bare hands. My own *Candombe* is just an homage to the genre, contrasting the broken rhythm with melodic turns. It was written especially for the recording with the Málaga Philharmonic Orchestra, which includes my three previous attempts at concert tangos.

WINDANCE, for strings (2019)

When planning a string-ensemble recording of music by Manuel de Falla, we encountered very few original works for strings and added music by his friends and contemporaries. I was asked to contribute an homage, and the result is this brief *Windance*. The title, combining the words *wind* and *dance*, was chosen because at the end I quote one of the short phrases from the "Ritual Fire Dance" by Manuel de Falla, and instead of fire I emphasize the wind.

THE YEAR 2020, for woodwind quintet (2020)

Two thousand twenty was an enigmatic, unforgettable year for everyone in the entire world, even more so perhaps than the world wars. Even as horrible as those wars were, they did not affect every human being on the entire planet as the pandemic of the year 2020 has. The title of the opening section in this quintet, "In Memoriam: The Death of George Floyd and Countless Others," speaks for itself. The middle section, *"Windance* Revisited," is a reimagined version of my *Windance* for strings, originally a tribute to the music of Manuel de Falla. This section is meant to provide a respite from the doleful first and last segments. The finale, "The Year 2020," is an elegy—a questioning cry.

NOSTALGIA, for solo viola (2020)

This heartfelt musical moment was written expressly for a BIS recording by Berlin-based violist Hiyoli Togawa. Her idea was to portray in sound the isolation felt by humanity during the 2020 pandemic, when life as we knew it suddenly stopped. We experienced helplessness but felt moved to look deeply into our souls and develop an enhanced sense of compassion. In the few brief notes of this song, aided by the special sound of the viola, I spontaneously tried to express the longing, and sometimes the hope, amid the seclusion experienced by everyone in the world.

THE SYMPHONIES

SYMPHONY No. 1, in one movement (1956)

The story behind my first symphony goes back all the way to my last years in Montevideo, Uruguay, before going to the United States to study at Tanglewood and at the Curtis Institute of Music in Philadelphia. Anxious to conduct, I had organized in Montevideo a youth orchestra, which gave concerts all over the country with ambitious programs. In our first concert we performed the four Bach orchestral suites! I convinced the teenage musicians to memorize the music, which took months of rehearsals. I was eleven years old at the time. Four years later, I read an announcement in the press about a composition contest for an orchestral work. The winning piece would be played by the national symphony, known as OSSODRE. I thought that, if I won, perhaps they would let me conduct it, which was by then my main interest. For some unknown reasons, the announcement was made at the very last moment, with only a couple of weeks' advance notice. I worked day and night on this, my first full orchestral work. Inspired by Thomas Mann's *Doctor Faustus*, which fascinated me at the time, *The Legend of Faust* was to be an overture-fantasy in the pattern of Tchaikovsky's works of the same genre. I remember my parents not actually worried but alarmed at seeing me work all day and night for the final five days to meet the deadline. Literally, I didn't sleep for four nights while working on my first orchestral essay. I finished the score in a taxi on my way to meet the deadline, which was on a Saturday at noon. Upon arrival, I was told I should have put my name in a notarized and sealed envelope with only a pseudonym on the score. The nice lady waited for me to run to a notary and return much later and accepted the application at the last minute with a welcome smile.

To my amazement, I won the competition, but being sixteen, the task of conducting this overture was given to a famous guest conductor, Eleazar de Carvalho, who had been Koussevitzky's pupil alongside Leonard Bernstein. It was a wonderful coincidence, because I had already been accepted as his conducting pupil at Tanglewood for later that summer.

In between, I had attended a lecture by Virgil Thomson. The *New York Herald Tribune* had just folded, and its famous music critic, composer Virgil Thomson, had been awarded a consolation prize in the form of a US State Department–sponsored tour of Latin America to conduct his own compositions. The only country that would not invite him to conduct, nor to include his music in concerts, was Uruguay. I remember the artistic director of the orchestra telling me that Thomson's music was "too simplistic." Later, when I got to know and admire his music, I could easily see that this apparent simplicity was no less than Satie's or, many decades later, many minimalists' "simplicity." Thomson knew very well what he was doing. Nevertheless, in Montevideo his appearance was relegated to giving a lecture. Organized by the US Embassy, the lecture was only attended by three people—it was a terribly rainy night—my parents and me. None of us understood English, and he must have sensed it, because after fifteen minutes he abruptly left the stage, mumbling something that sounded like, "This is absurd." I had my scores with me and was hoping to give them to him: a new saxophone quartet, a woodwind quintet, and my *Elegy for Strings*, which had already been performed in Paris by Radio France and in Brazil, conducted by my teacher, Guido Santórsola. Obviously peeved by the reception he had been given in Uruguay, and the poor attendance at his lecture, Mr. Thomson dismissed my offer of scores and refused to shake hands. The cultural attaché, James Webb, smiled and asked if he could keep my manuscript scores and give them to Mr. Thomson later. The Cultural Affairs Officer, named Elizabeth Taylor (!), said she would make sure Thomson looked at them in his hotel before his morning departure for New York. By midmorning I had a phone call. We had no telephone at home—which was not unusual in those days in Uruguay; you had to know government officials to qualify for a phone. We managed by using one of the nearby shops. This call came through the grocery store across the street. It was from Virgil Thomson, aided by Ms. Taylor, who translated. He wanted to know if he could take all my scores back home with him to show them to Aaron Copland, Eugene Ormandy—so he could recommend me to study at the Curtis Institute—and Howard Hanson to see if would be interested to teach me at the Eastman School in Rochester. I could not believe my luck!

Less than a month later, I had been accepted both by the Curtis Institute and the Eastman School, and I had to make a difficult decision. All of my father's side of the family had gone from Russia to Philadelphia, so that was a deciding factor. Besides, my composition teacher, the man who accepted me at Curtis, was Bohuslav Martinů, who wrote me amazing letters of welcome. By the time I arrived at Curtis in September 1956, Martinů had left and moved permanently to Switzerland, but that is another story. At Curtis I had a wonderful composition teacher, more like a friend, in Vittorio Giannini, who was also the main composition teacher at Juilliard. All that was made possible thanks to Webb and Taylor, who helped me apply for a US State Department fellowship to pay for my trip and studies. It was a one-year grant, which was generously renewed for a second year. Tanglewood also gave me a full fellowship and the Koussevitzky Award to study conducting with Eleazar de Carvalho and composition with Aaron Copland. One of my classmates in composition was Einojuhani Rautavaara, who would become a lifelong friend. My conducting classmate was Seiji Ozawa, also a longtime friend and colleague. That first summer at Tanglewood was idyllic. My English was still very primitive, so I didn't learn much, except by osmosis. At the end of the six-week summer experience, I went to New York for a month to await the start of my first year at the Curtis Institute in Philadelphia. During those four weeks I worked intensely and wrote my first symphony. I was sixteen. It was my second orchestral work, my first symphony. Together with my earlier saxophone quartet, the symphony went on to win a BMI—Broadcast Music Incorporated—Award in 1956. I had decided to write a one-movement symphony, with connected multiple sections in different speeds, since I felt that the idea of a multiple-movement symphony of largely unrelated sections no longer applied in the middle of the twentieth century. Anyway, that was the way I felt at the time. I had had very little exposure to contemporary music, except for the festival of American music I had organized in Montevideo the year before, in which I had included everything from Varese to Cage. They both fascinated me. Curiously, I had not discovered Ives just yet.

The following year—1957—while running late toward school, I bumped into a cellist, and my score fell to the floor. The cellist, Harvey Wolf, was on his way to the airport to join the Houston Symphony. He impulsively asked if he could carry the score along to show to Leopold Stokowski, who had just hired him as the last cellist in the orchestra. I had another copy, so I agreed, not expecting anything from this gesture. I suspected that few conductors would take such an idea seriously. A couple of days later, the Curtis telephone operator started giving me messages to call Mr. Stokowski. I was sure it was a joke, as I used to leave messages for other students to call Leonard Bernstein or Arthur Rubinstein. Eventually, the institute's director, Efrem Zimbalist Sr., called me to his office. "What are you doing? Maestro Stokowski called me to say he's been trying to reach you urgently for two days!" We called Stokowski from his office. There was this highly accented voice telling me, "We tried doing the premiere of the Charles Ives Fourth Symphony, but it proved impossible. Orchestra can't get past first bars. Need a premiere as replacement. Press invited: *Time* magazine, *Life*, UPI, the AP. We do your new symphony premiere instead. Please bring music. Rehearsals start in two days."

The premiere of my first symphony took place in Houston on November 4, 1957. The concert also included Debussy's *Epigraphes Antiques*, Rachmaninoff's *Rhapsody on a Theme of Paganini* with Leonard Pennario as soloist, and Stokowski's own orchestration of Mussorgsky's *Pictures at an Exhibition*—the first time I heard it; I recently recorded and filmed it. But another more momentous event took place that evening: news from Soviet Russia revealed that the USSR had launched the first manmade object in space, the Sputnik. Music and art therefore disappeared from the news for some weeks—although the symphony was a big success with the public and the critics. The interviews with *Time* and *Life* magazines never came out. Only space science filled the news for weeks and weeks.

This was the first time I ever heard the name Charles Ives. I did not see his music until four years later. One day, while conducting my first orchestra as music director—the Utica Symphony in upstate New York—I received a telegram from Stokowski, inviting me to become associate conductor of the maestro's soon-to-be-formed American Symphony Orchestra. During the second season, Stokowski planned once again the long-awaited premiere of the Ives Fourth Symphony. The first time I got to see the score was when the maestro, facing the orchestra and the score on the stage of Carnegie Hall, in front of music critics and Ives scholars invited to attend the first reading, asked me to approach the podium. "Let's start with the fourth movement. Please conduct it. I want to hear it." Being twenty years old, everything seemed possible, but opening the oversize score was the biggest shock of my life. I don't know how, but I "conducted" it. Afterward, I told Stokowski, "But, Maestro, I was sight-reading!" to which he replied casually and smiling, "So was the orchestra."

In 1962 Stokowski gave the New York premiere of my *Elegy for Strings* and in 1963 the world premiere of my *Poema Elegíaco* to open the Carnegie Hall season.

It was with great surprise and joy that I learned of the release on CD of the Stokowski premiere of my First Symphony, taken from the original broadcast so long ago. Incredibly, it coincided with my own first actual studio recording of this early work for Naxos, released in August 2010. This is the central piece in a CD that includes the first recording of *Nueve*, a concerto for double bass and orchestra, featuring the incomparable Gary Karr, for whom I wrote it a long time ago when I was composer-in-residence at the Cleveland Orchestra with George Szell. This rather unusual concerto includes recital of poems—an integral part of the score, performed with amazing artistry by the great Simon Callow—an offstage chorus, jazz drummers, musicians in the audience, and so on. The CD also includes one of my most recent works, *Music for an Imaginary Film*, which could not be more different from *Nueve*. Just prior, I had finished an extensive new Flute Concerto written for Sharon Bezaly at the request of BIS records, which was released in 2011. The amazing Australian Chamber Orchestra and its leader, Richard Tognetti, recorded it, as is their norm, without conductor. They also toured Australia with the concerto. I could not imagine a better performance.

SYMPHONY No. 2, *Partita* (1959)

Upon graduating from the Curtis Institute of Music in composition in 1958, I spent two years in the apprentice conductor position with the Minneapolis Symphony Orchestra—now called the Minnesota Orchestra—under a Doráti Fellowship while studying conducting with Antal Doráti and composition at the University of Minnesota. During the two years there, I wrote my most ambitious work, *Partita*, for large orchestra. The genesis of this large work, which I later retitled Symphony No. 2, *Partita*, was a commission from Mrs. Faith Smyth of Chicago, my first commission. *Partita* turned out to be a large four-movement work. The opening Prelude uses Latin American–sounding rhythms and colors. The second movement, "Funeral March" (*Poema Elegíaco*), is in a somber Slavic mood, in full contrast to the opening movement. The third is actually a transition, an interlude leading to a grand finale, an intricate fugue in which the theme of the "Funeral March" transforms itself little by little into an irreverent conga/candombe. The work ends with a jazz semi-improvisation, based on the same Latin mold.

Partita was performed by the National Symphony Orchestra, in 1960, under my direction, in the mammoth auditorium of the DAR Constitution

Hall. This was eleven years before the construction of the Kennedy Center. It was a success with the public, though not with *Washington Post* critic Paul Hume. The second performance in Washington was a very special night, November 8, 1960—the night that John F. Kennedy was elected president. TV sets had been placed in the lobby of the concert hall, and the scattered few people in the audience kept wandering out to the lobby to follow the results of the close election. When the concert ended, even the musicians ran to the TV sets backstage. At that time, by ten in the evening, it was still unclear if Kennedy or Nixon would win. The following evenings, the concert hall was completely full, and Hume wrote a follow-up review, in which he reconsidered his earlier statements, saying that the work gained with each hearing. I was impressed by his willingness to reconsider.

Some months later, Robert Whitney, music director of the Louisville Orchestra in Kentucky, called to say that he had decided to record *Partita*. On a grant from the Rockefeller Foundation, the orchestra had embarked on an ambitious contemporary American music–recording project. This would be my first commercial recording. But there was a catch: *Partita* was too long for a 1961 LP recording, and one of the movements would have to be omitted. I agreed to drop the "Funeral March," but I was not pleased, as this was an intrinsic section of the work—in fact, the one that my teacher Aaron Copland had favored. Though *Partita* went into the recording world without its slow movement, there was poetic justice. When Stokowski decided to open his 1963 Carnegie Hall season with the American Symphony Orchestra, he selected the "Funeral March," but he asked me if I would consider changing the title. That's how "Poema Elegíaco" was born. The recording of *Partita* received tremendous reviews worldwide. More recently I recorded the uncut version with the London Philharmonic. It has been released by Reference Records on LP and CD and also by Naxos on CD. It was premiered by the Louisville Orchestra in 1960, Robert Whitney, conductor. Performed on 8, 9, 10 November 1960 at the DAR Constitution Hall by the National Symphony Orchestra, under my own direction. Recorded by the Louisville Orchestra, Robert Whitney, conductor, on First Edition Records (LOU 641); London Philharmonic Orchestra, myself conducting, on Reference Recordings (RR-90CD); reissued on Naxos (8.559303).

SYMPHONY No. 3, *Symphonie Mystique* (2003)

I completely surprised myself when writing this work, in being able to complete it in a week. Part of the rush was the imminent recording deadline, but it came out of my pen as if I were simply transcribing something that had always been in my memory. Later I was reminded of a recent statement by my friend Einojunani Rautavaara: "Music exists in some other plateau, and we composers merely write it down." When he and I shared Aaron Copland's composition class at Tanglewood in 1956, we had struck up an immediate friendship. His music has almost always had a spiritual undertone, which has not been a regular characteristic of my music. An exception could be *George and Muriel*, which seems to have mystical undertones, and perhaps also *Momento Psicológico* and *Dorothy and Carmine!*

My third symphony is in the traditional four-movement format, but there the tradition ends. The opening is a rather brash, aggressive *motto perpetuo*, the only fast movement in the work, with obsessive, repeated rhythms. The Slavic-sounding melody of the second subject reappears throughout the other movements in several disguises, not necessarily as a leitmotif, but as a memory of things past. The opening is in the simple A-B-A format, while the rest of the movements are quite rhapsodic. The second movement opens with a long cello line, which builds in a dark climate, using the minimal diatonic interval, a semitone, sometimes broken across octaves. A haunting high violin line intercedes, like a voice from afar. It leads to succeeding interludes that have a feeling of unresolved conflict, ending quietly and questioningly. The third movement is also a fantasy or rhapsody like the pervious one, but quite different in character. It opens quietly with the second violins, soon joined by the violas, and soon followed by anxious, anguished sounds. It is eventually interrupted by a sad, cryptic waltz. This waltz keeps returning obsessively, over and over. Eventually it gives up, and the movement ends in resignation. The finale is perhaps the main reason for the subtitle. After a short introduction, again based on the second motive of the first movement, it changes character, leading to a repeated drone, like a passacaglia, serving as the backdrop for a distant voice, a disembodied sound, wordless and mystical. Echoes of that same recurrent second motive from the first movement make their final ghostly appearances, hidden under the string ostinato. It seems to have an outherworldly character.

The French subtitle may seem an affectation, but in fact it sounds better in French. Also, it was written for a French orchestra, the Orchestre de Chambre National de Toulouse, and it was the orchestra musicians who suggested the title, during the recording sessions. The recording had long been scheduled, and a cancellation just weeks prior meant the CD would be too short, at forty-plus minutes. Since the entire recording was devoted to my own music, I was faced with the task of composing a new work to complete the recording, and this symphony was born.

Paul Conway on the Music of José Serebrier

Composers who are also conductors and enjoy equal success in both branches are in short supply. Few musicians can reconcile the relentless demands of a hectic life on the international stage with the concentration and devotion to the craft required by a creative artist. José Serebrier has always regarded the two activities as being inextricably linked. His wide experience as an orchestral trainer has fed into the development of his own authentic musical voice, while the process of writing music has informed his approach to interpreting the scores of fellow composers. Hours of study of works at the heart of the mainstream repertoire and, notably, outside it, have not only helped Serebrier to crystallize his interpretations as a conductor but have also guided his decisions as a composer. His understanding of what works, and, perhaps more importantly, what does not work, is the product of years re-creating the music of other composers in performance. Serebrier's musical education is thorough and broad-based. Tellingly, the ramifications of his "experimental" era in the late 1960s and early 1970s are evident in works written long after his Cleveland Orchestra residency, including a highly imaginative use of offstage forces and other theatrical elements, such as lighting effects. Instead of following the trend set by several fellow composers of rejecting early avant garde tendencies outright as a youthful adventure, he has simply taken what he needs and values from the innovations of his formative years as a composer to expand and enrich his creative palette. Though Serebrier's output embraces the traditional forms of symphony, concerto, and sonata, in each case he adopts an intensely personal approach to the medium. All his scores are underpinned by the fundamental principle of communicating directly with an audience. They also contain a certain Slavic wistfulness in their harmonies, together with a predilection for singing melodic lines and a firm grasp of structure, orchestral balance, and proportion. If a piece of music can be regarded as the summation of its composer's series of choices, Serebrier's creative decision-making is both instinctive and precise. In his writing, a refined poetic sensibility is shaped by the pragmatism of an experienced performer: a big heart tempered by a cool head.

As might be expected, the composer's most recent works are subtle and concise, yet even his earliest pieces are remarkably compact and focused, without the slightest degree of self-indulgence. There is an acute sense in Serebrier's scores of all periods that the notes on the page have had to work hard to justify their existence. Just as Serebrier the creative artist is not easy to pigeonhole, so his music often defies simple categorization. Is *George and Muriel*, for solo double bass, double bass ensemble, and choir, a chamber work or a concertante piece or music for double bass and orchestra? Similarly, the *Symphony for Percussion* might be classed as chamber music, as it only requires a quintet of players. In making decisions regarding genre groupings, however arbitrary they may seem, the guiding light must surely be the music itself. *George and Muriel* might be a rare example of a double bass taking the spotlight in the role of orator and as first among equals, and the repertoire is not overburdened with similar examples, so it felt right to include it among the concertante works. The *Symphony for Percussion* is scored for an ensemble of five solo percussionists and has the breadth and logic, and indeed the title of a symphony, so for me it takes its place alongside the official numbered series. In all cases where the basic original material was conceived by another composer, those works have been classed in a separate, catchall category as arrangements, orchestrations, realizations, and transcriptions, no matter how elaborate Serebrier's re-composition of them.

THE SYMPHONIES

Though Serebrier's symphony output is modest in number, his contributions to the genre are, in their contrasting ways, entirely representative of his output as a whole, while highlighting different facets of his writing for the medium. Richly scored and meticulously constructed, they make an ideal place to begin an exploration of his music.

SYMPHONY No. 1, in one movement (1956)[1]

Serebrier's first symphony is cast in a single span of music divided into several unbroken sections in different speeds. Without preamble, there steals in an

eloquent, hushed passacaglia for strings, initially grounded in the lower instruments but gradually gaining in fluency and reach as the upper instruments
join in turn until the textures radiate with contrapuntal energy. A climactic
unison statement of the main idea, featuring first violins in their highest register, leads to a sobering reminder of the tenebrous opening bars. A rhythmic
variant of the principal idea for woodwind, brass, and timpani offers satisfying contrast, its staccato crispness shedding new light on the smooth, heavily
accented opening threnody. Calling a halt to this newfound sprightliness,
muted strings restate the opening idea. Then another section begins in faster
tempo, bright and fleet of foot. Gaining in weight and intensity as it unfolds,
this passage culminates in a climax for full orchestra. In its aftermath, a new
three-note idea is introduced on English horn. The rest of the symphony
consists of a thorough exploration of the harmonic, melodic, and rhythmic
potential of all the main ideas before they are united in the dramatic final
section. Though the peroration is emotionally committed and full-blooded,
it has been hard-won.

Although the score has all the virtuosity of a concerto for orchestra, it is
avowedly symphonic in intent. The basic material for the entire symphony is
stated in the opening lament for strings. In this sense, the work may be regarded as a quintessentially symphonic continuous development of the ideas
presented at the outset. On the other hand, the climactic restatement of the
principal theme, marked "Chorale" in the score, has an unmistakable feeling
of "arrival," as if all the previous sections, with their incomplete or distorted
presentations of the chorale, had been preparing us for this crowning moment
of catharsis. Whichever view the listener favors, there is a powerful darkness-
to-light trajectory in the narrative of this symphony, in the time-honored
traditions of the genre, exemplified by the fifth symphonies of Beethoven,
Tchaikovsky, and Mahler. Yet this naturally post-Romantic sensibility is
contained within a structure of neoclassical restraint. There is a concision
and concentration in the writing, completely unexpected in the first symphonic statement of a teenage composer. Already in this early piece, Serebrier
demonstrates that he is concerned primarily with the musical argument and
the logical working-out of ideas. The full orchestral passages may have the
heft of a natural symphonist, but the delicate, chamber-like textures of many
episodes and the frequent solo passages are arguably even more striking, Serebrier's expressive English horn writing being especially notable. This impos-
ing score resonates with the newfound confidence of a fully fledged creative
artist who has discovered his own voice. The seventeen-year-old composer
wrote this work just before starting his studies at the Curtis Institute, after a
summer course at Tanglewood with Aaron Copland.

SYMPHONY No. 2, *Partita* (1958)[2]

The opening Prelude establishes a Latin American feel by the timbres and pulse of the music's initial gestures. Here too outlined is the main material of the movement: a crabbed, two-note motif introduced by muted trumpets, an idea first heard on clarinet that ascends stepwise, and a suave, wide-ranging theme, divided into two phrases, which appears initially on oboe. From these straightforward ingredients, Serebrier builds a perfect structure in which the prevailing mood is one of wistful nostalgia. There is an open-air, distinctly Copland-like quality to the more extrovert passages of this opening Prelude, a tribute, conscious or otherwise, to Serebrier's erstwhile teacher, perhaps. A powerful climactic section in which all the thematic components are deconstructed ends in six tutti hammer blows, but the movement draws to a close in blithe contentment, as if nothing has really been amiss, and ends on an enigmatic dissonance, suggesting that the main symphonic argument has yet to be fully worked out.

The second movement, "Funeral March" (later titled "Poema Elegícaco") is the emotional heart of the piece. Tinged with Slavic melancholy, it begins and ends in hushed eloquence. Contrasting aspects of grief are mined, including raw anger in the extended central processional, as well as numbed disbelief in the lyrical outer portions. This poignant threnody unfolds with its own inexorable logic. Such is the music's integrity and self-sufficiency, its success as an independent piece, divorced from a symphonic setting, is unsurprising. Leopold Stokowski decided to open his Carnegie Hall season with the premiere of this work.

Marked "Interlude," the shadowy, atmospheric third movement takes the form of a transition. Growing out of tremulous, mysterious lower string chords, it proceeds calmly and sequentially, starved of expressive warmth. A brief passage in which boisterous outbursts for full orchestra intrude upon the strings' icy ruminations has a cinematic quality, as if the narrative is jump-cutting between scenes. An intensification of mood leads eventually, without pause, to the concluding fourth movement, an intricate triple fugue in which the theme of the "Funeral March" gradually transforms into an irreverent conga/candombe. The unselfconscious revelry of this finale, which also has the character of a whirling moto perpetuo, makes a satisfying counterpoise to the second movement's profound melancholy. As the merrymaking reaches fever pitch, there is a semi-improvised cadenza for percussion before this Dionysian work is rounded off decisively with a final Latin flourish.

Whereas Serebrier's Symphony No. 1 concentrates on the notes and on realizing all their implications, its more-unbuttoned successor embraces unblushingly a variety of styles and genres and displays a wider emotional range with conviction. It is arguably the earliest orchestral piece to feature the composer's musical language in all its diversity and fearless eclecticism.

SYMPHONY FOR PERCUSSION (1964)[3]

In this symphony, five percussionists play on an extensive array of instruments:

> Percussion 1: small suspended cymbal, small bongo drums, claves, cowbell, snare drum, large conga drum, maracas, tam-tam, giro.
>
> Percussion 2: medium-sized suspended cymbal, conga drums, bass drum, timbales, wood block, large tenor drum, xylophone.
>
> Percussion 3: timpani, xylophone, large suspended cymbal.
>
> Percussion 4: tam-tam, bass drum, snare drum, guiro, timbales (or South American tamboriles), wood block, maracas, cymbals, suspended cymbals.
>
> Percussion 5: suspended cymbals (medium), dance-band set, vibraphone. The dance-band set, or "jazz kit," consists of three snare drums of different pitch and a bass drum with a foot pedal, and two cymbals of different pitch and a foot-pedal cymbal.

In the opening movement, the prefatory Adagio section is scored almost exclusively for suspended cymbals. Serebrier is precise in his stipulations, requiring percussionist 1 to scrape a coin on the edge of a suspended cymbal before reverting to a conventional stick technique. The Adagio draws to a close with two sustained crescendos, starting *pianissimo* and ending triple *forte*, topped off with a tam-tam stroke. In the main conga section of the movement, the principal idea is presented by percussionist 1, beginning *allegro comodo* on the small bongo drum, played with bare hands; after contributions from conga drums and timpani, bass drum and the dance-band set become involved, and the music weaves an intricate web of semiquaver-patterned exchanges between the various players. A change of pulse signals the arrival of a fresh rhythmic motif in woodblock and dance-band set in 6/8 and 2/8 times. Before long, the other players also join, and the tempo increases as the maracas play a 4/4–time motif. After a further textural elaboration, the pace slows down with several bars of tremolando and trills and dynamics varying from one extreme to the other. This conga section has three different basic tempos, but Serebrier avoids awkward shifts in pulse by the subtle use of *accelerandos* and *rallentandos*.

The second movement is a short solo for percussionist 4, who moves in turn from snare drum to bass drum, tenor drum to suspended cymbals, and eventually tam-tam, which is finally gently hit with the fist. To give the performer sufficient time to get from one instrument to another, Serebrier builds in a variety of eloquent silences, which become an integral part of the music.

Marked "Moto Perpetuo e Cadenza," the finale provides the symphony's climax. Against a backdrop of 4/4 time, Serebrier offers an array of rhythmic subtleties, such as a lengthy passage for xylophone in triplets, accented in twos, and a variety of syncopations in the accompaniment of bongo drums, timpani, cymbals, and dance-band set. The xylophonist deftly transforms the triplet theme into semiquaver runs, and the music builds to a climax. After a short (written) cadenza for the dance-band set player, other members of the ensemble join in consecutively for a short race to the finishing line.

Rewarding for players and listeners alike, Serebrier's *Symphony for Percussion* is one of his most exhilarating pieces. Though not part of his "official" series of symphonies, it shares with them a concern for developing motifs within the context of a cogent, well-ordered musical argument. It also relates to the more venerable sense of the word "symphony," a sounding together of instruments, and provides a fine example of the more experimental side of the composer's art.

SYMPHONY No. 3, *Symphonie Mystique*, for string orchestra (2003)[4]

Serebrier's Third Symphony was completed in a week, partly due to an imminent recording deadline, but also because the composer felt he was merely setting down musical ideas that had always existed in his memory. He chose the French subtitle of the symphony because he believed it sounded better in that language. Also, it was written for a French orchestra, the National Chamber Orchestra of Toulouse, and it was the orchestra musicians who suggested the title, during the recording sessions. The subtitle reflects the spiritual aspect, which is new to his symphonic output but is shared with some other previous instrumental scores. There are four movements, but there the adherence to tradition ends.

The opening Presto is a vigorous moto perpetuo in simple ternary form. It is the only fast movement in the work, with agitated, repeated rhythms. The Slavic-sounding theme of the second subject, which is thematically related to the fast music, recurs in the other three movements in various guises, not as a formal leitmotif but rather as an echo of things past. The quick music returns, bringing this bullish movement to an astringent conclusion.

Three rhapsodic slow movements follow. The second opens with a long, dark cello line that occupies half the duration of the movement and makes deeply expressive use of the interval of a ninth, recalling the anguished, wide-spanning themes that open the *adagios* of the ninth symphonies of Bruckner and Mahler. Eventually, other instruments join in, notably a high violin line, sounding like a voice from afar. Various episodes follow in quick succession, one employing an array of string techniques, such as *pizzicati*, *tremolandos*, and playing near the bridge of the instrument. The movement ends softly and without resolution.

The third movement is another fantasy-like utterance but more fluent. It opens quietly with the second violins, soon joined by the violas. The music increases in intensity and is eventually interrupted by a wistful, enigmatic waltz, which recurs obsessively for the rest of the movement. Eventually the waltz is gone, and the movement ends in submission.

The symphony's subtitle arguably derives most clearly from the finale. After a short introduction, based on the second theme of the first movement, the music transforms into a hypnotic ostinato over which floats a distant voice, disembodied and wordless. Echoes of the recurrent second subject from the first movement are featured within the ostinato. It seems appropriate that this otherworldly closing movement fades into silence in the final bars, ending the symphony in an entirely different mood and place from its angry, aggressive opening tirade.

Serebrier's Symphony No. 3 makes a virtue out of the various restrictions he imposes upon it. As well as confining himself to strings only, he sets himself the challenge of writing no fewer than three slow movements in succession. In his creative response, he explores the full expressive gamut of string writing, and, especially in the two inner movements, he exploits the individual lyrical properties of each of the stringed instruments in turn. His varied use of the same basic theme for all four movements serves to bind them together so that, despite their undoubted stylistic diversity, there is an inescapable feeling that we are being presented with four different perspectives or properties of the same material.

THE CONCERTOS

Working so often with top-flight instrumentalists in his capacity as an international conductor, it is no wonder that Serebrier should have composed so many pieces for soloist and orchestra or ensemble. The musician for whom the score is written is generally someone he has worked with or whose artistry he admires. In these instances, the rewarding, idiomatically conceived solo part becomes a perfect vehicle for their musicianship. None of the following examples could be accused of shallow virtuosity and empty rhetoric, however. Serebrier never takes the easy way out. The numerous concertante pieces he has produced are serious attempts to reconcile traditional elements of display with such symphonic virtues as long-range tonality, rhythmic energy, and melodic growth. Rarely do soloist and orchestral forces lock horns, conforming to the archetypal combative scheme of the individual pitted against the masses. Instead, the soloist, while often negotiating challenging, bravura passages, interacts effectively with the other players within the framework of a convincing, organically conceived musical structure. It is surely no surprise that the solo parts of his concertos contain memorable ideas, fashioned and tempered by the particular demands of the featured instrument, when so many of his works in other categories include substantial, key solo passages for different instruments.

VARIATIONS ON A THEME FROM CHILDHOOD, for trombone (or bassoon) and string orchestra (1963)[5]

This challenging piece demands bravura playing from the soloist and the string players, who must negotiate some intense and febrile *tremolandos* and stratospheric writing for violins. Pyrotechnics aside, the soloist must also be an all-round musician with interpretative flair, not least when expounding the searching, deeply expressive opening solo. The work is monothematic, consisting of a series of varied restatements, rather than formal variations, on the melody. The theme itself appears in its most straightforward guise (played by the soloist, lightly accompanied by pizzicato strings) at the center of the piece, as if the memory of the tune has sharpened and the years have rolled away. Soon the melody becomes fractured and distorted, as though the memory is clouding again. An unexpected final burst of energy with a quickening of tempo brings this showcase for an orchestral Leviathan to a brilliant conclusion.

PASSACAGLIA AND PERPETUUM MOBILE, for accordion and chamber orchestra (1966)[6]

The *Passacaglia and Perpetuum Mobile* is scored for solo accordion and a chamber orchestra consisting of two horns, trumpet, bass trombone, suspended cymbal, tam-tam, tenor drum, bass drum, and strings. Serebrier uses his resources lightly and confronts the restrictions the solo instrument imposed upon him by using two strict musical forms. The tightly knit, slightly claustrophobic quality of the repeated patterns in both movements suits the solo instrument, which has a chance to show an expressive side in the passacaglia and a more virtuosic streak in the breathless concluding perpetuum mobile.

COLORES MÁGICOS, **Variations for harp and chamber orchestra (1971)**[7]

This atmospheric piece is scored for woodwind, brass and strings, piano, and two percussion players, one with tam-tam, the other with wind machine, and both with their own dance-band set. Timpani and celesta are optional. The work begins with a mysterious sounding "Invocation," scored for offstage voice and muted solo violins with contact mikes. Presently, other violins, tam-tam, and piano join in, the latter player running a fingernail over the strings of the instrument to form a glissando effect. A stroke from the bell chimes heralds the arrival of the second section, a study for solo harp that begins and ends with ominous repeated chords but contains more florid figurations at its center. The third section features a songlike theme for harp, which unfolds under a fusillade of pizzicato patterns from the main body of violins and rapidly repeated tattoos from the solo violins. There follows another study for solo harp, closely related to its predecessor. A "Variation in Gray" follows, setting up repeated patterns for divided strings with light percussion interpolations and repeated, arpeggiated figures on harp. A solo improvisation for the soloist follows, based on the two previous studies. Next comes an "Interrupted Variation," with strings playing recurring figures with the wood of the bow over a brisk theme for harp. Eventually, all the instruments initiate a massive crescendo that ends in a triple *forte* climax and the next section, titled "For Percussion." Both drum sets, cymbals, and harp improvise freely. Suddenly the piccolo players stand up, initiating their own ostinatos, before swapping their instruments for flutes. Another massive climax marks the start of ninth section, "For the Brass," with harp interjections. The final section begins with an eloquent harp solo before all the instruments join in. At the heart of a crescendo whipped up by wind machine, the voice reappears, sounding from behind the audience, but the singer soon walks off into the distance. Repeated instrumental figures, including the recurring harp chords, gradually fade into silence as the stage lights fade into complete darkness.

Colores Mágicos is a satisfying blend of avant-garde techniques contained within a traditional format. The variation structure offers leeway for a wide variety of musical articulation within a set framework, and there is a feeling throughout that Serebrier is enjoying the expressive freedom as well as ritualistic elements of the music. One feels this immersive experience needs a live performance to do it full justice. The score's dramatic qualities suggest that Serebrier is a born man of the theater, and it is a pity he has not yet added an opera or a piece of musical theater to his oeuvre.

Nueve: **Concerto for solo double bass and chamber ensemble (1971)**[8]

A companion piece to *Colores Mágicos*, the Double Bass Concerto is avowedly experimental in outlook yet retains much of Serebrier's natural lyricism, especially in the expressive, extended solo lines, and the music is always clearly communicative, however avant-garde the style. Serebrier's musical language has undoubtedly changed since those experimental days, yet he still feels an affinity with the piece. Rightly so. It remains one of his most immediate, unvarnished, and highly charged utterances.

GEORGE AND MURIEL, for double bass, double bass ensemble, and wordless offstage chorus (1986)[9]

This is the work in which Serebrier rediscovered his urge to compose after some fifteen years of creative silence. For his festival in Miami, Serebrier asked ten prominent composers to write new works, especially for Lucas Drew, one of the foremost double bassists in America. Drew insisted that Serebrier add his own contribution to the list. The result was *George and Muriel*, for the unusual ensemble of double bass, double bass choir, and, in the closing moments, wordless offstage choir. Serebrier found that writing this short piece, after so many years, was as if he had never stopped composing, and it encouraged him to continue. At that time, his close friends George and Muriel Marek were about to celebrate their sixtieth wedding anniversary, and Serebrier could not think of a more personal gift for them than a new composition. The work is not intended to be in any way a portrait. It is a piece that Serebrier may have written anyway. It reflects what was on the composer's mind at that moment, his most intimate thoughts, and as such it is his humble but deeply felt homage to George and Muriel Marek.

DOROTHY AND CARMINE! for flute and strings (1991)[10]

Though the roving flute steals the show in the second half, it is worth noting that a solo viola has a significant role to play throughout the first half of this unusual piece, with a sonorous introductory soliloquy and an obsessive ostinato that drives the music toward the point where the flute feels moved to join in. Though enigmatic, the work has a clear trajectory and would be most effective in performance, especially for audience members totally unaware of the musical narrative's unusual turn of events.

VIOLIN CONCERTO, Winter (1991)[11]

The concerto begins expansively with a deeply felt, freely expressive cadenza for the soloist, which the orchestral first violins eventually trail, vibrato-less and distanced. Toward the end of the slow introductory section, there is an eloquent duet between the soloist and the first violin from the orchestra, which ushers in the main body of the work, a bravura, unflagging Allegro featuring double-stopping and fleet-footed scalic and arpeggiated figures from the soloist. A gentle melody on oboe soon mutates into a brash processional. The quotations from Haydn, Glazunov, and Tchaikovsky are subtly woven into the music's fabric. A march-like episode initiated by timpani and percussion leads to a sudden moment of calm and a gathering of energy before the concerto powers toward a hectic conclusion.

FLUTE CONCERTO WITH TANGO (2008)[12]

Flute Concerto with Tango was commissioned by the BIS record label for Sharon Bezaly, who first performed it on tour in Australia. The American premiere took place in October 2012 at Carnegie Hall, with the American Composers Orchestra and Sharon Bezaly as soloist. The work is scored for solo flute and strings. Without preamble, the first movement bursts in with driving string rhythms and long, flurrying lines for the soloist. Virtuosity holds sway for a considerable period, and then the mood relaxes, and a wistful, songlike passage offers some respite before the energetic finale flourishes. Serebrier constantly varies the accompanying textures in this opening movement, mustering an array of string techniques to match his volatile soloist. The second movement opens with a long, eloquent solo line, with the orchestra providing punctuation. Entitled "Fantasia," the third movement has a capricious spontaneity. It begins in rapt lyricism, reveling in the rich low register of the alto flute, but gains in intensity before ending with a hushed coda. The intermezzo-like fourth movement provides the "tango" of the work's title. Sultry and sophisticated, this example of the Latin American ballroom dance takes the traditional ending of a strong dominant chord followed by a brief, barely audible chord a step further by leaving the music up in the air in the middle of a phrase. The space left by this inconclusive ending is soon filled by the whirlwind Allegro finale, sporting a breathless, wide-ranging, and memorable tune. A virtuoso Presto coda signals a race to the finish line, rounding off in considerable style a technically challenging and idiomatically written vehicle for flute and stringed instruments alike.

SYMPHONIC *B A C H* VARIATIONS, for piano and orchestra (2018)[13]

Serebrier's piano concerto consists of four unbroken variation movements, all based on the four notes B (B-flat)–A–C–H (B natural). The opening Allegro is fiery and combative, with bravura writing for both soloist and orchestra. There is a contrasting lyrical episode for strings that points forward to later variations. The second variation movement has a quirky, scherzo-like feel.

The piano's motoric ostinato eventually runs out of steam, and the movement ends quietly, preparing the way for the gentle threnody for piano and muted strings that opens the third variation. A stormy central Allegro that alludes to the seething subterranean whirring of the concerto's opening bars is eventually calmed, and the variation closes with a return to the measured pulse and serene lyricism of its initial section. The final variation is hushed and darkly elegiac. A baleful tuba hints at the "Dies Irae" plainchant, a sequence as widely quoted by various composers as the *B A C H* motif itself. The manically repeated ostinatos of the former variations are now transformed by the soloist into rippling scalic figures. A short orchestral outburst hints at a barnstorming peroration, but the calming piano figurations pour balm onto this disruptive element, and the concerto ends in deep contemplation. Punchy yet reflective, deft and elusive, it is one of Serebrier's most substantial pieces of recent years and one of his finest from any period in his long and varied career as a composer.

CANDOMBE, for flute and orchestra (2019)[14]

A superb showpiece, *Candombe* combines rhythmic exuberance with distinguished melodic invention to provide one of Serebrier's most instantly attractive works. The inventive instrumentation, notably for the strings, suggests that the composer's love affair with the orchestra is as strong as ever. There is also a gratifying concern for balance and proportion, with the lively sections offering a perfect counterpoise to the more reflective passages. After an impressive buildup, the demure payoff is deft and charming.

OTHER WORKS FOR ORCHESTRA

The orchestra is a natural medium for Serebrier. Yet remarkably few of his compositions are conceived for conventional forces. He has written prolifically for strings, bringing his own experience as a violinist to these richly scored works. Even in pieces for full orchestra, he often favors a chamber-like approach to the musical resources, highlighting various members of the ensemble in intimate, idiomatically written solos, duets, and other subgroupings.

ELEGY FOR STRINGS (1952)[15]

A concentrated, single-movement piece, the *Elegy for Strings* is a meditation on the opening viola strain. As the piece unfurls, it weaves richly contrapuntal lines and builds to a powerful climax before fading away to nothing.

"POEMA ELEGÍACO" (1956)[17]

The "Poema Elegíaco" was first conceived as the second movement of Serebrier's Symphony No. 2, *Partita*. After that work's successful premiere in Washington, DC, the Louisville Orchestra decided to record *Partita*, but the work proved to be too long for one side of an LP record, and the slow movement, then titled "Funeral March," had to be lifted out. A few years later, when Serebrier was associate conductor of Leopold Stokowski's American Symphony Orchestra in New York, Stokowski decided to open the first season at Carnegie Hall with a Serebrier premiere. The "Funeral March" movement from *Partita* was chosen, but Stokowski, at age eighty-eight, appeared uncomfortable with the title. Serebrier revised the work, giving it a new ending and a new title, "Poema Elegíaco." Stokowski conducted the premiere of the "Poema Elegíaco" in its present revised form at Carnegie Hall on October 13, 1963. Since then, it has taken on a life of its own with performances all over the world. A powerful statement, the "Funeral March" movement makes a satisfying standalone piece, and the title of "Poema Elegíaco" captures fully the music's imaginative power as well as its melancholic tone.

MOMENTO PSICOLÓGICO, for string orchestra with backstage trumpet (1957)[16]

This evocative short piece is scored for string orchestra and a ubiquitous distant (offstage) trumpet sounding a single note. It is a tribute to Serebrier's ear for timbre that, when the trumpet first becomes audible through the sinuous contrapuntal string lines, the listener feels as though the instrument has been present from the outset.

FANTASIA, for string quartet or string orchestra (1960)[18]

This work begins with a short, atmospheric introduction, after which a wistful, pastoral-sounding theme emerges, followed by an insidious violin solo, described by the composer as a "sort of devil's trill," and purposely incongruous. The music has a rhapsodic, spontaneous feel in keeping with the title. The ending, frenetic and strident, comes as something of a surprise in view of the lyricism elsewhere in the piece. The disorientating effect reminded me of the discordant clashes that appear unexpectedly at the close of Peter Warlock's *Capriol Suite*, for string orchestra, of 1926, but the two works are entirely different. The original version of *Fantasia*, commissioned by the Harvard Musical Association and premiered by members of the Boston Symphony, was written for string quartet, and a new version for string orchestra was conceived later. Both versions are published.

WINTERREISE (1999)[19]

Serebrier always felt that his violin concerto contained the seeds of a purely orchestral symphonic piece. The resulting work, *Winterreise*, focuses upon the ideas in the concerto's main section, including the quotations from Haydn, Glazunov, and Tchaikovsky. Serebrier also interpolates a reference to the "Dies Irae" plainchant toward the end, emphasizing the nightmarish aspect of this wild, white-knuckle train ride for orchestra as the snowcapped terrain outside flashes by. Ear-catching violin solos remind us of the work's dual derivation: the brilliant concerto and the precocious early sonata. Fast and furious, this vivid orchestral showpiece would make an impressive curtain-raiser.

TANGO IN BLUE (*Tango en Azul*) (2001)[20]

The fun the composer had writing this work is palpable in every bar. Grand but never grandiloquent, its richly scored gestures never descend into crude parody simply because the composer knows the genre and milieu he is drawing upon inside out. At his publishers' request, Serebrier has produced several other incarnations of the score for various forces, including one for flute and orchestra.[21]

CASI UN TANGO (*Almost a Tango*) (2002)[22]

Casi un Tango (*Almost a Tango*), written shortly after *Tango in Blue*, makes a satisfying foil to the earlier piece, being intimate and delicate. Exploiting the haunting quality of English horn with strings, it taps into the element of nostalgia inherent in the dance form and is much less of a public statement than its predecessor. More fluid in construction and meter, it has a natural, impulsive character. It is written for the salon rather than the concert hall and unfolds spontaneously in a simple ternary form. Like *Tango in Blue*, it adheres to the spirit and mood of the tango rather than being intended to accompany a dance. Though *Casi un Tango* suits the haunting quality of the English horn with strings, it also works perfectly well with other solo instruments, and Serebrier has provided alternative solo parts for flute, oboe, B-flat clarinet, bassoon, French horn, and trumpet.

THEY RODE INTO THE SUNSET: MUSIC FOR AN IMAGINARY FILM (2009)[23]

This music for an unrealized film project is colorful and evocative but retains a symphonic quality in that the music grows out of the eloquent opening soliloquy for contrabassoon. There are intimate solos as well as massive, cinematic tuttis, and the use of a wordless choir in the climactic closing moments provides an emotional lift. Stylistically this piece is palpably from the same creative artist as the symphonies, concertos, and other works written for the concert hall. Yet the picturesque qualities inherent in Serebrier's writing are allowed full rein in an attractive and accessible composition in which the composer's virtues as an articulate, born communicator are on display throughout.

ADAGIO, for string orchestra (2014)[24]

The mournful nature of this short piece is established at the outset by the main theme's sighing, falling phrases, which dominate the rest of the music. Muted throughout, the strings encompass some deft metrical and harmonic shifts as they build to a climax of considerable intensity. Veiled and bereft of warmth, the final halting chords die away into silence, terminating one of the composer's most austere utterances. This moving piece is an orchestration for strings from a choral work, *Vocalise*, composed in 1964.

LAMENTS AND HALLELUJAHS (2018)[25]

Inspired by the biblical story of Lazarus, this score covers a wide spectrum in terms of style and texture, from the heartfelt supplication of the extended clarinet solo at the outset to the communal celebrations incorporating jazzy rhythms of the central episode and the ringing, fanfare-capped paean in the uplifting, exultant final section. The unexpected appearance of a chorus in the closing bars evokes memories of Hollywood-style biblical epics, yet the rug is suddenly pulled out from under us, and we are left in contemplation as the work ends, shrouded in mystery with eerie, ethereal sounds echoing in the distance.

LAST TANGO BEFORE SUNRISE (2018)[26]

As with Serebrier's previous essays in the medium, *Tango in Blue* and *Casi un Tango*, this piece is intended to capture the spirit of tango. The element of nostalgia typical of most tangos is exploited by Serebrier in this sincerely eloquent piece, scored for strings only. It was written at the request of publisher, music critic, and entrepreneur Martin Anderson, who asked for a work in memory of the love of his life, Yodit, recently deceased. The febrile middle episode features some of Serebrier's most passionate and emotionally committed writing and makes a perfect contrast to the wistful, yearning outer sections.

WINDANCE, for string orchestra (2019)[27]

This homage to Manuel de Falla makes use of an impressive array of string techniques during its brief span. Contrasting effectively pizzicato passages with bowed articulation, and deftly combining trills and tremolandos, the latter played near the bridge of the instruments, it enchants the listener with its recurring, symmetrical patterns even before the crowning references near the end of a short but instantly recognizable phrase from de Falla's *Ritual Fire Dance*.

CHAMBER AND INSTRUMENTAL MUSIC

Serebrier's musical voice is sufficiently authentic, flexible, and multifarious to be convincing in small forms as well as in large-scale statements. Indeed, it is in these chamber and instrumental pieces that we encounter his muse at its most intimate and concentrated. His deeply felt piano concerto involves the listener emotionally as well as intellectually. His music is experienced at its purest and most immediate form in his scores for reduced forces. It is good that so many of the works considered below are available on disc and excellent news that Nadia Shpachenko has just set down Serebrier's Piano Sonata of 1957, but other instrumental works, such as his Sonata for solo viola (1955) and Suite for solo cello (2006), for example, remain in urgent need of a studio recording.

SONATA FOR VIOLIN SOLO (1948)[28]

A remarkable achievement for a young boy, this sonata is the product of instinct. It evolves naturally and spontaneously from the lyrical opening strain, to which the music returns intermittently throughout. A contrasting idea, resonant and deeply expressive, is also developed as the piece unfolds. In his writing, the young José explores the individual sonorities of the instrument's various registers and makes effective use of pizzicati, harmonics, double-stopping, and trills. These effects are entirely at the service of the material, which is distinguished and heartfelt. Though the piece is a challenge for the performer and demands a high level of virtuosity, the overall impression made by the sonata is that of an individual musical statement from a young person who has found his most natural means of expression.

QUARTET FOR SAXOPHONES (1955)[29]

This is one of Serebrier's most satisfying works. It begins with an introspective "Meditation" that draws upon the expressive, melancholic qualities of the saxophone. The following Dance has a Latin American lilt to its saraband rhythm. The following "Song" is an affecting slow waltz in the style of popular French chanson. The droll concluding Rondo finds Serebrier in exuberant and playful vein. At its core is a reference to "Chopsticks," wrong notes included!

PEQUEÑA MÚSICA (*Little Music*), for wind quintet (1955)[30]

This set of three movements for flute, oboe, clarinet, horn, and bassoon has proved to be one of Serebrier's most successful pieces, having been played by wind groups around the world, including the New York Woodwind Quintet. Marked *andante lamentoso*, the poignant opening "Elegy" taps into that vein of melancholy that pervades so many of Serebrier's early works. A change of mood comes with the central Dance movement, adorned with trills and permeated with sudden dynamic shifts. The ardent closing "Song of Love" has a graceful simplicity, with fervently lyrical solos for oboe and French horn.

SUITE CANINA (*Canine Suite*), for woodwind trio (1957)[31]

This piece is dedicated to Serebrier's faithful friend, his dog, who died while the composer was still a young boy. The work opens with an elegy of great dignity and restraint, with fluent contrapuntal lines. By contrast, the "Dance of the Fleas" is a jolly romp, packed with hints of popular American march tunes playing against each other, very much in the manner of Ives, even though, curiously enough, Serebrier had never heard a note of Ives when he wrote the movement. Following without a break, the "Transformation and Toccata" begins with a somber introductory section and concludes with a quirky, Latin American–style *allegro* dance. This suite is quintessential Serebrier, containing within its tiny movements all of the composer's preoccupations at the time, several of which, such as the tendency toward Slavic wistfulness and an unabashed, cheerful eclecticism, have remained part of his creative persona ever since.

SEIS POR TELEVISIÓN (*Six on TV*), for wind quintet and percussion (1965)[32]

During a successful assignment as music director for the American Shakespeare Festival, Serebrier accepted a commission to compose the music for three of William Shakespeare's plays presented as television specials. These three pieces, together with one more, were incorporated into a complete suite, scored for flute, oboe, clarinet, horn and bassoon, timpani, and modest percussion, consisting of celesta, castanets, tambourine, suspended cymbal, tam-tam, and bass drum. *Seis por Televisión* begins with a courtly, march-like "Mini-Overture," replete with formal repeats and processing stiffly in unison with staccato articulation. In "Sunaloiroc," the bassoon plays a key role, proceeding with stealth in the outer sections and presenting an expressive, cadenza-like solo passage before high spirits reach a dramatic climax. "Juliet" begins with lyrical, eloquently phrased lines for flute and oboe and then, heralded by trills that cascade down the instruments, a haunting tune in the manner of a popular song in its second half. The formality of the "Mini-Overture" returns in the final movement, but this time evoking a different kind of ritual altogether. "The Taming of the Bull" features castanets and tambourine, but Serebrier imbues the music with a sadness that precludes any stereotypical Hispanic gestures. This colorful and thoughtful suite stands up perfectly well as an engaging set of diverse movements, divorced from its original context as music for the small screen.

EROTICA, for wind quintet and offstage soprano (or trumpet) (1968)[33]

This was Serebrier's first twelve-tone work. It also incorporates aleatoric elements and uses the human voice atmospherically as a mysterious, wordless, disembodied sound coming from afar. The composer requests in the score that the wind players be seated at some distance from each other, this special separation being crucial to both the atmosphere and the tonal quality of the work. The title was suggested by musician friends of the composer after hearing the work performed. In some ways the title works against the piece, which is hypnotic and cabalistic rather than erotic.

After *Erotica*, Serebrier composed another work for winds, *TWELVE PLUS TWELVE* (1969). Written for the American Wind Symphony Orchestra, it was an amusing experiment in audience participation. Arguably the work belongs in the orchestral repertoire, as it is scored for twelve winds, twelve brass, and six percussion. The audience gets to choose the order of the variations, and the work is designed so that each variation can serve as either the beginning, middle, or end of the piece. No two performances are the same.

MANITOWABING, for flute and oboe (1970)[34]

The ravishingly beautiful land in the heart of Ontario captivated Serebrier's imagination at first sight. Staying with friends along the banks of the Manito-uwabing River, and grateful for the free time away from conducting, Serebrier completed several compositions, of which *Manitowabing* was the first. "Manitou" is a Canadian native word for "place of the Great Spirit," and Serebrier has attempted to reflect this spiritual element in the music, as well as the more playful side of his Canadian vacation. The work was written at the suggestion of oboist Michael Kamen, who went on to become an acclaimed composer of film scores; he participated in the first performance.

A series of vibrant vignettes, *Manitowabing* contains some of Serebrier's most straightforwardly expressive writing. The opening "Raindrops" has fun with repeated rhythms and a limited range of alternating notes for both instruments. Yet within these tight strictures, the composer fashions a cogent dialogue evoking the random patterns of light rainfall. "Cloud" is an airy, long-breathed flute solo, liberated from bar lines. "Canoe" flows along in triple time and in rhythmic unison, while "Tree" is a plaintive, remote oboe solo, counterbalancing the earlier "Cloud" movement. "Time" is a brief but satisfying finale, employing conventional gestures such as fanfares, ostinatos, and trills, but making them sound newly minted. Though it is a short piece for small forces, *Manitowabing* opens up a wealth of possibilities to performers and listeners. Dating from a time when Serebrier was adopting a more experimental approach to his craft, it uses a refreshing variety of means to create an exciting series of miniatures.

at dusk, in shadows . . ., Fantasy for solo flute (1988)[35]

Framed by two rhapsodic sections and incorporating faster outbursts and a waltz-like episode, this heterogeneous, variegated piece is tailor-made for its solo instrument. There is a powerful sense of unity about the score's disparate facets as they all derive from the flute's initial phrases. A veiled, tenebrous quality throughout justifies the evocative title. Despite the painterly aspects of its narrative, the work emerges as a compact and compelling study for solo flute.

NIGHT CRY, for brass ensemble (1994)[36]

In this very personal statement, Serebrier celebrates some of his musical passions. A predilection for instruments at the lower end of the orchestral palette (witness the many and varied solos for bassoon in his orchestral works) bears fruit in eloquent and expansive solo writing for tuba at the start of the piece and for offstage trombones and tuba in the closing paragraphs. Another leitmotif running through Serebrier's work since his experimental years of the late 1960s and early 1970s is his inventive use of spatial effects in general and offstage instruments. In this work the offstage instruments are integral to the score rather than merely adding a striking effect at a critical moment. The results are ear-catching and haunting. Satisfying though it is to hear the piece in a recording, experiencing it live in concert would undoubtedly reveal even more layers of this multifaceted, deeply considered score.

AIRES DE TANGO, for solo violin (2010)[37]

This piece was commissioned by Rachel Barton Pine for inclusion in her re-cording of short solo violin works for Cedille Records. Serebrier saw the oppor-tunity to write a bravura essay with the spirit of the tango as the inspiration—not, as he has put it, "an obvious tango but a work that evokes the perfume of the genre, the feel and color of the tango, its nostalgia, sadness, bitterness." The consequent piece is a powerful, multifaceted soliloquy that captures the essence of the Latin American dance while following its own carefully plotted path-way. It evolves logically, but never predictably, from the opening statements and brings into play the full gamut of technical devices available to violinists, without recourse to virtuosity for its own sake. After all the pyrotechnics have died down, the ethereal, meditative ending is entirely characteristic. Though the language may be more sophisticated, this piece for solo violin displays the same adventurous spirit and intuitive grasp of balance and proportion as the composer's boyhood sonata written more than six decades earlier.

SAMSON AND BUDDHA, for two flutes (2014)[38]

The composer writes about this short piece, "Samson, our beloved eleven-year-old Maltese, a very special dog, had a pet of his own, a stuffed blue hippo named Buddha. Samson played with it for hours, chased it, slept with it: they were inseparable. The news of Samson's death reached me while on tour in Boston. In my hotel room, I wrote this piece in his memory, in which two instruments follow each other closely and complete each other's thoughts."

There is effective imitative writing in this short tribute, but Serebrier takes care to ensure each instrument has its own character and individual material. The outcome is an intimate duet in which both performers are cru-cial to the musical narrative but are given sufficient creative freedom within the partnership to contribute their own musicality. The hushed ending has a quiet nobility, solemn but not mournful.

IF I CAN STOP ONE HEART FROM BREAKING, for horn in F, violin, and narrator (2017)[39]

Violinist Elmira Darvarova and French horn player Howard Wall com-missioned Serebrier to write a duet based on a poem by Emily Dickinson, which they selected. This poetry at once inspired the composer to write for this unusual combination, interpolating paragraphs from the poem to be spoken by a narrator or by the performers themselves. Elmira Darvarova and Howard Wall gave the world premiere at Carnegie Hall in New York in December 2019, and their recording was released the following month. Serebrier writes gratefully for both instruments, yet he also successfully blends their sonorities, skillfully intertwining them in an engaging narrative, guided by the spirit of Dickinson's words.

NOSTALGIA, for solo viola (2020)[40]

This heartfelt musical moment was written expressly for a BIS recording by Berlin-based violist Hiyoli Togawa. Her idea was to portray in sound the isolation felt by humanity during the 2020 pandemic, when life as we know it suddenly stopped. In the composer's words, "We experienced helplessness but felt moved to look into our souls and develop an enhanced sense of compassion." In the few brief notes of this song, aided by the viola's expressive timbre, Serebrier spontaneously attempts to express the longing and sometimes the hope amid the seclusion experienced by everyone in the world.

ARRANGEMENTS, ORCHESTRATIONS, AND TRANSCRIPTIONS

Another valuable offshoot of Serebrier's intense scrutiny of a wide range of scores in his role as conductor is his consummate skill in transcribing and orchestrating the works of other composers. In these arrangements there is a keen sense of partnership as Serebrier invariably retains his fellow composers' individual language and style rather than attempting to impose his own musical voice onto their ideas. He has brought his talents to a diverse range of music by composers of different nationalities. As well as the following selected examples, he has successfully arranged music by Gershwin ("Lullaby" and *Three Preludes*), Rachmaninoff (*Vocalise*), and Janáček (*Makropulos Case*), among other composers.

Silvestre Revueltas and José Serebrier: "MEXICAN DANCE," for symphonic band (1971)[41]

Mexican composer Silvestre Revueltas (1899–1940) composed the music to ten films made in his homeland, the first of which was a documentary called *Redes* (Nets). A moving social commentary on the economic victimization of poor Mexican fisherman in the 1930s, the film was codirected by Emilio Gómez Muriel and an Austrian named Fred Zinnemann, who would later rise to fame in Hollywood as director of such classic films as *High Noon* and *From Here to Eternity*. In 1946 conductor Erich Kleiber made a symphonic suite based on the music from *Redes*. Serebrier became intimately familiar with this music through Kleiber's version and has since performed it throughout the world. There is a brief but striking passage toward the end of the first part of the suite that in the film accompanies a scene in which the desperate fishermen make a large catch after an extended period of netting very few fish. Serebrier extracted this colorful music from the suite and expanded it to create an independent work for wind band, his first foray into the medium. In this spirited short piece, which he titled "Mexican Dance," Serebrier does full justice to Revueltas's variegated and vibrant music.

Grieg, arr. Serebrier: *FOURTEEN SONGS*, for voice and orchestra (1990s)[42]

Realizing that Grieg's songs constitute some of his most exquisite works, Serebrier took great care to orchestrate them idiomatically. He felt it essential to stay within the spirit as well as the letter of the music and to use only the instruments dictated by the character of each song. Serebrier's choice of songs for orchestration was dictated primarily by the character of the writing. For the most intimate songs with simple accompaniments, such as "The Time of Roses," op. 48, no. 5, and "The Mother's Lament," op. 60, no. 2, Serebrier uses only strings, whereas in other, more complex songs with a greater expressive range, such as "A Dream," op. 48, no. 6, he uses the full orchestration that Grieg himself employed in his own orchestration of his song "A Swan," op. 25, no. 2—namely, two flutes, two oboes, two clarinets, two bassoons, two horns, harp, and strings. Serebrier's orchestrations are superbly idiomatic and are always at the service of the music. At no time do these arrangements detract from the voice but serve to enhance its expressive power.

Tchaikovsky, arr. Serebrier: *ANDANTE CANTABILE* for string orchestra (1990)[43]

The *ANDANTE CANTABILE* from Tchaikovsky's First String Quartet from the start had a life as a separate work and is often performed as a separate work. Serebrier was unable to find a proper orchestration of it, however. Tchaikovsky, while in Paris in 1888, had arranged this movement for cello and strings, which for Serebrier helped to justify the idea of extracting this movement from the quartet. Serebrier wrote the string orchestra version with the greatest pleasure and, in the hope that his orchestration will, in his words, "provide orchestras with an enhanced opportunity to perform this wonderful music."

Bizet and Serebrier: *CARMEN SYMPHONY* (2004)[44]

The *Carmen Symphony* is one of Serebrier's most successful transcriptions, either in its orchestral guise or in the version for symphonic band, both of which Serebrier has successfully recorded. Decisions such as giving the "Toreador Song" to a trombone and the "Habanera" to a saxophone seem to have been dictated by the character of Bizet's music rather than by any attempt by Serebrier to impose his own instincts as a composer. The saxophone is a particularly happy choice, as Bizet's use of the instrument in the opening number of the first *L'Arlésienne Suite* was one of its earliest appearances in concert music. The chosen excerpts trace the opera's narrative effectively, and the "Gypsy Dance" makes a rousing and satisfying conclusion.

Erik Satie and José Serebrier: *TANGO PERPÉTUEL* (2003)[45]

In *Tango Perpétuel*, Serebrier has attempted an orchestral version of Erik Satie's solo piano work, no. 17, *Sports et Divertissements* (1914). As with a number of Satie's pieces, the pianist is asked to repeat the few bars over and over. Serebrier's version involves subtle changes in orchestration at each repeat. No matter how sophisticated his orchestration, Serebrier ensures that Satie's refined, elegant Gallic spirit pervades every bar of the score.

Tchaikovsky, arr. Serebrier: "NONE BUT THE LONELY HEART" (2017)[46]

"None but the Lonely Heart" is a song from Tchaikovsky's *Six Romances*, op. 6, for voice and piano. The song is a setting in Russian translation of Goethe's poem "Nur wer die Sehnsucht kennt," also set by many other composers—notably, Franz Schubert. This is Serebrier's second orchestration of music by Tchaikovsky, the first being the *Andante Cantabile* from his String Quartet no. 1. In all his transcriptions, Serebrier tries to make them sound as if they had been orchestrated by the original composer. In this case, Serebrier succeeds brilliantly, and it is easy to believe that the rich, authentically Russian–sounding sonorities in this piece have come from the same pen as Tchaikovsky's *Serenade for Strings*, for example.

José Serebrier's readily adaptable musical language has enabled him to contribute successfully to a number of different musical forms. A natural tendency toward eclecticism, including the quotation of other composers' works, never produces a confusion of styles but instead serves as a constant source of replenishment for his own original voice. His decision to not use opus numbers for his compositions helps avoid the potentially crushing cumulative weight of a sacred corpus of work and chimes perfectly with his essentially fresh and revisionist approach when tackling a new commission, free of any limiting preconceptions. Consequently, his music retains a genuinely contemporary spirit, revalidating received forms intuitively and, when necessary to realize his unique musical vision, creating his own unique genres, as in the practically unclassifiable *George and Muriel.* Though his musical voice has absorbed and adapted advanced techniques over several decades, these "progressive" innovations have always been a means to an end, broadening his expressive horizons. Scores dating from every phase of his creative career maintain a healthy equilibrium between the orthodox and the unconventional, the familiar and the unfamiliar, the expected and the unexpected. He remains extremely active as a composer,[47] and we can surely look forward to further works from him in the future, safe in the knowledge that these will be logically conceived, idiomatically written, and, above all, directly communicative.

NOTES

1. Naxos 8.559648 (Bournemouth SO/Serebrier) and Guild GHCD 2347 (Houston SO/Stokowski).

2. Naxos 8.559303 (London Philharmonic/Serebrier); First Edition records LOU 641 (Louisville Orchestra/Robert Whitney).

3. *Music for Percussion, Volume One*: GALE GMFD 1-76-004 Stereo LP (Tristan Fry Percussion Ensemble/John Eliot Gardner). Recorded by Elia Melikhov and the Gnesin Percussion Ensemble, Moscow, in 2019 on Reference Recordings.

4. Naxos 8.559183 (Carole Farley/Toulouse National Chamber Orchestra/Serebrier) and Naxos DVD 2110230 (Carole Farley/National Youth Orchestra of Spain/Serebrier).

5. Naxos 8.559183 (Laurent le Chennadec, bassoon/Toulouse National Chamber Orchestra/Serebrier).

6. Naxos 8.559183 (Yi Yao, accordion/Toulouse National Chamber Orchestra/Serebrier).

7. Recorded by Sara Cutler, harp, the Málaga Philharmonic Orchestra and Serebrier in 2020.

8. Naxos 8.559648 (Gary Karr, double bass/Simon Callow, narrator/Bournemouth Symphony Chorus and Orchestra/Serebrier) and Urlicht UAV-5985 (Gary Karr, double bass/Plainfield Symphony Orchestra/Serebrier).

9. Naxos 8.559183 (Toulouse National Chamber Orchestra/Serebrier) and Phoenix PHCD 144 (Lucas Drew, double bass/Festival Miami Doublebass Ensemble/Festival Miami Chorus/Donald Oglesby).

10. Naxos 8.559183 (Sandrine Tilly, flute/Toulouse National Chamber Orchestra/Serebrier) and Phoenix PHCD 144 (Royal Philharmonic Orchestra/Serebrier). Recorded by the Málaga Philharmonic Orchestra (2020).

11. Naxos 8.559648 (Philippe Quint, violin/Bournemouth Symphony Orchestra/Serebrier) and ASV CD DCA 855 (Michael Guttman, violin/Royal Philharmonic Orchestra/Serebrier).

12. BIS-2423 SACD (Sharon Bezaly, flute/Australian Chamber Orchestra/Richard Tognetti).

13. BIS-2423 SACD (RTÉ National Symphony Orchestra/Serebrier).

14. In the the 17th and 18th centuries, Africans sold as slaves took the candombe percussion patterns to Uruguay, Argentina, Brazil and even to Cuba where it developed different rhythms. It became adopted especially in Uruguay, later modifying into milonga, itself a predecessor of the tango. Candombe, milonga and tango originated from the same African roots, but tango adopted its name and pulsation from Spain. Candombe still exists in Uruguay, especially during Carnival, when amazing drummers parade with their collection of drums played with bare hands. My own Candombe is just an homage to the genre, contrasting the broken rhythm with melodic turns. It was written especially for the recording with the Málaga Philharmonic Orchestra, including my three previous attempts at concert tangos.

15. Naxos 8.559183 (Toulouse National Chamber Orchestra/Serebrier).

16. Naxos 8.559183 (Toulouse National Chamber Orchestra/Serebrier) and ASV CD DCA 785 (Royal Philharmonic Orchestra/Serebrier).

17. ASV CD DCA 785 (Royal Philharmonic Orchestra/Serebrier) and Urlicht UAV-5985 (Belgian Radio Symphony Orchestra/Serebrier).

18. Naxos 8.559303 (London Philharmonic Orchestra/Serebrier) and Naxos 8.559183 (Toulouse National Chamber Orchestra/Serebrier).

19. Naxos 8.559303 (London Philharmonic Orchestra/Serebrier).

20. Naxos 8.559648 (Bournemouth Symphony Orchestra/Serebrier).

Recorded by Nestor Torres, flute, the Málaga Philharmonic Orchestra and Sereb21. rier in 2020.

22. Naxos 8.559648 (Bournemouth Symphony Orchestra/Serebrier).

23. Naxos 8.559648 (Bournemouth Symphony Chorus and Orchestra/Serebrier).

24. BIS-2423 SACD (RTÉ National Symphony Orchestra/Serebrier).

25. BIS-2423 SACD (RTÉ National Symphony Orchestra/Serebrier).

26. BIS-2423 SACD (RTÉ National Symphony Orchestra/Serebrier) and Toccata Classics TOCC 0370 (Ukrainian Festival Orchestra/Paul Mann). Recorded by the Málaga Philharmonic Orchestra in 2020.

27. Recorded by Concerto Málaga String Orchestra and Serebrier in 2020.

28. Naxos 8.559303 (Gonzalo Acosta, violin).

29. Phoenix PHCD 144 (The Australian Saxophone Quartet).

30. Phoenix PHCD 144 (Australian Wind Virtuosi).

31. Phoenix PHCD 144 (Australian Wind Virtuosi).

32. Phoenix PHCD 144 (Australian Wind Virtuosi).

33. Phoenix PHCD 144 (Carole Farley, soprano/Australian Wind Virtuosi/Serebrier).

34. Centaur CRC 2775 (Claudia Anderson, flute/William McMullen, oboe).

35. Blue Griffin Recording BGR375 (Martha Councell-Vargas, flute).

36. Naxos 8.570727 ("The President's Own" United States Marine Band/Serebrier).

37. Cedille Records CDR 90000 124 (Rachel Barton Pine, violin).

38. Samson, our beloved eleven-year-old Maltese, a very special dog, had a pet of hisown, a stuffed blue hippo named Buddha. Samson played with it for hours, chased

it, slept with it: they were inseparable. The news of Samson's death reached me while on tour in Boston. In my hotel room, I wrote this piece in his memory, in which two instruments follow each other closely and complete each other's thoughts.

39. Affetto AF2001 (Elmira Darvarova, violin/Howard Wall, horn).

40. Recorded by Hiyoli Togawa (BIS 2533, 2021).

41. Naxos 8.570727 ("The President's Own" United States Marine Band/Serebrier).

42. SOMM Ariadne 5001 (Carole Farley, soprano/London Philharmonic Orchestra/Serebrier).

43. BIS-CD-1283 (Bamberg Symphony Orchestra/Serebrier).

44. BIS-CD-1305 (Barcelona Symphony Orchestra and National Orchestra of Catalonia/Serebrier) and Naxos 8.570727 ("The President's Own" United States Marine Band/Serebrier).

45. BIS-CD-1175 (Barcelona Symphony Orchestra/Serebrier).

46. BIS-2423 SACD (RTÉ National Symphony Orchestra/Serebrier).

47. One of his most recent works is *The Year 2020*, written for the Quintet of the Americas, who premiered it online in December 2020.

José Serebrier (left) with daughter, Lara (center), and wife, Carole Farley

José Serebrier's conducting debut at age eleven in front of the president of Uruguay and the entire cabinet

José Serebrier (left), George and Ira Gershwin's sister, Frances Gershwin (middle), and her son, Leopold Godowsky III

José Serebrier conducting the American Symphony Orchestra at Carnegie Hall

José Serebrier, age twelve, conducting his youth orchestra in the premises of the major newspaper in Montevideo

José Serebrier (left) with Samuel Barber after Serebrier's concert at Lincoln Center

Elliott Carter (left) with José Serebrier after the premiere of Carter's String Quartet no. 4, Serebrier's commission

José Serebrier (left) with Leopold Stokowski

José Serebrier, together with Leopold Stokowski, conducting the American Symphony Orchestra in rehearsal of the Ives Fourth Symphony, Carnegie Hall

José Serebrier (left) with Lorin Maazel, who is congratulating Serebrier after a Carnegie Hall concert

Morton Gould (left) and José Serebrier before Serebrier premiered Gould's new work at Carnegie Hall

· 6 ·

José Serebrier's Experiences and Anecdotes about Colleagues and Mentors

PIERRE MONTEUX (1875–1964)

His gentle nature, acute and constant sense of humor, and true camaraderie rendered him dear and unforgettable to the musicians who have known him. Monteux behaved in such contrast to the way famous orchestra dictators did at the time—for example, Toscanini, Reiner, Szell, or Stokowski. Things had not always been that way. Monteux sometimes entertained his audience with anecdotes of the times when he, too, had behaved as a despot. It was a great way for me to learn, just by observing him at work, especially his way of handling the musicians, as I must confess that I, too, showed a tendency to be unnecessarily harsh with some of the poor instrumentalists at the beginning of my career. In that sense, Doráti had not been a model. His frequent and violent tantrums could only match Szell's regular outbursts and bad moods. By today's standards, such behavior would not be tolerated by orchestra musicians. But in the early sixties, that is what was expected from certain famous conductors. To work as a musician in an orchestra was, at the time, a perilous situation. Absolutely anything could trigger the conductor's wrath.

Monteux was always quiet; his frequent sarcastic remarks were never— quite rightly—taken as insults. Admittedly, in private situations he could be quite sharp. When it was requested that he end his association with the Boston Symphony to be replaced by Serge Koussevitzky—in 1924—he declared that he was totally convinced that Koussevitzky had bought everything. I could not quite fathom what he had meant by these words, as I was quite ignorant about the way the music world worked when it came to orchestras, especially those whose existence solely relied on private donations, which is in fact the case for nearly all the American orchestras. For a student, as I was then, music remained an art and in no way a business. Monteux was ever so aware of the problems created by nonprofessionals who constituted a majority in a board of directors, a necessity when orchestras are not subsidized by the public purse. Monteux's teaching was a constant reminder of the basic rules of life in America at the time. After having criticized all of us as future conductors and having mercilessly mocked our efforts at conducting, we were impatiently dying to see him at work. But, in fact, he was very reluctant to let us do so. One day, when he was feeling particularly full of energy—he was eighty-eight at the time—he surprised us all by saying, "Today, gentlemen, I will be the one to conduct, and you will get to criticize me!" That was his best session. Well, he didn't show us anything particularly spectacular or surprising: simple and tiny gestures, but each of his arm movements made quite a difference. We understood where the mystery was coming from. He had an intimate and perfect knowledge of the score. Experience is a key factor. Orchestra conductors, like good wines, improve with age. Monteux was the most senior member among conductors at the time, and he had the precious memories of a rich and immense tradition. I can still remember, fondly, my first meeting with him when he came to conduct in Minneapolis. At the final rehearsal, he addressed the orchestra with these words: "Remember that we are playing first the overture, then the concerto, and, after the interval, the symphony." Taken aback, I asked him for the reason for this bewildering declaration. He simply replied that, in his long career, he had sometimes heard instrumentalists play the overture, while others had started on the symphony. He was a colossal triumph in Minneapolis, as had never been seen before. He brought the house down with applause, and the public would not let him go. He had to take bows for a long time. The following week, Doráti came back. He took great offense at Monteux's triumph with the public. I tried to calm him down as much as I could. "But why," he asked me, terribly offended and hurt, "is the public so fickle? They have never applauded me like that!" (Some members of the governing body had rushed out to call him and let him know about it). I replied, "What did you expect? Monteux arrived looking like an alien, different from most people. It was something the public had never witnessed before! And he is a legendary figure." He seemed quite satisfied with my answer. The next morning, at the first rehearsal, he felt uneasy, as if the orchestra had betrayed him, as if he had been the victim of an infidelity. He started screaming after just a couple of bars. "What are you doing? What is happening to you? Have you lost any sense of ensemble? After all those years spent with me, I no longer recognize you. You are now sounding like an orchestra of beginners!" It was pitiful. We ended up playing only a few bars at a time. He interrupted the musicians nonstop and tried to convince them that the progress they had made the previous week—with Monteux—had destroyed the orchestra. An hour later, he stopped the rehearsal and walked off the stage. I learned with stupefaction on that day that even the greatest artists can be subject to pettiness and jealousy. Doráti had absolutely no reason to be jealous of another conductor. In his better moods, with most of his repertoire, he was their equal or superior. That feeling of inferiority, which seemed to have brought on that violent reaction, was accompanied by a more pragmatic preoccupation. The public in large towns could be fickle, and to safeguard his position, his status, Doráti had to be regarded as the best. In his opinion, if somebody else was enjoying greater success, Doráti might be challenged by any number of people, especially by superficial and snobbish members of the governing board in those days.

Another conductor received, like Monteux, a similar triumph in Minneapolis: Hans Schmidt-Isserstedt (1900–1973). He was a talented and friendly gentleman. A few days after his performance, I had the opportunity to chat with Ronald Wilford, president of the Columbia Artists Management in New York. I confided to him the strong impression the legendary conductor had made on the Minneapolis public and especially on me. Wilford answered, "That's exactly his problem. He's his own worst enemy. Nobody wants to see him back, except the public. The other music directors are jealous of his success and of his talent. Nobody will invite him back for fear of being compared to him." He never came back to the United States. Wilford added his advice to me, a nineteen-year-old conductor at the time: "Of course you must do well when guest conducting but not so well that you completely overshadow the orchestra's music director who invited you there." Pierre Monteux, considering his age, was not representing a threat to anyone. But he was still in the game, after spending years without a permanent job. After leaving the Boston Symphony, many decades would pass before he would become chief conductor of the London Symphony Orchestra.

I thought that the hills in Tanglewood and the stunning view of the lake were the most beautiful landscapes in the world. But when I arrived in Hancock, Maine, in August 1958, the views over the lake were even more magical. I could have imagined I was on a film set or in a dream. Autumn had settled early in the north of Maine, and the early morning mist was adding a gentle touch, like a Renoir painting, to this utopian view. I had never seen anything as beautiful as this. I had not yet visited Europe and not yet gotten a chance to admire the snowy mountains in Switzerland. In fact, it was all new to me. I had first seen snow in Philadelphia at age sixteen. It had been a very bizarre experience: all my senses were on alert, as if multiplied tenfold. I reacted to every smell, every sound, with acute sensitivity.

I will never forget the sighting of Monteux walking down the hill, linking arms with Mom—the nickname we had given his wife. She seemed to be his perfect female replica: same size, same facial expressions. We never quite managed to know whether she was exploiting the old man or she had the will to keep him alive by making him work hard and constantly. He never stopped. His school was a good source of income. Most of the seventy young conductors were paying for their tuition. As for me, I was on a full scholarship, but I had to pay for my lodgings and food.

The orchestra, as it was made up of students, did not cost him a penny. When he was not teaching, Monteux would be conducting all the time, in America as well as in Europe. One of his students was David Zinman. He arrived at Monteux's summer school after me, in 1960. David decided to follow Monteux to Europe and attended all his rehearsals. In the end, he became the maestro's privileged protégé, and doors opened for him very quickly: an important and very influential manager in The Hague procured many contracts for him all over the world, especially in London. He was also entrusted with responsibility for the Netherlands Chamber Orchestra. When we were both students in Minneapolis, he had already decidedly demonstrated his talent and his will to succeed. I saw firsthand his abilities when he conducted, with utmost skill, the Broadway musical *Pal Joey* by Richard Rodgers [1902–1979], a student production from the University of Minnesota. Most concerts by the student orchestra in Minneapolis were under his direction, but he had never really had the opportunity to prove what he was capable of. To ensure that he would be noticed by Monteux, following him in Europe was a great opportunity that he seized on the spot. When we were both in Minneapolis, we were close friends. I really liked his first wife, Leslie. David learned a lot by just listening to and observing Monteux every day, and he was probably reminding him of his own youth. Claude Monteux, Pierre's son, attempted a career in conducting, but he did not go far and remained a flutist. He recorded Mozart's concerto with his father. Eventually David became like a second son to Monteux, a successor.

Another conductor who became close to the Monteux was Harry Ellis Dickson, one of the funniest gentlemen I have ever known. He had been a violinist—since 1938—for thirty-five years with the Boston Symphony Orchestra, and then he became assistant conductor for the Boston Pops and music director for concerts with their youth orchestra. He published a souvenir book in 1974, which was fascinating and hilarious, titled *Gentlemen, More Dolce, Please!* [Beacon Press, Boston]. He studied over a few summers with Monteux. They became close friends, and he used to visit him very often. He was a wonderful colleague and invited me to conduct one of my compositions—the "Prelude" of my *Partita*—with the Boston Symphony, in one of his youth concerts. I was introduced to his entire family. I used to go there from time to time, and I met his daughter, who later became wife to the governor of Massachusetts, Michael Dukakis, and could well have become first lady of the United States had he not been defeated by Ronald Reagan. Harry inherited Monteux's impeccable technique and his strong sense of humor.

ANTAL DORÁTI (1906–1988)

He was left-handed but taught himself to become perfectly ambidextrous. Still, his right arm seemed awkward, at best, when conducting. His gestures were hardly elegant. But the music filled him so strongly, as if it were part of his being, that he would get, nevertheless, marvelous results. Good orchestras could read his mind like a book.

During my two years studying with him, he never uttered a single word of advice on conducting gestures. The only things that concerned him were the structure of the score, the instrumentation, and the harmony.

We would meet every Monday evening, for hours on end, so we could study and analyze the compositions performed that week. It was beneficial to both of us. Everyone knows that teaching is a good way of learning. He was so sincere when he was saying that he wanted to pass his knowledge on to the next generation. He must have believed very much in me, because not only did he invite me to study for a second year with the Doráti Scholarship, which he subsidized, but he also announced to the press that from then onward he would never teach another student after me. Not long after that, he declared strongly that nobody else could ever be considered his student and successor except for me.

In retrospect, I cannot quite fathom what he saw in me to be so impressed. Considering my age at the time, I was quite unable to properly benefit from his teaching. Nevertheless, on his best days he was unique. His performance of the Concerto for Orchestra by Béla Bartók was an invaluable lesson, just as with Stravinsky's *Rite of Spring* or Copland's Symphony No. 3, which he also conducted superbly. But where he excelled most of all was with the symphonies of Brahms and Beethoven. He had the tradition in his blood. And what he was trying to transmit with all his heart was precisely that immense tradition, which was on the verge of being lost.

His teaching very often consisted of anecdotes of concerts that he had attended in his youth. After class, we would usually go to the dining room to join his family for dinner.

His first wife was a warm, marvelous lady who had supported his career with all her might, planning his timetable and supervising all the administrative work. Her mother was omnipresent. His daughter, Tonina, who was my age, was ravishing. Doráti was a very jealous father. One day, he noticed me seated next to her at a concert, and for weeks afterward he would not speak to me. For a few weeks, I kept my distance, but later, once he knew me better, he even set up dates for me to meet her. He would say sometimes after dinner, "Children, we are off to the movies!" He would come with us to buy the tickets, and then he would say, "Oh, I have just remembered that there is something that I forgot to do. Just go on your own!" and he would leave us, to our great satisfaction. In those days, a conductor in rural America lived in a glass house. Every one of his moves was watched, remarked upon by everyone in the community, as if he were their priest. The whole family would be under the same scrutiny. And Doráti was perfectly aware of that. That was Minneapolis in 1958.

One Monday morning, as I was walking to his home for my class, I noticed the headlines on the front page of the Minneapolis *Tribune*: "DORÁTI RESIGNED AND IS LEAVING." It insinuated that he had resigned. But we soon came to realize that, in fact, the board of governors had fired him and had leaked the information to the press before he could even react. He found out about his "resignation" from the newspaper. He was completely furious. This announced, obviously, the end of his American career for quite a few years, if not forever. For me, it came as the end of one of the best times of my life. Not only had I learned enormously from him, especially by observing him at rehearsal every day, but I had also received my Master of Arts degree in composition at the University of Minnesota. I had also enjoyed student life to the full.

I kept in touch with the Dorátis in Europe—first in Rome, where they rented a magnificent villa overlooking the Forum. We often used to all go down to the beach. At the time, he was conducting summer concerts in the Italian capital and renewing his ties with the London Symphony Orchestra. Not long after that, he was appointed principal conductor of the BBC Symphony Orchestra, with which he toured worldwide, including in the United States. His international status never ceased to grow after his departure from Minneapolis. He had brought that orchestra to a top level, as the most recorded of its time. Doráti endured constant fights with the administrative director, Boris Sokoloff, whose brother, Vladimir, had been my piano teacher at the Curtis Institute in Philadelphia. In the end, after many plots, Sokoloff won the battle. As a departing gift, the maestro left Sokoloff a recorded tape of himself yelling.

Doráti then concentrated all his energy in Europe and eventually accepted the music directorship of the prestigious Royal Philharmonic Orchestra, the jewel founded and conducted by Sir Thomas Beecham. It regained him such prestige that he was brought back to the United States, where he was offered the music directorship of the National Symphony Orchestra in Washington and then the Detroit Symphony, previously directed for a long time by Paul Paray, and which would be Doráti's last major position. We lost touch with each other for quite a few years. Once, however, he invited me to conduct a summer concert in Washington. It happened to be on the very same evening that Watergate was broken into, and of all the hotels in town, that was the one Doráti and I had chosen. It was right next to the Kennedy Center, the most convenient.

We would meet occasionally, when he would invite my wife, Carole Farley, to sing in one of his concerts, which he did on a regular basis. He was the one who suggested that she sing *La Voix Humaine* by Francis Poulenc—which would become one of Carole's and my workhorses. Soon he hired her for Haydn's *Four Seasons*, for Beethoven's ninth symphony, in London as well as in the United States, and for the recording for Deutsche Grammophon with the Royal Philharmonic. She became one of his favorite opera singers: he very much appreciated her musical talent and her precision.

I admired his second wife, Ilse von Alpenheim, a very fine pianist, and I invited her to be my soloist at the Worcester Festival, Massachusetts, to play Mozart. Doráti came especially from Washington, and we all had a great time together. I was then music director in Worcester, the oldest music festival in America.

LEOPOLD STOKOWSKI (1882–1977)

Although I never received one single word of advice from Leopold Stokowski, it is with him that I learned the most. Just observing him at work was a permanent master class. His rehearsals were simply magnificent. What he accomplished at the time is no longer even possible. It was extraordinary and unique. What conductor would get himself to rehearsal more than an hour early and wait for the orchestra on stage? Whatever time I turned up, he would always already be there on stage, seated on his stool, before me and before everyone else. We never discussed the reason for his unusual behavior. Conductors regularly arrived at the podium after the orchestras had been seated and tuned.

I didn't have to wait long for the outcome. Over time, musicians would start turning up earlier for individual practice on stage, under Stokowski's vigilant scrutiny. It seems he had a good idea of the incessant comings and goings of the members of the orchestra. He used a memo pad to note their arrivals. They would soon realize it and would then start to get there earlier and earlier.

Another one of his distinctive characteristics was to rehearse, every single day, the entire program in the exact order of the concert, obliging the soloist to attend all four rehearsals instead of just the last two, considered the usual procedure. What was the most useful for me was to see how he would very rarely stop the orchestra in the middle of reading a work. He would play the whole score, and only after that would he allow himself to make criticisms and changes, and then he would require that this or that passage be done again. Rarely would he lecture the musicians. His comments would always be very brief, precise, incisive—often ironic. Sometimes he would let mistakes go by and only correct them if after a few tries the musicians had not corrected the errors themselves. This way of working seemed to give the musicians a sense of confidence.

After any first meeting with an orchestra, he would quickly change its sound and color. He would not have uttered a single word or done anything that could easily explain that perceptible, radical change in sound. After a brief greeting, he would simply begin the rehearsal. What he had in mind was the extremely precise idea of the sound he was hoping for. His ample and original gestures and his facial mimics would have the power to transmit that very personal and fascinating sound to the musicians. He was not the only conductor with that special gift. I had already observed that same phenomenon with other great conductors. Similarly, it was not a rare occurrence to see a professional orchestra acquire some of the characteristic sound of a student orchestra after having worked with a school orchestra conductor; it works both ways. It has nothing to do with the strictly technical aspects of a performance, as we might be led to believe, but much more to do with this conductor's ability to reproduce the same quality of sound to the one inscribed in his inner ear, with any symphony orchestra. Most conductors have that ability, that level of influence being linked, partially, to the degree of sound impression in the conductor's memory. It seems obvious to us that if a conductor who has spent a few years conducting the Vienna Philharmonic then has contact with a student orchestra, the latter will soon sound smoother and more refined, perhaps even close to the one in Vienna. Although it can be said that, if motivated, focused students do their best when confronting a strong character, the change in the sound quality would be beyond their control. It is more of a natural reaction to the sound design acquired by that character after years listening to and practicing a specific sound quality.

There was a time when orchestras had a specific identity color that made them distinguishable from one another. These differences were mainly the result of many years spent with the same music director. That was not, however, the only decisive factor. Some symphony groups—let's take the Philadelphia Orchestra as a typical example—had hardly changed key players for many years, and more than half the musicians had been taught by the same teachers, at the same school. Nowadays, most orchestras sound similar.

Although techniques and criteria for interpreting have significantly improved, we notice a world standardization of the musical approach, which renders the interpretations almost interchangeable. Whatever happened? Do performers listen to their colleagues' recordings and imitate them unintentionally? Are they scared of taking risks? Do they only want to stay within safe traditions, excluding any personal feelings? Why a unique trivial sonority? And overall, boring. The idea of the orchestral sound universe that Stokowski had bore no resemblance to any other. It could not be mistaken for anybody else's. It stayed with the Philadelphia Orchestra for years after he had left. We nicknamed it the famous "Philadelphia sound." In fact, through his successor, Eugène Ormandy, who over the years made a few changes here and there, that "sound" remained a tradition, and a quality symbol to this day. A large part of what Stokowski demanded, trying to reach that exceptional coloring, came unconsciously. It would guide any of his gestures, even his approach to the scores. Nevertheless, with full knowledge, he would work hard to achieve the best possible sound. One of his famous requirements was to ask—or rather demand—that the strings play with free bows. When it was not his own orchestra that he was conducting, that demand would trigger anger and distress. I can vividly remember at some of the rehearsals, when he was conducting American or European orchestras, he would meet with strong resistance from the strings when explaining to them that they had to play with their bows in opposite directions from each other, and not together. Orchestras like the Philadelphia, the Houston, or the American Symphony, which worked with him on a regular basis, would understand and take advantage of this method. Although the explanation seemed simple enough, it was a complete reversal of what the string players expected, which is to perform with bows all in the same direction, and many instrumentalists understood it very well. In fact, the bows lose some of their power when they play downward and gain strength when going upward. By combining both simultaneously, the sound comes out as more united and constant. I personally believe that he went a bit too far, because he used it nonstop instead of using this technique only for necessary effects on a particular musical passage. However, we should recognize the fact that the sound that he was getting from the strings was lush, powerful, and of an undeniable beauty and inimitability.

Trying to find a proper balance for the woodwinds was another one of his pet hobbies. As Rimsky-Korsakov mentions in his *Principles of Orchestration*, a flute or oboe player finds it hard to compete with sixty string players. Trying to deal with this balance predicament, Stokowski changed the traditional placing normally given to these instruments, so these musicians could raise their volume and be more visible to the public. He realized that to make them play behind the large strings' semicircle, as universally accepted, could render them nearly inaudible. He then placed the woodwinds on the right, instead of the cellos and violas. The sound and general balance were radical. Sometimes he would place the double basses at the back on a high podium and the horns just in front. The result was a huge harmonic transformation for the orchestra, the double basses sounding like an organ, with the French horns bouncing their sound on the large bodies of the double basses. Stokowski was always experimenting with the placement of the orchestra to obtain the best possible balance. He had the brass perform on the same stage level as the strings, contrary to the usual way all over the world that has the brass on high risers. This contributed, to a great extent, toward the creation of the famous mellow sound of the Philadelphia Orchestra. Stokowski had a personal logic as to what he was doing to achieve a full, warm sound from the whole orchestra. Part of the results would have a perfect technical explanation. For the rest, I believe it must have been some sort of "magic."

As early as November 1963, as part of the educational activities with the American Symphony Orchestra, Stokowski organized concerts for young people, Teenage Concerts, that were extremely successful. He had realized that his ability to draw a large teenage audience had been key to his success in Philadelphia. Coaches full of teenage students, who were delighted to skip a few traditional school periods, pulled up outside Carnegie Hall. A concert would last about an hour. Two concerts were given in sequence for two different school groups, about thirty in total in a year, all co-sponsored by the school districts and Stokowski himself. He would conduct the first and the last pieces, and I was put in charge of conducting the middle part of the program. While I was conducting, Stokowski would sit on a stool next to me, scrutinizing my gestures and speaking to the students briefly before each piece was played. He never commented on my conducting, except for handing me over my baton with a sort of disgusted gesture, which reminded me how he felt about batons, as an inexpressive piece of wood. He preferred the warmth that could be communicated by the hands, and he proved it all the time with his hand gestures. I used a baton mainly to show him I wasn't being influenced by him—perhaps a natural reaction at age twenty-one. I always use one when conducting an opera so the singers can see it from the stage.

It was the same with the other two associate conductors. At the end of the first season, one of the three was fired. Stokowski kept David Katz and me. He needed Katz as unpaid contractor and personnel manager, and in exchange he let him have the title of associate conductor, same as mine.

Eugène Ormandy, who succeeded Stokowski at the head of the Philadelphia Orchestra, only used his hands. It was only toward the end of his career, on his doctors' orders, that he finally bowed to their advice and used a baton. He was suffering, in fact, from a serious heart condition, and the use of a baton would render his physical efforts less stressful—or so it seemed to his doctors. I must admit that conducting solely with the use of the hands can be hard work. Nowadays, I use that technique on occasion when certain slow music movements require delicate conducting. Hands are, no doubt, more expressive than a piece of wood. Of course, the instrumentalists placed at the back of the orchestra—percussion, brass section—prefer the baton because they can more easily sense the beat. When a problem arises, it's usually because the conductor is not using the baton properly—or, more precisely, not using it as an extension of the right arm. To point the baton upward doesn't allow the musicians to really understand where the beat is. Many conductors suffer from this inability. Somebody should really let them know about it. A baton should only be the precise extension of the right hand, whether it is pointing or moving, as if you possessed a long arm. It can, however, show legato or short staccato notes.

The first time I heard the name Charles Ives was when Leopold Stokowski informed me that he was going to premiere my Symphony No. 1 instead of Charles Ives's Symphony No. 4, which he found still unplayable. Five years later, I heard Ives's name mentioned again, when Stokowski announced that he was going to try, once again, to play that impossible piece, with the American Symphony Orchestra, as a pièce de résistance for the second season of his new orchestra. He invited me to his very posh home, situated on Fifth Avenue in New York, to talk about it, but he never showed me the score. Thanks to a generous donation from a leading national foundation, he could spend a few months rehearsing the orchestra, working only on this "impossible extravaganza," the Ives Fourth.

The parts for the orchestra had been copied and especially prepared by the Fleisher Music Collection in Philadelphia—the same organization that had helped me very efficiently with my symphony. Stokowski explained that Ives had originally written his composition with four conductors in mind, who would be leading simultaneously, but that after looking very closely at the score, he could probably do it with only three. I would be the second conductor, placed on a podium beside him, and David Katz would be the third, conducting the offstage percussionists in the last movement. Katz had the easier role, because the offstage percussion performs somewhat unrelated to what is being played onstage by the orchestra.

When I asked him if I could get a glance at the score, Stokowski changed the subject immediately. He seemed particularly nervous about that composition, having failed twice before to present it on stage. The first time that I finally got to see it was at the first rehearsal at Carnegie Hall, to which Stokowski had invited the press. Harold C. Schonberg, music critic of the *New York Times*, and a dozen of his most important colleagues had made the journey.

Virgil Thomson attended as well. He had been a distinguished and dreaded music critic—though personally, I owed him a lot—but he no longer reviewed concerts. A dozen of musicologists and specialists in Charles Ives's work were present. At the start of the rehearsal, for a few minutes Stokowski looked at the score, then looked at the orchestra, then back at the score. Nothing was happening. But he noticed me backstage: "Ah, Maestro," he said—he always called his assistants "maestro," perhaps so he did not have to remember our names—"please, come this way! Please conduct the last movement; I would like to hear it." He was starting the rehearsal with the last movement. I was flabbergasted. It was the first time that I was setting eyes on Symphony No. 4, and I was being asked to conduct the last movement, in front of a throng of critics and musicologists. It was an enormous score, so complex, that I found it difficult to read; but, somehow or other, I started conducting. That was the most difficult moment of my entire career. At the end, I told him, "You know, that was the first time I was reading the score. I was sight-reading." "So was the orchestra," he replied without emotion. Then he spoke to the orchestra: "Now, let's get to work!" and started with the first movement, one bar at a time. He didn't go back to the treacherous last movement for several weeks.

The Samuel Rubin Foundation, which had paid for the recording of the symphony for CBS records, sponsored the orchestra's second season at Carnegie Hall. Stokowski had met the Rubins on the elevator of his building on Fifth Avenue, where they also had their apartment. Stokowski paid for the entire first season of the American Symphony Orchestra, but that is another story. Summing up, the person who organized the orchestra and sold the idea to Stokowski escaped to Mexico with all the money from the subscription ticket sales, and Stokowski, with short notice, felt he had no choice but to pay for the entire season himself. He wanted to avoid an embarrassing situation and never notified the press of what had happened. All subsequent seasons had sufficient sponsorship.

My colleague David Katz, much older than me, had a disagreeable job: he was the one who had to hire, one at a time, the required musicians, all under the vigilant control of Stokowski. Katz was not getting paid for it; the honor of being an associate conductor was his only reward.

GEORGE SZELL (1897–1970)

The first time that George Szell invited me to Cleveland to become his assistant, such a desirable position, I had to decline the offer. I was working with Stokowski, and I thought that I should not miss out on the opportunity to work with such a great conductor and on having the luck to conduct every year in Carnegie Hall. Also, he performed my compositions regularly, often opening the season with a new work of mine. But in my fifth year with the ASO, Stokowski confided that he had decided to return to the UK, ending his American career. At that point I contacted Szell and asked him if the offer to be an assistant conductor with the Cleveland Orchestra still stood. Szell replied that he had a principal guest conductor, Pierre Boulez, in his first job, two associate conductors, and four assistant conductors and that I would probably not get many opportunities to conduct, but he instead offered me a position as composer-in-residence, with financial assistance from the Rockefeller Foundation. I accepted at once, and the offer was repeated the following year, Szell's last.

Szell, despite his reputation as unmercifully harsh, sometimes justified, could also be capable of generous gestures. He would show, alternately, these two aspects of his personality. It is how it went during my two years by his side. I was anxious, impatient to conduct in front of him, and to be able to do so, I invited him to my first concert. He answered that, unfortunately, he would have to decline my invitation, as he had to attend a meeting with the orchestra's governing board. However, he managed to leave the meeting early so he could come listen to me. He stood at the back of the auditorium, and I saw him smiling at the end. His last surprise deeply touched me: I received, not long after his death, his piano, a splendid Steinway, that he had left me in his will.

To watch Szell during rehearsals was a master class. He was capable of polishing, for months on end, a symphony by Haydn until it became a pure jewel, with the characteristic qualities of a chamber music performance. His knowledge was unique.

LEONARD BERNSTEIN (1918–1990)

I did not get the chance to get to know Bernstein very well. He had been, like me, a pupil at the Curtis Institute of Music in Philadelphia two decades earlier, in the conducting class of Fritz Reiner. After that, conducting was no longer offered at Curtis.

I met Bernstein a few times in New York during concerts and in Baltimore, when he was a member of the jury in a conductor's competition sponsored by the Ford Foundation. He would rarely phone me, but every conversation we had remains engraved in my memory. Once, more precisely two or three days before the presidential elections in 1976, he called to beg me to vote for Jimmy Carter. His voice sounded tired, as if he had been on the phone for days, calling everyone in his huge address book. Another time, just a few years before he died, he kept me on the phone for over an hour. He had programmed Charles Ives's fourth symphony with the National Symphony Orchestra in Washington and with the New York Philharmonic, four performances with each orchestra, plus a recording for DG. Bernstein called to ask me if I might be available to give him a hand with this difficult task, to be his second conductor, as I had done years before with Stokowski for the premiere of the Ives Fourth. He had my recording with the London Philharmonic, which I had done on my own without the assistance of a second and third conductor. Bernstein was very insistent. I remember that he started like this: "I am not sure if you would be able to do it now. You are a famous conductor at this point, working all over the world. If you don't want to do it, I can also ask Michael Tilson Thomas or John Mauceri, since both know the Ives Fourth very well." I think that he also mentioned Ozawa, who had long been his assistant and protégé, and who had recorded it in a specially prepared version for a single conductor, arranged by Gunther Schuller. I answered that it would be a great honor for me to help if my agent agreed. Next, his agent called mine to discuss it, and negotiations started, lasting a whole week. My agent did accept, but on one condition: that I could also conduct—on my own—a short overture (we suggested "Decoration's Day," also by Ives) on the same program. Unfortunately, the deal could not be concluded. That saddened me. Especially that Bernstein removed Ives's Symphony No. 4 from the eight programs and replaced it with Schubert's Symphony No. 4, a beautiful composition, indeed, but a strange substitution. Bernstein never conducted the Ives Fourth. He had championed the Second and the Third. I have always been sorry that my management at the time would not agree to my participation. Bernstein would have surely done a wonderful version of the Ives.

Bernstein called me once again, still hoping I would co-conduct the Ives Fourth with him. I did my best to convince him that he really did not need my help, as he had conducted much more complicated compositions. He was of a modest disposition, or so he seemed (!), or very anxious and full of uncertainty. I have always felt sorry that he did not get around to conducting Ives's fourth symphony. He would have, assuredly, given a new and fresher view to it and imposed his personal vision onto this mad and nearly impossible puzzle of a work. He had been one of the first and most ardent defenders of Charles Ives's music. It is mostly thanks to him that Ives's music was taken seriously. Bernstein attended the first performance of the fourth symphony and had come with Seiji Ozawa to congratulate Stokowski and thank him for his invitation. He saw me at work there. What had made him ask for my cooperation was reading my liner notes for the RCA recording I had done on my own with the LPO. In those notes I described what I had had to do to make possible a recording in two days of a work that, for the premiere in New York, had taken many weeks to rehearse. In my notes I explained how I had slaved for six months to fix the musicians' parts to make it practical. Bernstein was asking for my set of the orchestral parts.

SERGIU CELIBIDACHE (1912–1996)

I was, like many, quite impressed with his perfect pitch, his demands for many strict rehearsals, his vast knowledge, his refusal to compromise. I was, however, somehow disillusioned when I saw him rehearse at Carnegie Hall, conducting the Curtis Music Institute Orchestra. I was disappointed to see him talking, and talking . . . nonstop, instead of rehearsing properly. It seemed as if he was trying to hypnotize the young musicians. Also, when he first started on *Tristan und Isolde* [Wagner] he could not manage to get the wind and brass sections to play the opening chords together, after the expressive entrance of the cellos. His right hand seemed incapable of making the wind section start together. After many unsuccessful attempts, he explained to the instrumentalists that it was a frequent occurrence and that there was no need to begin together. His movements were far too extreme, and he could not really control the ensemble. It was, I am quite sure, the consequence of having spent so many years conducting mediocre orchestras, which required large gestures, after he'd had to leave Berlin. Celibidache ended up in Lima, Peru, which in those days did not have an orchestra of international quality, to put it gently. Today Lima has one of the best orchestras in Latin America.

WILLIAM STEINBERG (1899–1978)

I first met Steinberg in Pittsburgh, where he was music director of the orchestra. I had won a competition sponsored by the League of American Orchestras. My prize was conducting part of a concert with the Pittsburgh Symphony. I chose *Quiet City* by my teacher Aaron Copland. The next day, Steinberg conducted a wonderful version of Verdi's *Requiem*. I was astonished to not see him sweat at all. Taken aback, I asked him how this could be. He answered in a rather sarcastic way: "I do not sweat. I am a cold-blooded conductor!" He was frequently criticized for his detachment—readily apparent—and his coldness—

all external. His performances were strict and sober but uniformly great. He was the antithesis of Bernstein, who used to literally sweat blood on every rostrum.

CHARLES MUNCH (1891–1968)

I met Munch when I was a student at Tanglewood. He was then music director of the Boston Symphony Orchestra. I attended many of his rehearsals and concerts. I would sit in the front row, next to Ozawa. I admired Munch's work, his sincerity, his enthusiasm, his ability to create lively and exciting performances. His hectic and exhilarating rendition of *Daphnis and Chloé* by Ravel remains forever in my mind. I sang under his direction at Tanglewood with various choirs, especially Beethoven's ninth symphony and *A German Requiem* by Brahms. Wonderful memories.

PAUL PARAY (1886–1979)

I was only fifteen when I was introduced to Paray in Montevideo. He was a major conductor, barely appreciated nowadays. His extraordinary performances in the French repertoire greatly influenced me. In the first instance, his magnificent and powerful version of Chausson's Symphony in B-flat. It was a composition that I discovered thanks to Paray and Monteux and that later I added prominently to my own repertoire. I recorded it in Brussels, one of my earliest recordings for Chandos.

JEAN MARTINON (1910–1976)

Although Martinon used to come to Montevideo on a regular basis, as he was married to an Uruguayan pianist, we finally met in Chicago—when he became music director of the Chicago Symphony Orchestra—and we soon became close friends. We used to meet frequently, especially in New York, and mostly outside the music workplace. Eleanor Morrison, who was our common agent, was our main link. She unfortunately died quite young, just a few years later. She was an adviser to Martinon when he worked in Chicago. We had met him thanks to pianist Philippe Entremont. For years, she had worked exclusively for Entremont, spending all her time and energy helping him build a career in the United States. I became closer to Martinon when he was chosen to be director of The Hague Residentie Orchestra. He invited Carole, my wife, to sing Gustav Mahler's Symphony No. 8—possibly the first and last time he conducted that monumental score. The following year, he invited Carole again, to Düsseldorf, for Mahler's Symphony No. 4. Martinon was a charming and very pleasant gentleman but also a prolific and ambitious composer, who truly deserves to be much better appreciated.

ERICH LEINSDORF (1912–1993)

It was in New York that I was introduced to Leinsdorf. We briefly acknowledged each other, but we never kept in touch after that. He was a great musician, gifted with a prodigious memory. His technique was baffling, and his repertoire ever so vast. He had succeeded Munch as music director of the Boston Symphony Orchestra. Previously, he had been the conductor for the Cleveland and the Rochester orchestras, after having been Toscanini's assistant in Salzburg in 1936, along with Solti.

MORTON GOULD (1913–1996)

I became acquainted with Morton Gould during the years I worked with Leopold Stokowski. Gould asked me to orchestrate some of his compositions. He had been commissioned by the producers of the TV series *World War I* filmed in 1964 and 1965, to write the background music, a monumental task for which he desperately needed help. I was rather busy at the time, and I had to work hard and very quickly. He wrote the basic theme, sometimes in just a few sketches, as quickly as he could, and he would then pass the scores over to me at my desk so I could orchestrate them, at maximum speed as well. Later, after Stokowski's return to England, I was invited every season to conduct the American Symphony Orchestra at Carnegie Hall. It was there that I conducted the premiere of Morton Gould's *Fanfare*, which he wrote especially for me to perform at the opening of the symphony season in 1990.

RUDOLF FIRKUSNY (1912–1994)

During my childhood in Montevideo, I frequently heard the name Rudolf Firkušny. He had been on many tours in South America in the fifties, and

I remember listening to him year after year. In those days, music students would treat him with the same respect as another famous pianist, also named Rudolf, Rudolf Serkin. When I arrived in the United States in 1956, his name appeared less and less, then gradually disappeared from the daily vocabulary in the world of classical music. Firkušný was living a quiet life in New York, where he carried on teaching just a few privileged students at the Juilliard School. His concert career didn't stop completely, since he did make a few appearances here and there, but not what he deserved. The best plausible explanation of this for me was simply deplorable management, but he was not, unfortunately, the only great artist in that situation.

When I first launched Festival Miami in 1984 and 1985, one of my main ideas for the program was the *Choral Fantasy* for piano, choir, and orchestra by Beethoven, with the great Philharmonia Orchestra from London, which came to my Festival Miami with Rudolf Firkušný as soloist. I can still picture him clearly when he arrived at the Hotel Grand Bay on Coconut Grove: an elegant, smiling, and impressive gentleman, one of the nicest colleagues I have ever met. He was so grateful to have been invited to perform. We had already become acquainted in the corridors of the Juilliard School, where I had been conducting the orchestra for several years, and we had met again in Fort Worth, Texas, where we had both been members of the jury at the Van Cliburn International Piano Competition in 1977. I clearly remember how interested he had been in my opinion of the candidates because he wanted to get a new, unprejudiced view. He was convinced that since I was a conductor and a composer I would be interested in other qualities besides technique.

Performing the Beethoven *Choral Fantasy* with Firkušný was one of the best music experiences in my life. His art reminded me, in one way or another, of Pierre Monteux. What they were both accomplishing was simple, without unnecessary complications, but rather, following an unstoppable logic. Their secret was the intimate knowledge they had of the compositions they were playing. Everything that Firkušný performed sounded natural.

By the end of the eighties, he started to come back onto the scene, with his wonderful and unforgettable performances of Janáček's piano works. It is at that point that my friend Richard Freed, a major music critic, made the decision to try to help that amazing artist, who was rather ignored at the time. Freed contacted the president of RCA Records in New York and hassled him until he finally signed a new recording contract with Firkušný, and he did not have to wait long for a meaningful result, as his career never stopped moving forward from that point. His last recordings, not long before he died, were a great success, and the same goes for the international tours that kept coming his way. A true miracle.

LORIN MAAZEL (1930–2014)

We met in Berlin, when Maazel was the director of the Berlin Radio Symphony Orchestra—the RIAS. He invited me to conduct that marvelous ensemble for one of the very first concerts I did in Germany. Maazel repeated his offer later in Cleveland, this time for one of the summer concerts during the Blossom Festival. The other event that brought us together again was when he bought from an art dealer, for his apartment in New York, a large painting by the Uruguayan artist Carlos Páez Vilaró. I was delighted to introduce him to this great painter, who was living in New York at the time.

I have always had the firm conviction that Maazel was one of the most important and complete artists of our time, a true Renaissance person, with a vast knowledge and many talents. He was a famous conductor, but he could equally have had an international career as a violinist, and even as a pianist. To celebrate his seventieth birthday, he went on a world tour performing Brahms's violin sonatas, therefore starting a new career at an age when others may think about retiring. When he left his position with the Pittsburgh Symphony Orchestra to spend more time composing, quite a few people were surprised. Nobody knew he was a composer. He might have tried his hand from time to time, but now it had become a serious undertaking. Within a short span, he composed an impressive list of scores for violin, cello, and flute, as well as many scores for orchestra. These compositions revealed an original and expansively creative mind. He wrote an opera, which I fortunately heard at Covent Garden. In the short history of conducting, not many have possessed Maazel's brilliant technique. Because of his great knowledge, photographic memory, and dedicated work, he became one of the world's musical giants.

SAMUEL BARBER (1910–1981)

He never went to concerts, especially in the last ten years of his life. He had become a sort of recluse. But when meeting personally, he remained the same, warm, like his music. However, his public image, his relationship with people, had changed. I remember him at the Van Cliburn International Piano Competition when I was a member of the jury. He had been invited to Fort Worth, Texas, where the competition took place, and he had composed a special score for the event. All competitors had to play his short, beautiful score he'd titled *Ballade*. Barber went to many evening receptions in Fort Worth but only spoke in French. That only reinforced the exotic image that the public had of him. I have never quite understood why he did that. He spoke, indeed, perfect French, but why do that in Texas?

When I conducted the New York premiere of his ballet *Souvenirs* with the American Composers Orchestra at Lincoln Center—after a tour from Washington to Philadelphia and New York, in which we performed it alongside other American works—I assumed that he would attend the concert. I was informed by his music publishers that it would not be possible for him to attend, as he had been unwell, and that he never went out to listen to his own music. Far from being convinced, I decided to phone to invite him. He was absolutely delighted and answered, "It has been a long time since anyone has bothered to invite me. I will be happy to attend. I have your recording of my ballet with the London Symphony Orchestra, and I very often play it for friends." Of course, he came and received a magnificent long standing ovation from the audience at the end of the performance. The photo that appears in this book was taken in the foyer of the concert hall, just after the performance at Lincoln Center. He was extremely happy.

The first time I ever met Barber was when my wife, Carole, and I had gone to his country house, where he lived with Gian Carlo Menotti, just an hour outside of New York. Carole had just been hired to sing a major role in one of Menotti's operas, and for my part, I had agreed to record *Souvenirs* by Barber in London. A total coincidence. They had invited us for lunch, unaware that Carole and I knew each other, much less that we were married. We had a lovely time and spent a long time talking about the Curtis Institute of Music, where the three of us had been studying at different times. Our meeting forever remains engraved in my memory. I had brought the score of his ballet with me, and when I wanted to talk about it with him, he simply said, "But you know exactly what you've got to do! The recording you made with the London Symphony Orchestra says it all."

GIAN CARLO MENOTTI (1911–2007)

I first heard his music when Eric Simon, an enterprising German-Uruguayan musician, presented and conducted Menotti's opera *The Consul* in Montevideo, its first performances outside the United States. It was a revelation. I was in my early teens, still learning the basics of music, but the music and the contemporary subject made a lasting impact. I heard more of his music when studying at the Curtis Institute years later, but when I was assigned at the last minute to record the ballet *Sebastian* with the London Symphony, it was a welcome surprise. The only previous recording had been conducted by Stokowski, and being limited by timing on LP records, it had only included highlights of the ballet. My recording was to be the first complete version. Years later, I programed Menotti's short opera *The Telephone*, which I admired for the freshness, the melodic beauty, and the outright fun of it. I presented it with my first orchestra, the Utica Symphony, in 1961. Long after, I conducted it for a Decca/BBC co-production as a companion opera to *La Voix Humaine* by Francis Poulenc with Carole Farley and the Scottish Chamber Orchestra. It was an amazing project of early recording and filming technology: the two singers were at the BBC Scottish studios in Glasgow, and since the producer did not want the distraction of having musicians at the same venue, the orchestra and I recorded simultaneously in Edinburgh, while the recording engineer and producer were in their London studio, all connected via direct cable. I was concerned at first, because I felt strongly that the musicians needed to hear the singers, not just follow my beat. This was achieved by installing tiny speakers behind each musician's head, small and soft enough that the sound would not be heard by the tall microphones recording the orchestra. It worked. The film was shown on BBC TV on a Sunday afternoon in place of a regular sporting event. I can only imagine the disappointment of soccer fans when turning on their TVs. I happened to be conducting in Edinburgh when the DVD came out, and I contacted Menotti, offering to show him the film of his short opera. Menotti had recently fulfilled one of his lifelong dreams and purchased a castle in Scotland. He sent a chauffeured limousine to pick me up, and after a short ride I found myself in a small town outside Edinburgh, facing an old castle on top of a hill, obviously centuries old. Menotti introduced me to the family, and we all had a lovely lunch, served by white-gloved waiters in formal tails. We watched *The Telephone* on his diminutive TV set, and he was thrilled. I left the DVD with him. It was the last time I saw Menotti.

JAMES LEVINE (1943–2021)

I first met "Jimmy" when we both received the Ford Foundation American Conductors Award after a grueling competition in front of a star-packed jury. He had just graduated from Juilliard as a pianist. We all lived in the same hotel in Baltimore as did John Canarina and Lawrence Smith (who later changed his name to Lawrence Leighton Smith, Smith on its own being too short and common). John and Larry were co-winners of the conductor's competition in Baltimore. I met Jimmy a few years later in Cleveland. He was an assistant, and I was composer-in-residence. Once again, we all lived in the same hotel, near Severance Hall, the concert hall of the Cleveland Orchestra. Pierre Boulez, principal guest conductor, lived in the same hotel. We met very often.

We had different aspirations, and our sole common point was our passion for music, but of course we saw each other every day at rehearsals and at concerts. Ever since our time in Baltimore, Jimmy had shown an instinctive talent for conducting. I can clearly remember his performance of *A Midsummer Night's Dream* by Mendelssohn and of symphonic passages from *Romeo and Juliet* by Berlioz. He rarely had the opportunity to conduct in Cleveland, as Szell had a plethora of assistants and associates besides Boulez. Levine conducted the Cleveland Institute of Music orchestra, made up of students plus a few members from the Cleveland Orchestra. He also set up a few performances of operas in concert version, with the most famous singers at the time as soloists and in smaller roles—extremely expensive undertakings. This caught the attention of Ronald Wilford at Columbia Artists. The following year, Levine joined the Metropolitan Opera. His operatic concerts in Cleveland were financed by one of his friends, who was young and must have been obviously extremely rich and who believed in Jimmy's talent. I felt lucky to witness the beginnings of a young artist. I can remember very well his last concert as an assistant with the Cleveland Orchestra where he conducted a composition at random and using the improvisation technique of John Cage. A short or long score, depending on the audience's preference. Jimmy told the audience, "You can also decide not to have it performed at all!" That triggered a wave of applause from a witty audience. Jimmy smiled and played it twice. Since then, he accomplished a remarkable ascension. In his first year with the Metropolitan Opera, he would call us before each performance and would kindly offer us invitations. I was able to witness the progress he had made when, at the last minute, my wife, Carole, replaced Teresa Stratas in the Met production of *Lulu* by Alban Berg. A first for the Met, he had assimilated Berg's complex musical language and was able to get from the orchestra, as well as from the singers, very refined performances. Years later, Carole sang Berg's *Wozzeck* under his direction—also at the Met. What happened with Levine at the end was sad but not unexpected. The rumors that had widely circulated in the musical circles for many decades all the way from the early Cleveland days had finally taken their toll.

SAMUEL ADLER (1928–)

During a busy week of concerts in Glasgow with the Royal Scottish National Orchestra, I received an e-mail from Sony Classical in New York, marked "urgent," asking if I would be interested and available to make a recording with the London Symphony Orchestra in three weeks' time. I replied, asking for details, for exact dates, and especially about the repertoire, which had not been mentioned in the message. The reply from Sony seemed as puzzling as the original one. The project was to record a Symphony No. 5 by a thirteen-year-old composer, Jay Greenberg, and the companion work would be his string quartet, to be recorded by the Juilliard Quartet. This was a project that had been initiated by the IMG artists management in New York, and Sony had agreed to invest heavily in it, feeling that it could be a best seller. Jay had already appeared on *60 Minutes* on TV, which was interested in featuring him again during the London recording sessions. Furthermore, there were indications that Oprah Winfrey might be interested in interviewing Jay if I agreed to accompany him. I was next told that this was only an inquiry, not an invitation, since other conductors were being considered as well. I replied at once that I wished to be taken off the list, uninterested in being in a sort of competition for the recording. Minutes later, I received another urgent message indicating that I had been "chosen," to which I felt the need to write back, "Not until I see the music." They managed to get me the score of the symphony within twenty-four hours, and I devoured it so I could decide. The score seemed at once remarkable for a thirteen-year-old and a good vehicle for me to make music. The next weeks became extremely busy, during which I was making some minor adjustments to the score, putting string indications in the parts, balancing the brass, and working around the clock with two young Juilliard graduate students to apply my changes and indications on scores and parts. To find out more about the project, I called one of the London Symphony administrators, and she asked, "Isn't it amazing?" I of course assumed she meant a thirteen-year-old composer and his fifth symphony. "No, I meant Sony is making a recording." British humor.

Before accepting the Sony recording proposal, I called Dr. Samuel Adler, whom I had only met briefly at Juilliard, to ask for clarification about his young student. Adler was supportive of the idea and encouraged me to agree to the proposal. We became instant friends. His kindness and fatherly help toward his students seemed apparent. Years later, Adler approached me with his own request for me to record some of his own orchestral works. The main work was his 6th Symphony, which had a history. Originally commissioned by the Baltimore Symphony to be conducted by David Zinman, it wasn't able to happen before the conductor ended his Baltimore tenure. The piece was inherited by Jury Termikanov, who looked at the score and, it seems, found it too complicated to prepare within the usual limited number of rehearsals in Baltimore. Next in charge at the Baltimore Symphony was Marin Alsop, very experienced in contemporary music. Perhaps for similar reasons the symphony once again was passed along to the future. Upon seeing the Sixth Symphony score, I realized at once why it had escaped three major conductors. While Adler's manuscript was neat and clear, it was nevertheless a manuscript, which is always harder to read than a printed score. I suggested to Adler that it required the investment of having score and orchestral parts computerized, which would make it easier for orchestras to read. I also put in bowing indications for the strings and anything else that would facilitate the reading of the music. While not in any way comparable in difficulty with the Ives Fourth Symphony, the Adler Sixth presented technical challenges, somewhat like the Roger Sessions Sixth had presented. My previous work on the Ives and the Session symphonies proved useful when planning the Adler recording. The Royal Scottish National Orchestra had no problems with the Adler, and we were able to tape most of it on the very first reading of the work, which sounded at once brilliant and inspired, a true masterpiece that should be an integral part of the contemporary music repertoire. One of the added bonuses of this experience was a new great friendship with Sam Adler. After the recording sessions in Glasgow, the first trombone player came over to tell Sam that he had won his audition to join the orchestra years earlier by performing Adler's work for bass trombone. Sam was not surprised. He replied with his usual modesty that "very few works are written for bass trombones so it was not surprising that this work was the chosen one." The CD released by Linn Records and wonderfully produced by Philip Hobbs became an instant success and received a nomination from the Latin GRAMMY Recording Academy for best recording of the year.

NED ROREM (1923–)

While visiting my New York apartment to rehearse his songs with Carole Farley for a recording they were making together, Rorem approached me about recording some of his orchestral works, which were not receiving much attention, even after Leonard Bernstein had promoted them. Looking at the music, I decided at once to program and record them, and Naxos agreed, as did the Bournemouth Symphony Orchestra. Ninety-seven years old as of this writing in January 2021, Rorem had produced an amazing array of music, best known for his countless songs, but also including music of every genre. I first recorded Rorem's three symphonies with the Bournemouth Symphony Orchestra, which received multiple GRAMMY nominations. Then a CD of concertos with the Royal Liverpool Philharmonic—the concertos for piano, violin, cello, and flute. This is music that should be part of the orchestral repertoire across the world and should be appreciated by musicians and the public alike. It has the power of communication, and, as André Previn used to tell me, the music has a perfect sense of structure. While it didn't break new ground, that won't matter in the long run. Not all new music needs to be revolutionary.

JOHN CORIGLIANO (1938–)

When Leonard Bernstein conducted the world premiere of Corigliano's amazingly original Clarinet Concerto, I was struck by the spontaneity of the music and the hypnotic effect of the brass responses situated in various parts of the hall. Shortly after, I included it in one of my concerts in Italy, with the Rome RAI Symphony Orchestra, and more recently in China at the Beijing Modern Music Festival, both times an instant audience success. Long before hearing the Clarinet Concerto, I had conducted the European premiere of Corigliano's Piano Concerto in Spain with one of the Madrid orchestras. Since those early days, Corigliano has become an iconic presence in the world of music, equally successful in the worlds of opera and chamber and symphonic music, as well as in major feature films. Beautifully constructed, his music communicates at all levels.

$$\cdot\ 7\ \cdot$$

Articles by José Serebrier

JOSÉ SEREBRIER ON *SCHEHERAZADE*

It seems extraordinary that some of the most imaginative orchestrators of the nineteenth century were practically self-taught. Berlioz, who was many decades ahead of his contemporaries with his inventiveness, never quite learned to play an instrument, and his schooling was rather sketchy; Wagner had a similarly rushed learning experience. Rimsky-Korsakov managed to get himself a job teaching theory at the Saint Petersburg Conservatory before he knew much about the subject. He then learned it by correspondence, keeping just a step ahead of his students. With such genius, there are no rules.

Rimsky-Korsakov's musical language is simple and direct, even basic in content and harmonic structure. One could even think of the *Russian Easter Overture* as an early minimalistic essay, basically playing around with the same three chords over and over, just changing keys for occasional variety. It is through the vivid, brilliant orchestration that Rimsky-Korsakov maintains the interest. Using the simplest elements, he achieves the most colorful musical paintings. The unity of the piece and its impact are marvels of craftsmanship. I find it extraordinary that his most popular composition, *Scheherazade*, is also his most sophisticated work, a fountain of unending imagination. The orchestration is novel and surprising even today. Almost every page contains an inventive new orchestral coloring and an unexpected use of the instruments. While he composed his works in a relatively short time, everything has been carefully planned to work. And work it does. Pure magic.

I hesitated to accept the assignment when Reference Recordings proposed this repertoire. I knew that Stokowski had recorded it six times—three times in Philadelphia and three times in London, with different orchestras. I had been present during some of the London Symphony Orchestra sessions.

While I did not have any of these recordings, or any other versions, I had heard that landmark recordings had been made during the early stereo era by Beecham, Ansermet, Monteux, and Reiner. I did not see any reason to record it again. I was curious, however, to hear several of Stokowski's versions to try to discover why he would do it again and again. I heard four of his versions. I am not attempting to write a review of the recordings, but I think I may have found a reason for the persistence: *Scheherazade* is a very *elusive* work. One may never be completely satisfied with the results. "Next time I'll do it better," Stokowski muttered after his last LSO session, and these were prophetic words. A decade later, in his mid-nineties, he attempted it one last time. It was with the Royal Philharmonic Orchestra, in 1975. This time, surprisingly, he deleted most of the orchestration changes he had previously made, removing the tam-tam from one of the early climaxes in the finale, leaving the original orchestration alone at the end of the work, and so on. Still, exaggerations abound. While his performances were most imaginative and poetic, Stokowski seemed to miss the lighthearted character of some of the playful dance sequences. His pulling and stretching of the famous phrase in the slow movement has so many imitators that one can hear second-rate Stokowski performances all over the world. Perhaps this is the kind of music that allows such personal touches of "interpretation." What it does not permit are changes in Rimsky-Korsakov's scoring. His two-volume book on orchestration, a musical bible for me during my childhood, cites numerous examples from *Scheherazade*, indicating some of the options he could have chosen and the reasons why he made a final decision. The clarity of his creative process is so rational and businesslike as to give the impression of a genial craftsman rather than a pure genius who may act by some divine intuition or sudden inspiration. Like Wagner's and Berlioz's treatises on conducting, Rimsky-Korsakov's advice on orchestration may seem a little naive today. For example, his explanation of the volume of a single flute: "One flute matches the volume of the first violins." The basic principle, however, remains valid. In the early sixties, Stokowski encouraged me to keep in touch with my family in Kiev and St. Petersburg—then Leningrad. I had not been back to Russia for many years, so I decided to follow his advice. The visit to St. Petersburg was most revealing, especially because of the legacy of Pavel Serebryakov. He had become a celebrated pianist and dean of the famed conservatory. I was able to see and study many manuscript scores of Rimsky-Korsakov and Tchaikovsky, an experience that proved invaluable. The first versions of composers' works are not always the best ones. (There is no doubt in my mind that the revised and final version of Tchaikovsky's *Romeo and Juliet Overture* is far superior to the earlier, "original" version.) Stokowski had tried combining the two versions by performing the final one, with the quiet, slow ending of the first version, which was more in the spirit of the tragic end of the play, perhaps the best of both worlds. Rimsky-Korsakov's manuscript was neat and methodic. To me it seemed second only to Ravel's in its neatness and clarity. The conviction with which he indicated every dynamic marking seems to indicate that no changes should be necessary.

While the genius of Stokowski is unmistakable in all his recordings of *Scheherazade*, none of the versions seemed fully satisfactory, and he must have known it. The freedoms he took are refreshing, but one could argue the taste and the distortions as well as the repeated alterations of the score. I remembered Monteux talking about his own two recordings, one with the San Francisco Symphony and the other with the London Symphony Orchestra, during my summers of study with him in Hancock, Maine. He often spoke about the hundreds of performances he had conducted of it for the Russian Ballet. I had never heard before his recordings of this work, and the first hearing of the early San Francisco version made a wonderful impression on me. It was short-lived. How could Monteux's version be more than six minutes shorter than Reiner's? Perhaps it was because he had to do so many ballet performances of it, and maybe the dancers required a fast-moving third movement. It was in this single movement that the difference in duration took place. Compare Monteux's eight minutes, ten seconds, to Reiner's twelve minutes. Monteux did do a healthy thing: he removed all the contortions from the slow movement, but in doing so—in giving it a cold bath—he also managed to take away some of its charm and beauty. I had no problem with the speed he chose but with the musical statement, which transforms into prose what was obviously a very poetic verse. Surely there could be a middle ground, a poetic rendering that didn't automatically imitate the banal "traditions." Then, puzzled, I moved on to Beecham's and Ansermet's versions. While Ansermet had a few lovely touches in every movement, there was nothing distinctive, and the old Suisse Romande Orchestra could not quite cope with the great demands of the work. I eagerly looked forward to listening to Beecham's recording, having always admired his great musicality. But here again the elusive *Scheherazade* didn't quite respond to Beecham's instinct and intuition. There was no brilliance, even with a Royal Philharmonic Orchestra playing in top form, and there was no lasting impact. I particularly disagreed with the opening of the slow movement, which was played *non espressivo*, but there were constant reminders in the other movements as well that this was indeed a problematic work.

Next, I found a Bernstein recording made in Carnegie Hall in 1959. Unfortunately, it was made a little too early in Bernstein's career, before he had blossomed into the great conductor he undoubtedly became, so this version doesn't do him justice. Nevertheless, here and there one can already hear

Bernstein's interpretive genius, especially in the handling of long phrases. In those years, the tendency was to use a barrage of multiple microphones, and the result, in this version, is a distortion of reality, with highlighted flutes, oboes, or clarinets sounding louder and more present than the entire brass section together. I then heard the Reiner/Chicago version. He had always been a good role model. Yet he remained a mystery. How could this dictatorial Hungarian conductor with the smallest gestures imaginable bring such passion and authentic flavor to Spanish music—Manuel de Falla and Isaac Albéniz—and Russian music—his unequaled version of Prokofiev's *Alexander Nevsky* Cantata? The only negative I could find—at first hearing—was that, for all its brilliance and marvelous brass, this *Scheherazade* was too "calculated," not sufficiently spontaneous or poetic, neither quality being Reiner's strongest point. An ideal performance could have been a combination of Reiner's precision and drama and Stokowski's fantasy, freedom of phrasing, and sense of color. They both made orchestration changes that I found totally unnecessary. And both had some puzzling similarities in "interpretation." Did they listen to each other's recordings? In that case, it would have to be Reiner imitating Stokowski, who had done it first. Perhaps Stokowski started it because the cellos and basses could not be heard clearly—in the dubious acoustics of the old Philadelphia Academy of Music—after the loud ending of the previous bars. Or perhaps Reiner heard a live Stokowski performance in Philadelphia. (Reiner had taught conducting at the Curtis Institute of Music before he went to Chicago.) There certainly were quite a few similarities all along. But I could find no musical justification for that drastic change in dynamics or for other major changes from the original score. Like Toscanini, Reiner acquired a reputation for total fidelity to the scores. (Toscanini, however, sometimes made almost as many alterations as Stokowski, especially in a Tchaikovsky work that Stokowski never conducted, the *Manfred* Symphony, and in many other works as well.)

Finally, after all the research into previous performances, I decided to agree with Reference Recordings' choice of repertoire. At once I requested the LPO's old set of orchestral parts. With recording time being so limited in London, I have always ensured that the music is marked to the teeth, with every dynamic indication, every string bowing, sometimes even fingerings, clearly indicated. I was shocked when I had a first look at the LPO's set of parts of *Scheherazade*: every conductor's "interpretation" had been faithfully inscribed into the individual parts, often in conflict with one another. The same passage was indicated both *p*, *mf*, and *ppp*, the result of the diametrically opposite "interpretations" of many conductors. The opening of the third movement in the strings had been penciled *flautando, non espressivo*—echoes of Beecham's ideas, another "tradition"? Some of the more drastic indications or orchestration changes had the name of the conductor and date clearly marked—in case he ever returned? out of admiration? not to be played that way with the other conductors? for posterity? Every one of the eighty-plus parts had the indication "*In four!*" before the very first bar, in spite of the obvious fact that the composer clearly indicated it to be in 2/2, to beat it in two. To beat it in four distorts it. And then there were the numerous cuts all over the music. The only recordings I had heard with any cuts had been a couple of the earlier Stokowski versions and Ormandy's—an unnecessary cut of one bar, at the climax of the finale, which disrupts the binary concept of the phrase. The cuts in the LPO's music seemed to have been done for children's concerts.

Part of the problem with this work, I was beginning to see, was going to be making the orchestra forget the previous performances and "traditions." Fortunately, the British orchestras are notoriously flexible and adaptable. (They often record the same work several times in the same month, with different conductors.) When I finally agreed to this recording project and proceeded to clean the orchestral parts one by one, it brought back memories of doing something similar with the Ives Fourth Symphony, with the same orchestra, twenty-five years before. (At the end of the last recording session, I asked how many LPO members had been in the orchestra at the time of my Ives recording: four sets of hands were lifted, followed by recollections of vivid memories from each musician. How could they forget the endless sectional rehearsals, an entire week, twelve hours per day?)

The cleaning and remarking of the *Scheherazade* music took nearly a month of concentrated work, all day and night. Yet it was essential to use the LPO's old set (the first markings were dated 1955!). With it, musicians tend to feel comfortable, so the "good" and practical markings were left unchanged. Many of the string bowings made sense and were left unchanged, as well as the long-practiced fingerings, some breath marks in the woodwinds, pedal indications in the harp part, and so on. What was erased were all the cuts, all the orchestration changes, the "interpretations" of countless other conductors, the conflicting alterations in dynamics. The musicians appreciated having a set of parts that felt familiar while having clear new indications of what was expected. The result was that the first rehearsal, which was "unofficially" recorded, became the basis and model for the actual final recorded version. The RR recording is in fact a live performance, with very few edits.

While all the instruments in *Scheherazade* are made to play in their best registers, and while the writing, while novel, is always logical, the work remains a tour de force for even the most accomplished orchestras. Familiarity with the work does not make it easier to perform it. During the weeks before the recording, when I was conducting the LPO in a series of concerts of Spanish music, I overheard the trumpet section doing an impromptu rehearsal of the demanding sections of the *Scheherazade* finale, the repeated note sequence before the last climax. The piccolo and flute section constantly practiced the virtuoso staccato passage in the same movement, and the violins kept trying out the impossible short segment from letters S to T. The LPO seemed to be really enjoying the recording sessions. During these sessions, I had one of the great satisfactions of my recording career. After the second session, having declared the second movement finished, and with some thirty minutes left before the end of the session, I bid the orchestra goodbye and wished them a good lunch. But no one moved! Some of them spoke out: "We have the time; why don't we read through the third movement?" I was quite moved. How often do professional orchestras ask to play on?

JOSÉ SEREBRIER ON THE NINE GLAZUNOV SYMPHONIES: AN APPRECIATION OF AN OVERLOOKED TREASURE

When Warner Classics and Jazz approached me with the proposal to record some Glazunov symphonies shortly after our recording with the New York Philharmonic, I was both flattered and puzzled. As the Glazunov project evolved over the years, I grew more and more enthusiastic about it, as did the wonderful musicians of the Royal Scottish National Orchestra. As we delved deeply into the scores, we discovered a mostly untapped wealth of wonderful late-Romantic music that had been largely neglected.

Was Glazunov a truly major composer? Only time can decide his eventual fate. Not to compare them in any way, but we must remember that Bach was mostly forgotten for a very long time until Mendelssohn championed his music, while Mahler was widely performed but did not become standard repertoire until Leonard Bernstein found his music to be an expression of his own innermost feelings and championed it with revealing, passionate performances. Glazunov's music doesn't carry its heart on its sleeve like Mahler's, and it doesn't explode hysterically like Tchaikovsky's. Like a Russian Brahms, it has deep emotions that are contained and controlled, sophisticated and subtle. A perfect compositional technique is obvious in every bar of music, as is the brilliant orchestration in typical late-nineteenth-century style.

Glazunov's inventive and constant harmonic shifts, abrupt changes of tempo, and short contrapuntal canons established his personal style of writing from his earliest works and remained with him throughout his life. The youthful First Symphony already shows most of the characteristics that appear in his later work; it is already unmistakably Glazunov. Pairing it with the truncated Ninth Symphony reveals the steadiness of his musical thinking.

Great composers are not only the ones who led us along new paths and took chances with experimentations. Music history is also filled with composers who did not try to move forward but wrote beautiful, meaningful, and communicative music. A quick glance at any Glazunov score, from the earliest ones, reveals a mastery of form and harmonic progression and an absolutely professional mind at work.

I found early on in this recording series that I could communicate through this music; I found a soul mate in its inner logic and sensibility. I could not bear to listen to other recordings, because I sensed that the scores cried out for a freedom of expression that some had missed. I shall explain. At that time, Gustav Mahler was writing passionate, personal music. Being an active conductor, he wrote constant performance directions into his scores, obsessively indicating every few bars what had to be played a little faster here, much faster there, to slow down for a few notes "but only a little," and on and on. Glazunov did not indicate any such directions, so most of the time his music is played almost metronomically, tending to lose the life between the notes. For me, it is not a question of taking liberties but just a matter of discovering the music's meaning and its human message. The page of printed notes is but a pale representation of the actual sounds. It's up to each individual performer to imagine him or herself in the composer's mind and thus to try both to re-create the desired feelings and to make the music communicate to the listener. This process of understanding the meaning behind the black and white notes on the page is different for every composer. Glazunov's music cries out for it.

The Violin Concerto joined the standard repertoire early on, and some of the ballets remain in the dance repertoire, but the large body of Glazunov's music has made only cameo appearances in concerts over the past seventy years. During the composer's lifetime, and for a few decades after, his music was a more regular element in concerts around the world. Most of the great Russian soloists of the twentieth century performed Glazunov's Cello Concerto and piano concertos on a regular basis and, judging from reviews of the times, with enormous success. Glazunov's music is, of course, not the only example of an artist's work that is passed over by history for a while. There are quite a few such neglected composers being given a new chance all the time, going back to the early Baroque era. We always rediscover them with wonder.

I am frequently asked if I can understand why Glazunov stopped composing, except for minor essays, two-thirds into his life. Some have suggested that becoming head of the Saint Petersburg Conservatory and teaching large composition classes robbed him of the time to compose, but this would not explain the musical silence of his many years in Paris after leaving the Soviet Union. My own interpretation is that Glazunov found himself in a similar predicament to his friend Rachmaninoff—who made two-piano reductions of his symphonies—and Sibelius, both of whom stopped composing long before the end of their lives. Concert music changed so drastically from the early days of the twentieth century that these and other composers still immersed in the late-Romantic tradition found themselves out of place. After long lapses of time, most of them returned hesitantly to composing, as Rachmaninoff did in his final decade, but still remaining true to themselves rather than being carried away by fashion.

It had happened before. Bach was considered hopelessly old-fashioned by his own sons. He was still writing Baroque music well into the start of the totally different Classical era. Eventually, as time has proven over and over, it did not matter. Today we perform Rachmaninoff and Sibelius alongside Schoenberg and Stravinsky, and the date when the works were written is no longer relevant to their value.

JOSÉ SEREBRIER ON KODÁLY

My fascination with the music of Zoltán Kodály started while I was working under the tutelage of Antal Doráti, during my early years as apprentice conductor of the Minneapolis Symphony—now the Minnesota Orchestra—a time during my early student days that is filled with wonderful memories. While our weekly lessons concentrated mostly around the Classics and Romantics, not a day went by when Doráti didn't mention his teacher Kodály. Doráti seemed to hold all the secrets to Bela Bartók's music, which he knew intimately, but I think it was the music of Kodály that seemed closest to his heart. We spent countless hours looking at the Kodály scores, most of them inscribed with the composer's penciled markings. Some of the first works I conducted in Minneapolis in those days were by Kodály, at Doráti's suggestion. He found that I had a kinship of spirit with Hungarian music and was amused by my explanation that my mother, while born in Poland, had spent her entire youth in Budapest and that I'd grown up on a constant dose of Hungarian cuisine.

During my years with George Szell—as composer-in-residence with the Cleveland Orchestra—I heard him rehearse and regularly perform the *Háry János* Suite. It was a spectacular display of virtuosity every time. The work is not that difficult to perform, but it does require a special sort of orchestra for maximum effect, a virtuoso orchestra with technique to spare, and lots of rehearsal time. In London, where I work most often, the orchestras have all the technique in the world but absolutely no rehearsal time. Because these musicians are such incredible sight-readers, recordings are done in London in the shortest time imaginable. I have done so myself innumerable times, with all the London orchestras. They regularly obtain great performances and brilliant recordings in spite of these working conditions, but for this particular recording I had something else in mind. I wanted a situation that permitted the orchestra to live with the music for a while before recording it. When a decision had to be made regarding the choice of orchestra for the Kodály project, the wonderful SWF Symphony Orchestra of Baden-Baden seemed the perfect choice for the *Háry János* Suite. We had performed it on tour with great success, and they seemed to identify with this music, which they knew well from previous performances. A live-performance recording from one of my concerts had already been issued by the Bodensee International Festival. It was exhilarating playing. The virtuosic displays seemed to enliven the orchestra soloists. The musicians had fun with it. So *Háry János* was assigned to them without hesitation. As for the other three works, I was looking for special considerations: a particular clarinet solo sound and color for the *Dances of Galánta*, and similar, specific requirements for the other two works. Having worked regularly with the Brno Orchestra in concerts and recordings, I decided to complete the Kodály CD with them, despite the fact that these three works were unknown to them. My instinct was proven right. The solo clarinet sounded just as in my dreams. From the very first reading, the orchestra members played it as if they had known this music all their lives. After all, Hungary is next door.

To me it seemed interesting to record the *Dances of Galánta* with a Czech orchestra. Kodály had spent seven childhood years—from ages three to ten— in the village of Galánta in northwestern Hungary. Later on Galanta became part of what was then Czechoslovakia. The Czechs of the Moravian region feel this music like the native Hungarians. There is, however, a certain amount of detachment, which arguably gives them an advantage. The Brno Orchestra of course has a direct line of tradition from Janáček—who lived in Brno most of his life—and their folkloric Moravian roots but also for all the music inspired by the rich folklore of the surrounding areas, especially Hungary.

Each one of the four works I chose for my Kodály recording has different problems for the orchestra and for the conductor—and by implication for the recording team. For the *Háry János* Suite one of the most obvious challenges is how and where to place the cimbalom so that it sounds realistic. Under normal concert conditions, the cimbalom can hardly be heard above the orchestra, regardless of its position on the stage. But Kodály was after the color, the "taste," more than an obvious presence. We tried to make the recorded sound as natural as possible, resembling a concert situation. In fact, as a model we used our own live recording at the Bodensee Festival. We were fortunate to have one of the world's experts on the cimbalom, who had come especially from Hungary for all the performances, and later for the recording. We treated the recording as a live performance, with no edits. The movements are short enough that we felt free to rerecord them several times until we could confidently feel that at least one of the performances had the right spirit as well as the technical accuracy.

I mentioned before the crucial clarinet solo in the *Dances of Galánta*. There are no real technical difficulties in it, just a natural instinct for the folkloric roots of the melodic turns and the special phrasing and color that the melody requires. The *Dances of Marosszék* are equally beautiful but lesser known. The Brno musicians told me during the recording sessions that these dances reminded them of Janácek's early Lathian dances, which we had recorded for RR the previous year. Both sets of dances follow the same principle of stylizing folkloric material from nearby regions. However, the Janáček dances are "set" pieces, individually constructed. Kodály made a sort of continuous suite instead—both in *Galánta* and in *Marosszék*—moving fast and freely from dance to dance, creating an ingenious, unique free form. The same principle was used by Kodály in constructing the "Peacock" Variations. Each set of variations moves smoothly into the next one, creating a seamless musical form. Once again the folkloric elements made the Brno musicians feel at home. I am delighted that, since the recording and their discovery of this wonderful music, they perform it regularly and often in their tours. This is music that has strong and immediate appeal to all sorts of audiences and is also respected, admired, and loved by the professionals in the field.

JOSÉ SEREBRIER ON THE SONGS OF EDVARD GRIEG

There are some composers who appeal only to a minority, and there are those few who reach and touch everyone. Edvard Grieg was unique in many ways. Admired and respected by Brahms and Tchaikovsky, he became a source of inspiration to Delius. Unlike these three masters, Grieg came from a land without a long tradition of great composers. He exemplified the sound of Scandinavia until Sibelius came along. The sense of beauty that Grieg's music exudes has few parallels, and while there is nothing simple about it, it reaches listeners at every level. It is easy to like the music of Edvard Grieg. It communicates directly to the heart of the listener.

While Grieg composed over 180 songs, he only orchestrated a very few of them. The idea to orchestrate several of his other songs came to me only after a frantic search for orchestrations proved to be fruitless. The Swiss label Dinemec Classics was intent on having an orchestral recording of Grieg songs, but the idea did not seem possible at first. The Norwegian Music

Information Center in Oslo was most helpful in locating an orchestration of the op. 48 songs. At Peters Music Publishers we found the Max Reger unusual orchestration of *Eros*, op. 70, no. 1, and at the BBC library a 1943 Frederick Byl arrangement of *Eit Syn*, op. 33, no. 6. The BBC also had a few other arrangements from the same era, ranging from stock orchestrations for small radio ensembles to orchestrations of Wagnerian proportions. *Eit Syn* was the only one that came close to Grieg's sound. I soon came to realize that if we believed in this project, I would have to orchestrate the songs myself. Realizing that the songs were among Grieg's most exquisite works, I took great care to orchestrate them idiomatically, approximating his sound world. Some of the orchestrations that we found in libraries seemed overblown and bombastic. I wanted to stay with the spirit as well as the letter of the music and to use only the instruments dictated by the character of each song.

The original Dinemac Classics plan was to do a Delius/Grieg album, but it became apparent that we had accumulated enough material for two full recordings, one by each composer. There are similarities of approach and yet great differences between the two composers. One of the poems, "Twilight Fancies" (Abendstimmung), was used by both Grieg and Delius, with totally different results.

On July 17, 1900, Grieg had written to his American biographer, Henry Finck, "I do not think that I have more talent for composing songs than for any other genre. Why have songs played such a prominent role in my music? Simply because I was once in my life endowed with genius, and that flash of genius was love. I loved a young woman with a marvelous voice who also had a great gift as an interpreter. This woman became my wife and has remained my companion to this day . . . my songs come to life spontaneously, and all of them were written for her." Grieg, however, dedicated his collection *Sechs Lieder (Six Songs)*, op. 48, to the singer Ellen Nordgren (Ellen Gulbranson), who was becoming known for her Wagnerian roles. This might give an indication of the type of voice Grieg was looking for. Toward the end of his life, Grieg accompanied this singer in several recitals of these songs. Grieg admired very few singers, and most of them met with his scorn. There has been a tendency lately to perform Grieg songs with a white, sometimes vibrato-less tone, sometimes resembling altar singing, which hadn't been the case at all when Kirsten Flagstad had sung them. Grieg songs became a specialty of Flagstad, and she rendered them as warm, full-blooded songs. Nevertheless, these are universal songs that can withstand individual approaches.

My choice of songs to orchestrate was dictated primarily by the character of the writing. In most cases, the orchestration seemed so obvious, it literally jumped out of the page. The first two I attempted were the everlasting "Zur Rosenzeit" (by Goethe), op. 48, no. 5, and "Moderen Synger" (by Krag), op. 60, no. 2. The simple accompaniment seemed to require only strings. "Der Skreg en Fugl," op. 60, no. 4, and "Liden Kirsten," op. 60, no. 1, thus completed the cycle. There followed in quick succession "Die Prinzessin" (by Bjornson), "Til Norge," op. 58, no. 2; "Den Bergtekne" (a folk song), op. 32; "Ein Traum" (by Bodenstedt), op. 48, no. 6; and the Ibsen cycle, op. 25, "Spillemaend" (no. 1), "Stambogsrim" (no. 3), "Med en Vandlilje" (no. 4), "Borte" (no. 5), and "En Fuglevise" (no. 6). "En Svane" (no. 2) was the only one of this cycle orchestrated by Grieg, thus becoming the most famous of the group. The other five romances are equally brilliant, and hopefully these orchestrations will contribute to their popularity.

Grieg and Ibsen knew each other for a long time without ever developing a close friendship. Once in Rome, in 1884, Ibsen attended a soiree during which Nina Grieg sang some of the op. 25 songs, and he was reported to have been moved to the point of tears. Ibsen's poems did inspire Grieg to produce some of his most beautiful music. In 1876 Grieg composed the *Six Songs*, op. 25, capturing the introverted mood of Ibsen's poems and reflecting their drama as well as their innate lyricism. While Grieg obviously loved all the poems, "A Swan" touched him deeply, and it could be a reason why he decided to orchestrate it. His biographers, Benestad and Schjelderup-Ebbe, reflected that, "for Grieg, the strange poem of the swan that sings only before dying seemed to be an image of his own situation: the greatest tribulations of life are overcome only through art."

Small but subtle differences in orchestration give each of the songs their own special color and character. For "A Swan," the second song in op. 25, Grieg used only one oboe, two bassoons, two horns, harp, and strings. The Norwegian Music Information Center sent me Ragnar Søederlind's orchestrations of the *Six German Lieder*, op. 48. They seemed appropriate, except for the last two, which had extra trumpets, horns, trombones, tuba, and percussion, thus making them sound, in my view, larger than the more intimate the Grieg palette required. In fact, for "Zur Rosenzeit" I used only strings, and for "Ein Traum" the maximum "basic" orchestration of two flutes, two oboes, two clarinets, two bassoons, two horns, harp, and strings.

JOSÉ SEREBRIER ON STOKOWSKI'S SOUND

The sound of an orchestra would change within moments of its first encounter with Stokowski. There was nothing that he would have said or done to make such an obvious change, other than to start rehearsing after a minimal greeting. One explanation could be that Stokowski had a special sound in his mind, and his gestures and facial expressions had the ability to communicate this sound to any orchestra. This was not a talent unique to Stokowski, and we have noticed it elsewhere. It isn't unusual for the sound of a professional ensemble to acquire some of the characteristics of a student group after it has spent some time working under the direction of a school orchestra conductor. This has nothing to do with the technical aspects of performance. It has to do with the sound the conductor has imprinted in his inner ear and the conductor's ability to produce that same sound quality from any orchestra. Almost every conductor has that ability. The degree to which it produces a dramatic influence is related, partially, to the sound that has become imprinted in the conductor's memory. It seems logical that if a conductor who has spent years directing the Vienna Philharmonic has an encounter with a school orchestra, this group will soon sound smooth and refined. While it can be argued that the students would sit up, concentrate, and do their best when confronted with a known personality, the change in the actual sound quality they produce would be involuntary. It would be a natural reaction to the conductor's idea of sound, acquired after years of listening to a specific quality of sound.

This theory works in both extremes and also in the present reality of music making around the world. There was a time when orchestras had a distinctive quality that set them easily apart. These differences were partially the result of conductors spending long decades with their orchestras. But conductors were not the only decisive factors. Some ensembles, such as the Philadelphia Orchestra, had very few changes in personnel, and a vast majority of the musicians had been trained by the same teachers, in the same school. Sadly, most orchestras today have acquired a similarity of sound. While technique and performance standards seem to have improved, there is a worldwide unanimity of approach that makes many performances redundant copies of each other. What has happened? Do performers listen to each other's recordings and unconsciously imitate one another? Are today's performers afraid to take chances and want to be literal to the point of excluding personal sensibility? Why has the sound quality of many orchestras become so similar?

Stokowski's idea of sound was so unmistakable, and so special, that it remained with the Philadelphia Orchestra for many decades after Stokowski's departure. It became known as the "Philadelphia sound." In fact, with Eugene Ormandy, this sound continued in the same tradition but naturally acquired some changes over the many years. Part of what Stokowski did to obtain his kind of sound must have been unconscious, a reflection of his gestures and approach. But he also made conscious efforts to request specific playing from his orchestras to shape the overall sound. One of his most famous habits was to demand that the strings play with free bowings. When guest conducting, this request caused orchestras the greatest grief and displeasure. I remember

Stokowski's rehearsals with a few famous orchestras, both in the United States and in Europe, and the resistance he encountered when requesting that each stand of strings play with opposite bowings and not write bowings down. Orchestras such as the Philadelphia Symphony, and later the Houston and the American symphonies, which played all the time with Stokowski, understood the principle and learned to use this technique to advantage. Stokowski's explanation was rather simpler than the fact, but it helped the string musicians realize there was a method at work. Because bows naturally lose power as they descend, and similarly gain in power as they ascend, combining bows simultaneously in both directions would in principle produce a more even sound. In my opinion, Stokowski carried this good idea too far, using it in every instance rather than for specific effects or specific passages. In any case, it did play a great part in obtaining a lush, powerful, and unmistakable string tone. Balancing the woodwinds was another Stokowski hallmark. As Rimsky had noted in his orchestration book, a flute or an oboe has a hard time competing against sixty strings. Stokowski experimented with changing the traditional placement of woodwinds to try to enhance their volume and to make the performers more visible. He felt that, having to play behind the large body of strings, the winds were hidden from the audience and that their sound had to pass across the string barrier. For a while, Stokowski experimented by placing the woodwinds to his right, in place of the cellos or violas. This drastically changed their sound and the overall balance. Sometimes Stokowski lined up the basses in the back of the stage on high podiums, with the horns directly in front, to produce a soundboard for the horns and for the entire orchestra. It also gave the basses an organ-like quality. Stokowski would constantly make the brass softer than indicated in the score, to better balance the strings and winds. This, added to his specifications to not use podiums for the brass, contributed in large measure to form the smooth "Philadelphia sound," with a glorious string tone and audible woodwinds. Stokowski made sure that the sound had beauty, sometimes by smoothing the edges. There was logic to everything he did to obtain a rounded, warm tone from the orchestra. Some of it can be explained, but much of it can only be called magic.

How I Was in Two Places at One Time

Gary Karr

INTERNATIONAL DOUBLEBASS ASSOCIATION

"How would you like to record *Nueve* with the Bournemouth Symphony in June of next year?" Before giving my answer to the composer, José Serebrier, several thoughts popped into my mind. I had to tell him that I no longer traveled anywhere by plane with my bass and that I had retired in 2001. Also, it had been several decades since I last performed *Nueve*, and I couldn't remember the music. I hated saying no to Serebrier, but I couldn't come up with a polite response that would reflect my great joy in having been asked. So, after telling him about my retirement, I said, "Give me a few days to think about it, and I'll get back to you." I then pulled out my score of the aleatoric, twelve-tone-like piece and was struck once again, after all these years, by its inherent lyricism and long phrases (which is my cup of tea). I really wanted to be involved in the project, but the thought of traveling all the way to England with my bass was a strong deterrent. The increasing problem of flying with my instrument was one of the main reasons why I had taken early retirement.

Since *Nueve* was written specifically for me, Serebrier had my sound in mind, and it was that soloistic double bass sound that he wanted on the recording. He urged me to think about it some more. So, for several weeks I gave the matter considerable thought. Then the phone rang. It was Serebrier, and I've never heard him so excited! My first thought was that, in his inimitable style, he had found a way to bring the entire Bournemouth Symphony to Victoria, Canada (where I live), to record *Nueve*. He said, "I was talking to Carole, who had a great idea." Carole Farley, his wife (I played at their wedding!), is a Metropolitan Opera star who became famous in her soprano roles in *Salome* and *Lulu*. Carole had said to José, "Since much of the solo bass writing is without orchestra accompaniment, perhaps

181

Gary would be willing to record the solo line in the comfort of his own private studio?" I was trapped. How could I say no to such a logical and easy solution? "Okay," I said to José. "I'll record my part, send it to you for your expert opinion, and then you can decide if it might work." Later, this is what Serebrier had to say: "After discussion with the production team, we agreed that it"—multitracking in various locations—"was a great idea for this particular work. By the way, my friend Thomas Shepard, ex-CEO of RCA/BMG and producer of some five hundred recordings"—mostly with the Philadelphia Orchestra, including Ormandy—"recently made an opera recording with the London Symphony Orchestra and added all the singers later in New York! You cannot tell the difference. What matter most in recording are the final results." He also told me that the recording engineer would be Phil Rowlands, with whom I had worked before and who is regarded as one of the top people in the business.

There were still two problems that I wanted Serebrier to address. I suggested that a real actor instead of me should read the Shelley poems included in *Nueve*. His response was, "You recited the words wonderfully in many of our concerts together in Cleveland, New Jersey, Cape Town, et cetera, but I'll ask Simon Callow, the great British actor, if he'll consider doing it." Fortunately for me, since I was a big fan of his, Callow loved the idea and eventually recorded, in London, six versions of the poems from which Serebrier could choose for the recording. My other concern was the short pizzicato sections that I felt should be done by another bassist at the recording session who could work in conjunction with the drums. To my delight, Serebrier said, "It's a brilliant idea, because the Bournemouth Symphony Orchestra is blessed with one of the best bass players I have ever encountered." He then later e-mailed me, "I am delighted to tell you that the wonderful, brilliant solo bass of the Bournemouth Symphony Orchestra, David Daly, is quite happy to record the jazz passages in *Nueve*. I know you will be pleased." And indeed I was!

As they say in the UK, I'm "gobsmacked" and absolutely delighted with the finished product. It's an engineering and musical tour de force.

This is what José Serebrier wrote about *Nueve*:

> Commissioned by the Plainfield Symphony Orchestra for their fiftieth anniversary, I wrote *Nueve* for and in homage to Gary Karr. He was living in Plainfield, New Jersey, at the time. We premiered *Nueve* there and played it in Cleveland and even in South Africa among other places.
>
> I wrote *Nueve* during my two seasons as composer-in-residence at the Cleveland Orchestra. It was a companion piece to my harp concerto, *Colores Mágicos*. Both concertos have much in common: aleatoric writing, distance between the musicians, and, most disturbing for conductors, no

bar lines at all. In *Nueve*, conductors could not do what they basically do—beat time. The harp piece became a ballet with the Joffrey Ballet and toured the United States. In it, the only musician on the stage was the harp soloist, with the orchestra in the pit, like in an opera. In *Nueve*, the solo bass is surrounded by the string orchestra, while the only woodwinds, two clarinets, are "incognito" in the audience. During one of the variations, a jazz segment, the two clarinetists stand up and play along and surprise the unsuspecting audience. At the climax of the jazz variation, the brass erupts in the balcony. All along, the soloist is reading poetry, a poem by Shelley. In the concerts, Gary Karr did the poetry reading beautifully. For the recording, he suggested that an actor do the reading. We had the great fortune to have the incomparable Simon Callow. At the end of *Nueve*, while the orchestra reaches a tremendous climax on one note in unison, a choir emerges in the distance and can be heard in an ethereal chant, adding an element of timelessness and perhaps eeriness. This is in direct contrast to the noisy jazz variation in which two opposite jazz drummers undergo a sort of "combat," alternating and finally joining in the game. The work has nine variations and uses mostly nine notes. The reason for the title and the concept was that my New York apartment was, and remains, on Ninety-Ninth Street, on the ninth floor. *Nueve*, of course, is Spanish for nine. While *Nueve* may be a "period piece," unsurprising at the time it was conceived, something about its concept remains close to me, and when compared to previous or later works, it is not different in its ultimate message, regardless of the different language used.

Miscellaneous Press Interviews

GRAMOPHONE MAGAZINE

By James Jolly, Gramophone *Editor-in-Chief (reprinted with permission)*

Last summer, I was in Moscow introducing the piano categories of the Tchaikovsky competition for Medici TV, and you got in touch with me, when it was obvious that Alexandre Kantorow was doing very well. And he clinched the gold medal, and then went on to win the Grand Prix. Then you sent me a sound file of a recent recording of your new piano concerto. I listened to it, and I wrote to you: "I really enjoyed your piano concerto. It sounds incredibly Russian," to which you answered: "Well, if you heard more of my music, you may hear a Slavic bent in it. My mother was Polish and my father Russian. But I did not grow up listening to Russian music, so it must be in my genes, in my soul, I guess, to write music that sounds Slavic and the piano concerto reflects it. Sometimes I write music that has a Latin flavor because I was born and grew up in Uruguay."

How did your parents wind up in Uruguay?

My father went to Philadelphia where all my family lives. In fact, I have about 600 relatives there. Whenever I do a concert in Philadelphia, it sells out immediately, and they are all my cousins, uncles and aunts. My father was an engineer, and his company sent him to Uruguay to start a company. I happened to be born there, which was lucky, because many great musicians had immigrated to that part of the world from Italy, Germany, Spain and Russia. My violin teacher, Jasha Fidlon, had a picture in his study of himself with Heifetz. When Leopold Auer was busy, he told Fidlon to coach Heifetz. Fidlon escaped while on tour with a Russian orchestra and quietly requested asylum in Uruguay, where he started a marvelous school of violinists. When I started to study with Fidlon, it must have been painful for him to hear me doing beginner's scales on the violin, but for me at age 9 it was a great experience.

**If you listen to the opening of your piano concerto,
there is a sort of flavor of Mussorgsky in the opening bars.**

Indeed. I will call it post-Mussorgsky!

**Post-Mussorgsky, absolutely. So how did it come about, this commission?
Basically, it's not actually called a piano concerto, is it?**

No. I called it Symphonic *B A C H* Variations.

But it's in four movements, although they're not performed separate.

Yes. They link into each other. B-A-C-H are the German letters for the notes B for B flat, A for the note A, and then C for the note C, and H is B natural. Si-La-Do-Si. So, the whole concerto, or whatever you call it, is variations on these 4 notes. Many composers have done that including Bach himself, but I purposely stayed away from looking up any other versions so I would not be influenced. My work plays around constantly, obsessively, with those four notes.

Was this written specifically for Alexandre Kantorow?

It was a commission. The idea came from BIS Records, because they had been promoting him long before he won the Tchaikovsky competition. And the owner of BIS, Robert von Bahr, wanted to commission me to write something to help promote him further, long before we knew he will win this fantastic competition. At the same time, American Composers Orchestra, based in Carnegie Hall, wanted to commission me for a second time to write something. When I wrote it, long before I met him, it worked out like we were brothers, because he has the most phenomenal technique, as we saw at the Moscow competition.

I noted technique, stamina and musicianship.

I didn't have to explain a single phrase. By instinct or whatever, he knew exactly how to phrase the delicate passages and the octaves, which he told me they are quite difficult. He played them like it was simple and easy. The piano is like a toy for him. Alex is an unbelievable pianist.

We first tried it out in Costa Rica, with their National Symphony Orchestra. Of all the orchestras in Central America, it's my favorite. Costa Rica doesn't have an army. It's one of the few countries in the world that doesn't have an army. Whatever funds they have from tourism and other things, they use for theater, culture, medicine and, of course, music. So, we tried the concerto out there, a 'pre-premiere'. Then we played it in Dublin, before recording it for BIS. And most recently, we did it in Lima, Peru, which has the best orchestra in that part of the world, and a marvelous hall. In fact, Alex arrived the morning of the concert and went straight to rehearsal. I had prepared the orchestra before. He rehearsed like it was an everyday event, played the concert that night, and left the next morning. I still can't get over what he did at the Moscow competition. He played the Tchaikovsky Second Concerto beautifully, walked off stage, and within minutes he was back to play the formidable Brahms Second Concerto.

It was quite incredible. Well, he is 22. He probably would not have to do this often in his career, to play two enormous concertos in a row.

This new recording of yours, not only has the first recording of your piano concerto, the symphonic *B A C H* variations, but also a flute concerto, which you wrote for Sharon Bezaly. Is this another commission from Robert von Bahr of BIS, who happens to be Sharon's husband?

Indeed. And she did a premiere with me, with the American Composers Orchestra at Carnegie Hall. And it's an incredibly difficult work, but it all works. It's very practical for the instrument, but it requires an amazing technique. And then Sharon played it all over the world with other conductors. I wasn't at the recording. This was done with a marvelous chamber ensemble, the Australian Chamber Orchestra and Richard Tognetti. He directed it, and it sounds fantastic. So, BIS added this recording to the piano concerto.

It's a totally different piece from the piano concerto. I am very proud of that, because it's very easy to imitate oneself, for composers (or writers) to fall into that. But this one is a totally different piece.

And it's called "Flute Concerto with Tango."

I must say I was influenced by the title "Orkney Wedding with Sunrise."

Oh, the Maxwell Davies work.

Yes, Maxwell Davies's "Orkney Wedding with Sunrise." I thought, "What a great idea." I was inspired by that unusual title, and I called mine "Flute Concerto with Tango." There is a tango in the middle. It fits, because it leads right into the finale. And, it's not finished, purposely, it leaves you up in the air. The reason is, tangos traditionally end on the dominant chord, not in the final tonic, and they leave you up in the air, all tangos. And maybe not the Piazzola ones, but the original tangos. So instead of doing that, I left it, literally, in the air. When the music arrived for Sharon Bezaly in Stockholm, Mr. von Bahr wrote back saying, "It's not finished. Something's missing."

There is a page missing.

I said, "No, look at the title. The title is *Tango Inconcluso* in Spanish; "unfinished tango." And then, the finale comes and it's a fiery piece, very different from the piano concerto, but it's one of my best pieces.

And there are other pieces in the Super Audio SACD as well.

Yes, there are three more tango-related pieces on the BIS recording. The first one I wrote is "Tango in Blue." The National Symphony of Uruguay, OSSODRE, has a great tradition. Erich Kleiber was the conductor—Carlos's father—for about five years. That was before I was born, and he established a great tradition, which is why Carlos was given a Spanish name, why my parents gave me a Spanish name So the orchestra in Uruguay was becoming 75, and the members invited me to do their anniversary concert. From New York to Montevideo it's a 12 hour flight. I thought I would bring a gift, and this "Tango in Blue" was my gift to the orchestra.

And you wrote it on the flight?

Yes, I do that often. The third one I also wrote on a flight, "Last Tango Before Sunrise," a very romantic and evocative piece.

Well, you obviously are a very spontaneous composer. Do you think, "I am going to write something" and always travel with a good amount of music manuscript paper?

No. In fact, I was on a cruise last month, and I didn't have music paper with me. I had no intention of writing, but suddenly I realized I needed to add one more piece to the new recording of my music, sponsored by my publishers, Peermusic, but we felt the recording was too short. And they asked me, "Could we have one more piece?" So, I wrote to a student of mine from Julliard, and she sent me one page of music manuscript paper by email; I made copies, and I wrote a new piece and sent it. So, yes, I write spontaneously, but everything is planned somehow in my head. I don't just write, and then think, "what should I do next?." Somehow the architecture of it is all planned. And then, it is just being fast enough to put all the notes down.

And some of the music on here, you've gone back to pieces that you wrote many, many years ago, and have revisited for a new arrangement.

Yes. There is an Adagio for strings which I originally wrote for choir long ago. Then, when I made a recording with St. Michael Strings in Finland, and they wanted to include a work of mine I arranged it for strings. That CD includes music by my friend Rautavaara. We had studied together with Aaron Copland. Rautavaara and I became lifetime friends. In fact, he brought me to Finland to record his music; that's how I started a continuous relationship with Finland.

When you've written a piece of music and it's published, and it's out there, does it feel like you've sent your children out and they are making their own way? Do you like hearing your own music coming back from someone else?

Indeed. I feel that way about painters. I have several painter friends, and I wondered how do they feel when they sell a painting and never see it again? A composer doesn't have that problem. I was lucky that Sir John Eliot Gardiner, whom I have not met in person, recorded my "*Symphony for Percussion*" a long time ago, and I only found out when I heard it on the radio. It was on a short-lived label before CD, can you imagine how long ago? It was "Direct to disc." I went to buy a copy and it was incredibly expensive because it was on thick original vinyl, and it came with a 10-year warranty. But shortly after, two years later, that record company ceased to exist because CDs took over, but in between the LP and the CD there was "Direct to Disc."

So, I am lucky that other conductors play my music, and not only Sir John Eliot Gardiner; Stokowski premiered three of my works. It's a wonderful satisfaction to see one's music being played by other people. I seldom play my own music in concerts because there is so little space in concerts for new music, that I feel I should play other contemporary composer's music.

RITMO MAGAZINE, SPAIN, NOVEMBER 2020

José Serebrier

To Feel the Music

by Gonzalo Pérez Chamorro (reprinted with permission)

Talking with José Serebrier is like reviewing the history of music of the last seventy years, of which he continues to be a great protagonist. In fact, Seiji Ozawa himself extols Serebrier in his recently published book by Tusquets, *Absolutely on Music*, which collects Ozawa's conversations with writer Haruki Murakami. He is a great Serebrier admirer.

"As a conductor, I could define my artistic moment as eclectic, since it embraces music from all centuries and in all styles; I am not in favor of specialization," says Maestro Serebrier, who conducts the Málaga Philharmonic Orchestra on December 3 and 4 in a program of classical works. "This beautiful program replaces the original program that included works for large orchestra, and given the need to reduce the number of musicians on stage, we looked for a program that can be performed with fewer than fifty musicians." Who else has had such close contact with personalities like Aaron Copland, George Szell (when Serebrier was composer-in-residence for two years during Szell's glorious time in Cleveland), and Leopold Stokowski, among others? Stokowski premiered and recorded the Serebrier First Symphony when he was seventeen years old, studying at Curtis. Serebrier, who has a voice as both performer and composer, and whose works are recorded and performed throughout five continents, offered a rather curious statement: "When I play my own works, on recordings and rarely in my concerts, it is as if they were the works of some other composer—a strange experience . . . I feel detached from it." Or as he also tells us, regarding his relationship as conductor and composer, "One of the problems that seems to occur if one is both a composer and conductor is that other conductors generally do not program one's works, with rare exceptions." This is José Serebrier, an essential personality of the music world, feeling it so deeply that it appears to be an inescapable part of his DNA.

Maestro, you have two concerts in our country with the Málaga Philharmonic on December 3 and 4, with a program dedicated to Classicalism that culminates with Beethoven's Eighth. Can you tell us about the program and why these works?

The simple truth is that this beautiful program replaces the original one that included works for large orchestra. Given the need to reduce the number of musicians on stage these days, requiring separation between them, we looked for a program that can be performed with fewer than fifty musicians. These are extraordinary works of Classicism, and I have recorded them several times.

How would you define the artistic moment that you are in at this time?

As a composer, I feel liberated, because in these times there is no longer the dictatorship of having to write experimental or twelve-tone music. When I was composer-in-residence with the Cleveland Orchestra, invited for two extraordinary years by George Szell, it was a time of experimentation, and I composed works of the time, a Concerto for Harp and Orchestra, *Colores Mágicos*, which uses projections, and the score does not include bar lines. Just a few months ago we recorded this work for the first time with the Málaga Philharmonic Orchestra. During my time in Cleveland I also composed a Concerto for Double Bass and Orchestra, *Nueve*, for Gary Karr, recorded in Naxos. I have other experimental works, such as *Erotica*, for wind quintet and soprano, in which the musicians play separately from each other, in various parts of the theater, and the singer is offstage. But my music has evolved, and works like my new Concerto for Piano and Orchestra, *Symphonic Variations on B A C H*, could be classified as neoromantic. The recording, on the BIS label, was made with the extraordinary twenty-two-year-old French pianist Alexandre Kantorow, who shortly thereafter won the Gold Medal at the Moscow Tchaikovsky Competition. And as a conductor, I could define my artistic moment as eclectic, since it embraces music from all centuries and in all styles. I am not in favor of specializations.

Are you a composer who conducts, a conductor who composes, or does each of the two facets complement and enrich the other?

That is an extremely interesting question. I have always thought that being a composer helps enormously in preparing the scores for conducting, because after studying them thoroughly and digesting them, you see them as if you had composed them yourself. In addition, to be a composer you need to have studied music theory, counterpoint, orchestration, piano, and so on, all of which are essential for the conductor. Both facets complement each other, since the experience of conducting other works, from all periods, is invaluable for composing. I never conduct my own works in concerts, because I want to dedicate the little space allowed for new works to the music of my colleagues and not usurp that short span of time with my own music. In recordings, however, I have frequently conducted my own works. But it's great when conductors of the stature of Leopold Stokowski and Sir John Eliot Gardiner record my works. Stokowski premiered and recorded my First Symphony when I was seventeen years old and studying at the Curtis Institute in Philadelphia. Five years later, when I was Stokowski's associate conductor at Carnegie Hall, the maestro conducted my "Poema Elegíaco" and my *Elegy for Strings*. Sir John, whom I have not met in person, recorded my *Symphony for Percussion* long ago. I found out about it when I heard it on the radio in New York. One of the problems that seems to occur if you are both a composer and conductor is that other conductors generally do not program your works, with rare exceptions. The same thing happened to Mahler in his time, for example. There are good exceptions. Here in Spain, Maestro José Ramón Encinar conducted my Symphony No. 2, *Partita*, a couple of years ago. The Russian National Orchestra programmed my *Symphony for Percussion* last year, and they recorded it for a new CD of my works released by Reference Recordings. This RR CD was recorded in Malaga, Moscow, New York City, San Francisco, and Miami!

Can you tell the readers why you don't use the baton when conducting?

There was a period of years when I did not use a baton, as the hands are much more expressive than a wooden stick, but in opera I use a baton so that the singers can see my gestures from the stage, and lately I also use a baton in concerts. It is better for large orchestras so that the brass and percussion, at the back of the stage, can see the gestures clearly. For slow movements, I often give up the baton and use my hands.

**Of Russian and Polish origin, of American birth, and residences
between New York and London . . . Does this panoramic vision
of the world and culture help you better understand the situation
we are going through—politically and regarding health—
as well as better understand the great masterpieces of music?**

Another extremely interesting question. My panoramic view of the world
is due to my constant international tours with orchestras, and although the
stays in each city are extremely short, you get something tangential from each
place. Having a home in New York and London is practical. What the world
is going through this year is a new experience that has affected everyone. I recently composed a new piece for wind quintet titled *The Year 2020*, in which
I have tried to express in sounds the uncertainty that we all feel.

**Of your works, which do you feel most attached to?
Or do you love all your children equally?**

When we play my own works, on recordings and rarely in my concerts,
it is as if they were works by some other composer, a strange experience
. . . But there are certain works with which I identify more than others—early
works like the *Elegy for Strings*, the "Poema Elegíaco," the Third Symphony,
which we programmed in my European tour with JONDE and which can be
seen and heard on YouTube, since Naxos released a DVD of the tour; and my
three tangos, *Tango in Blue*, *Almost a Tango*, and *El Último Tango del Amanecer*
(*Last Tango before Sunrise*). A recent piece in this genre is *Candombe*, and we
recorded the four of these a few months ago with the Málaga Philharmonic,
my third recording with this orchestra. I have previously recorded several
times with the Barcelona Symphony Orchestra, and one of those recordings
on the BIS label won the Latin GRAMMY for best orchestral recording of
the year. That CD contains the *Carmen Symphony* by Bizet-Serebrier, a work
to which I am also quite attached.

**You have an extensive discography, and the accolades are continuous.
In fact, you recently achieved the Diapason d'Or for a CD of
French music with your wife, soprano Carole Farley.
What value do you place on these awards?**

It is always flattering to receive awards, but for me they are not very important. The GRAMMY and Latin GRAMMY awards and nominations have

very special meaning since the votes come from our colleagues, and being appreciated in such a way by colleagues is heartwarming.

On Naxos you not only recorded a large part of your own works but have also tackled a diverse repertoire of many other contemporary composers . . .

Naxos owner Klaus Heymann has been a friend since before he founded his record company, when his wife, a gifted violinist, toured Australia with me. Naxos's support for artists is enormous, and Klaus Heymann continues to consider new repertoire without prejudice and always with great enthusiasm.

Is there something you have not done in life that you still wish to do?

A lot. The list is quite long.

If you could go back to the past, what would you rectify?

That is a philosophical question. I imagined, back in my childhood when I decided to dedicate myself professionally to music, that it wouldn't be at all easy, and yet I made the decision anyway—but with some trepidation, because I had no idea what would happen without a "safe" profession. Thinking back, I don't think I would change any of the key, basic, and important decisions that defined my career and personal life.

As an international figure who has worked with Leopold Stokowski and George Szell, among other great names, how has the world of classical music evolved?

The evolution has not been satisfactory in the sense that much of the individuality of many artists has been lost—perhaps because the recordings of others are listened to.

I have been a juror in competitions for pianists, violinists, and conductors, and most of the participants sound rather similar. A long time ago I recorded Mendelssohn's Symphonies No. 3 and 4. A great musicologist, composer, and critic offered to send me some forty recordings of these extraordinary works. Those that were recorded before 1950 showed different contours, but many of the following renditions sounded like mirrors of one another. From time to time, artists emerge who feel the music individually.

Are you more of a concert or opera theater conductor?
Where do you feel most comfortable?

In both. They are different experiences.

Contemporary American composers are indebted to you for
your constant dedication, including premieres, recordings, and
performances of the highest quality. Do you think that a gap
has opened between today's audiences and composers,
or is there still a strong connection between the two?

Thank you for noting that I have constantly tried to schedule new works. It is sad that this is not usually the case, because many artists feel comfortable programming works that they know in depth and that are guaranteed to be successful with the public. Stokowski constantly programmed new works of all styles. It was one of the reasons he lost his position in Philadelphia. The same happened with Brazilian conductor Eleazar de Carvalho, who was my teacher and teacher to Zubin Mehta, Claudio Abbado, Seiji Ozawa, and many others. This great musician had to leave his post in St. Louis, as the board of directors could not tolerate so much contemporary music. The public in many cities expects and wants to hear new works. Concerts must not become museums.

Your relationship with Spain is intense, but how do you see our
country from its international position and from other countries?

Spain has always had extraordinary musicians and composers. Its music and its artists are admired and respected throughout the world. Spain is one of the most musical countries in the world.

Asking you about your next projects is like asking a river to stop pouring
water, since you tirelessly confront new goals, but can you tell us a few?

Nineteen years ago, French music critic Michel Faure decided to write a book about me and my experiences with Copland, Martinů, Doráti, Stokowski, Szell . . . and the book, which is still available on Amazon, has been acquired by a major publisher in the United States and has now been updated and released in English. Much has happened in these two decades, and the publisher has asked for my assistance to bring the book up-to-date, which has taken months. But regarding concert projects, there are many for 2021, including tours of South and Central America with the English Chamber Orchestra, a tour in the United States with this same orchestra, and new recordings, in particular the complete cycle of Schubert's symphonies, an old dream of mine.

A wish for the year 2021?

Peace in the world. Vaccines available to all to stop the virus. Return to normalcy in our lives. Love.

MUSICWEB INTERNATIONAL

Recording Glazunov and Serebrier

by Gavin Dixon (reprinted with permission)

I visited José Serebrier at his London residence. We discussed his recording sessions for the final installment of his brilliant Glazunov Symphony cycle with the Royal Scottish National Orchestra and later moved on to the recordings of his own music with the Bournemouth Symphony Orchestra.

You are just back from recording in Scotland. How did it go?

Fantastic—the best recording sessions ever! Such a great orchestra. The more they are challenged, the more they respond. In the past I have always done one or two symphonies per recording. This time I wanted to finish the Glazunov series, so I decided to do the last remaining symphonies: numbers one, two, three, and nine. At the end, I told the orchestra I was delighted we were finished but also sad that it had come to an end. But we are planning other recordings, CDs of music by Samuel Adler and Robert Beaser. Adler wrote the orchestration manual that has been translated into thirty languages and has been the teacher for hundreds of composers in America. Beaser is chairman of the composition department at Juilliard. I promised them long ago I would record their music, and I am delighted that Linn, the thriving and imaginative Scottish record label, will be releasing them.

Did it feel like a continuation of the earlier Glazunov sessions, or does each of his symphonies pose specific challenges?

Each one of the Glazunov symphonies is a challenge. Numbers one, two, and three, being his earliest symphonies, present the greatest challenges. The biggest problems, technically speaking, are the constant tempo changes. It is as if you turn the page in a book and suddenly, from one page to the next, you are in a completely different book. That was his way of being different, of being himself. This is very tricky, but I have found a way to make it happen naturally. Some other conductors, friends, heard some of the previous recordings where these tempo changes take place, and they asked if we did this in separate takes. But that wouldn't work. What I do is first rehearse with the new slower tempo—it usually goes from fast to very slow—and I tell the orchestra that the trick is to be able to go from a *presto* to this *adagio*. Usually, they get it right away.

You were a teenage symphony composer yourself. Did this help you to get a grip on Glazunov's early teenage symphony?

It just so happens that by sheer coincidence we both wrote our first symphonies when we were sixteen. Mine was premiered by Stokowski, and I am recording it with the Bournemouth Symphony Orchestra. Leopold Stokowski recorded it long ago. But this has not helped me with Glazunov, because Glazunov's First Symphony is totally mature. It is unbelievable. It is no different in structure or orchestration from his most advanced later symphonies. This is why the First Symphony had such a big impact at the time. It is a huge work, almost forty minutes long, and it is a masterpiece. But the coincidence of having written my own first symphony at the same age didn't help me all. However, being a composer always helps me conduct other people's music. It helps me to look at it from the inside. The best conductors are usually the ones who also compose—or at least who know how to, which means they have studied orchestration and harmony. I know some conductors who don't know much music, so they don't know what's really happening. When I study a new composition, I analyze it, and by the time I conduct it, I know it as if I had written it myself. Like the RSNO and most British orchestras, I sight-read very quickly, which is also helpful. But people who are good at sight-reading tend to be lazy about studying and going deeply into the piece, so I tend to do it methodically. But British orchestras, as you know, are famous for their incredible sight-reading abilities, and the Royal Scottish National Orchestra is fantastic at it. And so is their concentration. The way I record is not easy for them. I make them concentrate for the whole session, recording from the first to the last minute, not just when the red light is on. In fact, I never use a red light. Sometimes the first reading is the best. Then, if you keep on trying it, sometimes the standard drops. I play long sections like in a performance, and it shows in the recordings. You know, it's already edited. We had an experienced producer-engineer, Phil Rowlands, who has done half of my Glazunov series. Three days after the sessions had finished, it was edited. Sometimes waiting for an edit can take as long as a year, so we were quite lucky.

Glazunov's mature music is credited with reconciling the nationalist and European tendencies in the Russian music of his day. Is this balance already evident in his early symphonies?

Yes—the combination of European and Russian traditions is there from the start. The melodies are very Russian, with many minor sevenths. I mentioned Glazunov to a friend of mine, Turkish pianist İdil Biret, and she said, "Ah, the Russian Brahms." I had never thought of it that way, but he is very much like a Russian Brahms, because the music is very emotional but also contained . . . unlike Tchaikovsky, who was emotional but with his heart in his mouth. Glazunov is more like Brahms; the emotion is there, but it remains introverted.

The First Symphony is dedicated to Rimsky-Korsakov and the Third to Tchaikovsky. Are there any stylistic connections?

Rimsky-Korsakov was Glazunov's teacher, and he lived in the Rimsky-Korsakov household. In those days, students sometimes lived with their teachers. He was influenced by Rimsky-Korsakov in his orchestration. One passage in the First Symphony reflects a great orchestration trick—if you can call it that—that Rimsky-Korsakov used in the *Russian Easter Overture*. It's not imitation; it's just the idea of scoring the flutes with pizzicato strings, which is beautiful. That is the only relation to Rimsky; otherwise, from the beginning his music was influenced more by Tchaikovsky. Just as Rachmaninoff was influenced by Glazunov, you hear echoes. A different world, but there are influences there in the orchestration, in the harmonic relations.

Moving on to the Ninth Symphony, which is an incomplete work, is it satisfyingly incomplete, like Schubert's Eighth, or frustratingly incomplete, like Mahler's Tenth?

It is a satisfyingly incomplete work, so much so that I do not know how he could have continued it. It's an entity. He called it a symphony because he planned it to be his ninth, but the single movement has an *adagio* beginning, a main middle section based on a similar motive, and an *adagio* ending. It really would have been hard to continue that, and, anyway, at that time he stopped composing for many years.

Glazunov himself did not complete the orchestration of the symphony; it was done by Gavril Yudin. Does Yudin's work measure up to Glazunov's mastery of the orchestra?

Not really. That was the only thing I was sorry about. It is heavier. Glazunov could really orchestrate so that everything can be heard. Although comparison with Brahms makes sense, Glazunov's music is much denser. This can make it difficult to communicate, sometimes even with Glazunov's orchestration. And Yudin didn't really get the idea. Everything the double basses and cellos play, he doubled with the tuba, which is nonsense. But otherwise he followed Glazunov's directives in terms of orchestration, which the composer had written into the short score. The tuba was unnecessary, so I used it judiciously; otherwise I made no changes for my recording.

How has your approach to performing Glazunov changed over the course of this symphony cycle?

Glazunov's music was heard regularly in the early part of the twentieth century, but then his music went out of fashion. Nowadays it is played more, but there is a serious problem with the way it is often performed. If you play the notes metronomically, nothing happens; it's just square. Mahler was a contemporary of Glazunov, and Mahler's scores are full of indications on tempo flexibility: "slightly faster, but not too fast" or "a bit slower, but not too slow." Glazunov did none of that, so there is a temptation to play his music in strict tempo. But if you do so, the results are boring. So without taking liberties with the music, I have found a way to make it breathe by imagining what the composer would have liked, as you do with other Romantic composers, like Tchaikovsky, and not playing it with a metronomic beat, which destroys it.

Now that you've reached the end of the cycle of Glazunov symphonies, how do you feel the symphonies relate to each other as a cycle?

They are very much united in style. Although some of the symphonies have a definite independent personality, the Fourth Symphony, for example, is very much an entity, as are the Eighth and the Seventh. But they are all related. After two notes, you know it's Glazunov. There is continuity there. He didn't develop in the same way as Beethoven, who is in any case unique. You can hear that it is Beethoven from the First Symphony, but it is totally different from the Ninth or the Eighth. Glazunov is more like Brahms in that sense. Unlike Beethoven, who was an experimenter, constantly advancing music to the next stage, Glazunov and Brahms were much more steady. Glazunov's First Symphony is not that different from his Ninth. He was sixteen when he wrote it, but he had already established a pattern. Mozart is another good example: he stayed the course throughout his life. But his was a short life, so each composer is different.

Do you have any plans to continue recording Glazunov's other orchestral works?

We are hoping—and this is not an announcement, just a wish—that we can do the complete concertos, which are very interesting. Very late in his life—in fact, in his final year—Glazunov wrote a Saxophone Concerto, a work that I am hoping to record. He wrote it for an American saxophonist who had commissioned it, Sigurd Raschèr. And, in fact, I played it with Raschèr when I was very young. He played it with me in upstate New York, with an orchestra I used to conduct, the Utica Symphony. It was my first orchestra, I was eighteen or so, and Raschèr was then at the height of his fame. He had commissioned Glazunov when he was a very young man, and he later became a very famous saxophonist. When I met him, in about 1962, he was already an older man. So he came to Utica and played the Glazunov, and that was the first time I'd heard the name Glazunov. Since then, I have played it many times. There are also two piano concertos, which were famous in the early part of the twentieth century. The Rubinstein brothers played them, as did many other Russian pianists. His Cello Concerto is almost unknown, unlike his Violin Concerto, which is his most famous work.

Do you have any ideas about possible soloists you might want to work with?

It's all under discussion at the moment. It's a balancing act between Russian soloists—winners of the Tchaikovsky competition—some great British soloists, maybe an American soloist. We're talking about it.

I understand that you will be in Bournemouth recording some of your own works.

Yes—I was studying the scores as you arrived. Some of the works I wrote a long time ago and have to relearn. It is more difficult to relearn my own music than somebody else's. I do not study my own music; nor do I have much time to compose. But I've had some great opportunities. I was once composer-in-residence with the Cleveland Orchestra under George Szell. I won a conducting competition, the Ford Foundation American Conductors Award. I shared the first prize with James Levine. Szell was in the jury, and he invited us both to come to Cleveland as his assistant conductors. But I looked at the roster at Cleveland, and he had two associates, three principal guests, and four assistants. I thought I would never get to conduct. So I thanked the maestro, saying I was very honored, but stayed in New York as Stokowski's associate conductor. Jimmy went and was assistant conductor there for two years. The next year, Szell came back once again and asked if I'd like to come instead as composer-in-residence. By then Stokowski had announced that he was leaving America and was coming back to the UK; he was already eighty-six. It was a great opportunity, especially since Szell offered me the conductorship of the Cleveland Philharmonic—Cleveland's second orchestra—as an incentive. I had to write music, although the critic with the local paper wrote an article saying that instead of sitting in Cleveland and composing, for which I was being paid, I was going all over the world conducting. So, to prove myself, I wrote two concertos, one for harp and one for double bass. The double bass concerto is one of the works we're recording next week. It was written at a time of experimentation for me and includes a choir and has the orchestra spread across the hall and among the audience. Only the double bass is on the stage. It has a narration part, which for the recording will read be Simon Callow. The soloist will be Gary Karr, who premiered the work and who plays the

Koussevitsky's bass, which is a fantastic instrument. We will be recording this, my First Symphony—the one that Stokowski premiered—and a third piece.

I noticed the score of your Flute Concerto at your piano.

That is my latest work, which is funny to say because I hadn't written anything before it for a long time. It was a commission from Sharon Bezaly for the BIS record label, and it's being recorded in October by the Australian Chamber Orchestra. They play without a conductor, so I'm not going.

But you say that the Flute Concerto marks a return to composing . . .

It's my second work in the last year. Sharon Bezaly has been asking me for three years. But what broke the ice was a commission from Mumbai. A film company wrote to my website and told me this incredible story: The producer and director of a film were driving through Mumbai in the middle of the night, listening to a classical station. They heard my music, and they said, "Ah, that is what we need for this film." They stopped on the highway when it was finished, hoping to hear the announcement, but it just cut to the news. They called the station in the morning, who said their late-evening programs were taped ahead, and that if they wanted to know what the piece was, they would have to check themselves at the studio. So they went personally; they had to really research. They found out that it was my music and came to see me in New York. There were two scenes that they wanted me to write before the filming. It is about a Western-style composer who is blind and dictates his music. I wrote the music, but then the crash came, and they couldn't make the film. They might do it eventually, just not now. I have this music, which I have retitled *Music for an Imaginary Film.*

José Serebrier's recordings of Glazunov's First, Second, Third, and Ninth Symphonies with the Royal Scottish National Orchestra were released by Warner Classics in 2009. His recordings of his own First Symphony, Double-Bass Concerto *Nueve*, with soloist Gary Karr and actor Simon Callow, and *Music for an Imaginary Film*, with the Bournemouth Symphony Orchestra, were released by Naxos in 2010. —Gavin Dixon

Awards Received by José Serebrier in the United States and Abroad

BROADCAST MUSIC INC. STUDENT COMPOSERS AWARD

Serebrier received it in 1956 for his Symphony No. 1 and Quartet for Saxophones. BMI is an organization that controls the rights of composers. A jury of musicians makes the decision to award this prize. The music is submitted under pseudonyms. This was the first prize that José Serebrier was awarded in the United States.

INSTITUTE FOR INTERNATIONAL EDUCATION FELLOWSHIPS

Based in New York City, the IIE award made it possible for Serebrier to travel to the United States and study from 1956 to 1958 at the Curtis Institute of Music in Philadelphia. The fellowships were awarded on the recommendation of Aaron Copland, Virgil Thomson, Bohuslav Martinů, and Eugene Ormandy.

KOUSSEVITZKY FOUNDATION AWARD

Tanglewood in 1956, in composition classes with Aaron Copland, and in 1957, in conducting classes with Eleazar de Carvalho.

SODRE NATIONAL COMPOSERS COMPETITION PRIZE

Award for *The Legend of Faust* Fantasy Overture in 1954, premiered in 1955 by the National Symphony of Uruguay, OSSODRE conducted by Eleazar de Carvalho.

JUVENTUDES MUSICALES/MUSICAL YOUTH ASSOCIATION' COMPETITION AWARD

First prize in 1955 for Saxophone Quartet.

PAN AMERICAN UNION PUBLICATION AWARD

Shortly after arriving in the United States, the Washington, DC–based Pan American Union awarded Serebrier a publication award for his early *Elegy for Strings*, distributed by Peermusic.

DORÁTI FELLOWSHIP AT THE UNIVERSITY OF MINNESOTA

After an audition in New York, Antal Doráti awarded Serebrier, upon his graduation from the Curtis Institute in 1958, the Doráti Fellowship, which included composition studies at the University of Minnesota toward his Master of Arts degree, weekly private conducting studies with Doráti, and a position as apprentice conductor at the Minnesota Symphony Orchestra.

HARVARD MUSICAL ASSOCIATION COMMISSION AWARD

Serebrier writes, "I heard about its existence thanks to Antal Doráti, not long before we both left Minneapolis, and I entered the competition at once. The prize was a commission to write a String Quartet. I composed *Fantasia* [1960], which I would later also arrange for string orchestra. I recorded it in 1999 with the London Philharmonic Orchestra."

The premiere took place at the Harvard Musical Association's premises in Boston by members of the Boston Symphony Orchestra. (The Harvard

Musical Association is the oldest music association in the United States.) A second performance took place in Washington, DC, at the Inter-American Music Festival. On that occasion, the *Washington Post*'s review headline was "Serebrier's *Fantasia* Is the *1812* of String Quartets."

THE GUGGENHEIM FOUNDATION FELLOWSHIP GRANTS

Sponsored by the foundation created by John Simon Guggenheim, this grant remains one of the most important and prestigious awards in the United States. A substantial subsidy, aimed at artists of all sorts, writers, scientists, and other creative persons, to help bring their projects to fruition, the fellowship—or prize—covers a whole year's expenses so that the recipient can reserve full time for the project without depending on another job for income. It is an extremely difficult award to obtain, nearly impossible. Some famous people have applied and not manage to get it. This was the case for Arnold Schoenberg, a very regrettable example. Serebrier writes,

> I was nineteen years old when I was awarded the first of two consecutive Guggenheim Fellowships, and I remain the youngest to ever have received it in all the categories. Most of the beneficiaries were well over forty, and some were fifty or older, because the award criteria is aimed at professionals already accomplished, in addition to personal and confidential recommendations from influential people in their field. My first Guggenheim Fellowship [1958] coincided with the Doráti Fellowship [University of Minnesota] I had received to study conducting with Doráti and to take my postgraduate Master of Arts degree in composition at the University of Minnesota at the same time. The Guggenheim Foundation could not accept the fact that I would be receiving a second simultaneous grant. I appealed to them for an unusual arrangement: to split the fellowship into several separate months, to be used outside my time spent in Minneapolis. I did not hold out much hope that the foundation would accept that proposition. To my amazement, they agreed. When that fellowship ended, I unashamedly applied for a second one. The Guggenheim Foundation very rarely awards a second fellowship to the same applicant. However, they agreed once again.

Note by Gabriel Faure: The difference between a student or university fellowship and a bursary offered by a foundation resides in the fact that the first are exclusively reserved for students and the second is for experienced and prestigious professionals.

THE ROCKEFELLER FOUNDATION AWARD

For a few years this powerful American institution initiated a coveted composer-in-residence program with the most prestigious orchestras in the United States. The Rockefeller Foundation administration and the orchestras themselves jointly selected the composers. Serebrier writes,

> I benefitted from that program in 1968 to work alongside George Szell, music director of the wonderful Cleveland Orchestra. Szell had been in the jury of the Ford Foundation American Conductors Competition, which I won alongside James Levine. Szell invited us both to join him in Cleveland as assistant conductors. Levine accepted, but I declined because at the time I had a wonderful position as associate conductor of the American Symphony at Carnegie Hall with Leopold Stokowski. The following year, when Szell renewed his offer for me to be composer-in-residence with his Cleveland Orchestra, and the added incentive to become music director of the Cleveland Philharmonic, I accepted at once. The Philharmonic was a semiprofessional orchestra that included a few members of the Cleveland Orchestra, plus students and amateurs. The Rockefeller Foundation agreed. In 1969, I enthusiastically agreed to a second season as composer-in-residence of the Cleveland Orchestra and conductor of the Philharmonic. When Szell died, the Rockefeller Foundation program was discontinued, but the idea was taken up later by other institutions. To compensate for this financial loss of income, a new organization in New York, called Affiliate Artists, granted me some unexpected help. It allowed me to do a third season in Cleveland. They granted me the same allowance I had received as music director with the Plainfield Symphony Orchestra. This is another semiprofessional orchestra that boasts a solid tradition as the oldest orchestra in the state of New Jersey. At the same time, from 1966 to 1968, I was also teaching violin and conducting in Ypsilanti at Eastern Michigan University, as associate professor, commuting weekly from New York City.

THE FORD FOUNDATION AMERICAN CONDUCTORS COMPETITION PRIZE

Peter Mennin, the very talented American composer—later on Serebrier conducted the first recording of Mennin's Symphony No. 9, with the Adelaide Symphony Orchestra in Australia—was president of the Peabody Conservatory of Music in Baltimore. He had an original and vivid imagination and inventiveness. One of his numerous successful projects was to establish a competition for young conductors in Baltimore. This prize was not simply a financial award. He had the following idea: every year, four young winners would spend three months with the Baltimore Symphony Orchestra, working at rehearsals and at concerts under the guidance of internationally acclaimed conductors. Serebrier writes,

> I asked Stokowski's permission to take part in the second year of this competition, in 1965, taking a leave from my position as associate conductor of his orchestra. The jury included George Szell, Leonard Bernstein, Max Rudolf, Alfred Wallenstein, and Fausto Cleva. The winners that year were Lawrence Smith, James Levine, John Canarina, and I. It turned out to be a most unique experience. For months, every single day, I had the opportunity to conduct the orchestra under the supervision—and corrections—of the great professionals mentioned above. Mennin's project proved to be beneficial to all of us. The Ford Foundation paid for the winners' scholarships, the orchestra's expenses, the teachers' salaries, and the members of the jury. In those days, the Baltimore Symphony Orchestra only worked for some thirty weeks a year. The competition increased the working time by another twelve weeks a year for the musicians. During three seasons, it worked perfectly well. Then Mennin left for New York to become president at the Juilliard School, and the Baltimore conducting-competition project came to an end.

THE ALICE M. DITSON CONDUCTOR'S AWARD FROM COLUMBIA UNIVERSITY

At the beginning of his career, José Serebrier received the Alice M. Ditson Conductor's Award from Columbia University, delivered at the Kennedy Center in Washington, DC, during Serebrier's concert tour with the American Composers Orchestra. This award is allocated to the conductor who has performed the greatest amount of contemporary music. Among the previous recipients was Leopold Stokowski. Serebrier donated his cash award to the ACO.

THE NATIONAL ENDOWMENT FOR THE ARTS COMMISSION AWARD

In the first year of its creation, the National Endowment for the Arts commissioned Serebrier to compose a ballet score, intended for the Joffrey Ballet. He used his Concerto for Harp, *Colores Mágicos*, as a basis for his new score. The premiere took place in New York at the City Center of Music and Drama, under his direction. The Joffrey Ballet then presented it on tour across the United States, conducted by Seymour Lipkin, music director of the Joffrey. That ballet was titled *Orpheus Times Light* and was inspired by the legend of Orpheus. The original score, *Colores Mágicos*, was recorded in 2020 and released in 2021 by Reference Recordings.

GRAMMY NOMINATIONS

In 1974 Serebrier received the first of many consecutive GRAMMY nominations from the Recording Academy in the United States. The first nomination was in 1974, in the category of best classical recording of the year, for the Symphony No. 4, by Charles Ives, on RCA Victor with the London Philharmonic Orchestra. This work usually requires three simultaneous conductors. Serebrier recorded it and performed it in London at the Royal Festival Hall as the sole conductor. Previously, he had filmed it in Poland with the Polish Radio Symphony Orchestra in Katowice, and the film was shown regularly on NET, the public television predecessor of PBS in the United States.

LATIN GRAMMY AWARD

In 2004, soon after the Latin GRAMMY originated, Serebrier won the award for best classical recording of the year with the Bizet-Serebrier recording, *Carmen Symphony*, recorded with the Barcelona Symphony Orchestra on the BIS label. Since then, almost every Serebrier recording has been nominated for a Latin GRAMMY or an international GRAMMY.

GRAND PRIX DU DISQUE, FRANCE

The prestigious French recording award was given to Carole Farley, soprano, and José Serebrier, conductor, for their recording of Aubert Lemeland's music.

UK MUSIC RETAILERS ASSOCIATION AWARD
FOR BEST ORCHESTRAL RECORDING

For the Mendelssohn symphonies with the Scottish Chamber Orchestra, recorded on the ASV label.

DEUTSCHE SCHALLPLATTEN AWARD
FOR BEST ORCHESTRAL RECORDING

For the first of three CDs of Shostakovich's film suites, with the Belgian Radio Orchestra, on the Chandos label.

AUDIOPHILE MAGAZINE'S AWARD
FOR BEST ORCHESTRAL RECORDING

For Serebrier's rendition of Rimsky-Korsakov's *Scheherazade*, with the London Philharmonic Orchestra, on the Reference Recordings label.

CIUDADANO ILUSTRE DE MONTEVIDEO
(ILLUSTRIOUS CITIZEN OF MONTEVIDEO)

In 2016, after Serebrier conducted a benefit concert for Teatro Solis, the mayor of Montevideo awarded him the Ciudadano Ilustre medal, the highest civic honor awarded in Uruguay, in a special public ceremony held at the Solis Theater.

REACHINGU MEDAL

At a fundraising celebratory gala dinner held at the Pierre Hotel in New York City in 2019, Serebrier was honored for his services and career. ReachingU is an international charity devoted to raising funds for Uruguayan children in need.

• *11* •

At the Dawn of the Twenty-First Century

The last years of the twentieth century saw the disappearance of several orchestras around the world.

I remember my work in the nineties with the RAI Orchestra of Rome (I recorded the three Borodin symphonies with them for the ASV label). It seemed at that time unthinkable that Rome's Symphony Orchestra would be endangered. Every major Italian city had a large orchestra and choir under the tutelage of RAI—Radiotelevisione Italiana. The same in England with the BBC, Australia with the ABC, and with the vast majority of German radio stations. This was the fabulous legacy of musical culture in the first half of the twentieth century, when most state-sponsored radio stations had created their symphonic ensembles, professional choirs, and theater companies to make maximum use of their media. Even in the United States, and without any government assistance, NBC, a pioneer in radio broadcasting, had formed its own orchestra and called upon Arturo Toscanini to be its conductor. The advent of television did not thwart this tremendous expansion. Although radio seemed like a better vehicle for the dissemination of classical concerts, the early days of black and white television were a powerful popularizer of culture. Dozens of years later, when every household had a color set, television adapted itself to the lowest common denominator. Televised concerts became rarified events, and those aimed at "the popular masses," such as "The Three Tenors" or New Year's Eve concerts in Vienna, became the norm. European radios began questioning the need to finance full-time symphony orchestras and choirs.

As I had just conducted the famous RAI Orchestra Alessandro Scarlatti in Naples, its members solicited my help. RAI, without their having requested it, had granted them a two-month leave in the middle of the season. This decision seemed quite strange to the players and made them suspicious. Was this the beginning of the end? The explanation given by RAI? "It is less

211

costly to only pay musicians' salaries, even when they do not play, rather than present concerts and pay guest conductors and soloists." RAI realized that this sudden interruption of the orchestral season was badly perceived both by the public and the press. RAI therefore proposed to the members of the Scarlatti—a chamber orchestra of approximately forty-five musicians—the possibility of an early departure, either by transferring them to another of its orchestras or by asking them to accept a different position, while remaining within the organization, in an office, in a bookstore, or as drivers. The musicians opposed it with a fierce determination bordering on hysteria. Like many of my colleagues, I tried my best to help them, but their fate was already sealed. Alas, this ensemble, which had been great in the past, had so deteriorated that it had become an embarrassment. The behavior of its members, the discipline, had become terribly slack. Finally, when their dissolution became a reality, the musicians tried with all their might to play as best as possible and to improve the general state of mind, but it was too late. At each concert, they read a letter to the public, imploring their help, mentioning all the messages of support received from many artists, including my own letter of support. But the concert hall, almost empty, responded with apathy. Then the musicians tried to get help from other orchestras within RAI—Rome, Turin, Milan—seemingly still stable and with secure futures. I guess these orchestras did their best to support them in their fight, never imagining that they could be next on the list and disappear in turn. When RAI realized that the simplest thing was to end the existence of the Scarlatti Orchestra once and for all, it did so as quietly and discreetly as possible. Simultaneously, it made the decision to get rid of its Rome choir, which by then had devolved into complete chaos. What had been once a magnificent choral ensemble had become politicized to such an extent that it was barely employable. Its partner, the Rome RAI Orchestra, tried to help. Once again, it was too late. The choir broke up without making waves. Few people thought then that the orchestra would soon suffer the same fate. In fact, first it was the RAI Milan orchestra that was dissolved. I conducted this ensemble's penultimate concert in the auditorium of the Verdi Music Conservatory in Milan. Unlike their colleagues from Naples, the Milanese musicians accepted their fate with resignation, not even trying to save themselves with alternative jobs within RAI. One of two things may have happened: either they understood that it was impossible to fight RAI, or they had been offered a favorable financial arrangement for early retirement. This orchestra, once great, had started to decline over the prior ten years. But once their fate was decided, and without the possibility for appeal, they did their best and adopted an attitude both dignified and professional. As for the program of their next-to-last concert, I agreed to conduct a French program with, among others, the *Bacchus and*

Ariadne Suite by Albert Roussel and the opera *La Voix Humaine* by Francis Poulenc, with my wife, Carole Farley, as soloist—a challenging program.

The Rome orchestra seemed safe and stable until they too realized that their unions were completely unable to reverse the trend, and within months it disappeared. RAI kept only one of their original multiple orchestras, in Turin, long regarded as its best, the only one that had maintained strict discipline and a sense and taste for hard work. Today it's better than ever!

The rest of the musical world had watched these Italian events unfold with great interest. The BBC, for its part, had tried years earlier to get rid of one of its orchestras. There had been such an outcry on the part of associations and musicians' unions around the world, and so much criticism from the press, that the BBC eventually decided, tentatively, to keep things in their present state. The BBC had made, in the last years of the twentieth century, many drastic cuts, especially to TV, and did not want to trigger the wrath of the entire world of music. It tried to merge the Scottish BBC Orchestra, in residence at Glasgow, with the Scottish Opera Orchestra, but without success, as no acceptable formula could be found. Meanwhile, numerous German radio stations were trying to reduce their number of large symphony orchestras by any possible means. South Africa, in turn, terminated some of its oldest and most outstanding orchestras, those of Cape Town and Johannesburg, which I knew very well, having led them often. The explanation given was once again economic: it was too great an expense for the benefit of a tiny minority, classical music being the expression of a European culture and not that of the country.

Similarly, in England the Bournemouth Sinfonietta disappeared completely, without raising the slightest protest or hardly a mention in the national newspapers. An alarming precedent.

In the United States, in the mid-eighties, it became common practice in most medium-sized cities for orchestras to slow down or stop their activities the moment tax benefits for private sponsorship stopped (this was replicated in museums). This may have contributed to the disappearance of the symphony orchestras of New Orleans, Kansas City, San Diego, Oakland, and even Sacramento, the capital of California. Some of them were subsequently reborn, managed by the musicians themselves, but with shortened seasons and modest budgets. The musicians had to fight hard, turning themselves by night into accountants or administrative agents, searching for funding, scheduling the concert seasons, engaging conductors and soloists, in the image of the big London ensembles that functioned similarly. Most succeeded but always with the sword of Damocles hanging over their heads.

The general public's interest in symphonic concerts differed from country to country. However, in general, attendances dwindled in large cities during the last two decades of the twentieth century—even in those in the United States, which had some of the best ensembles in the world. In Cleveland, for example, the public became much older. The musicians attributed the cause to the lack of musical education in schools. Chamber music societies had become scarce or else ceased their activities altogether. Recitals, especially vocal recitals, had become rare and infrequent events in most American cities. Opera, on the contrary, although a much more expensive art form, enjoyed a tremendous expansion. New companies sprang up everywhere around the world. Few operas composed in the twentieth century remained on the program after their first performance, but most of the Classical and Romantic repertoire was sufficient to attract a wide public, which asked for it again and again. While orchestral and chamber music concerts attracted meager audiences, operatic performances were regularly sold out.

With the invention of digital recording and then, shortly thereafter, the CD, record companies all over the world experienced a stunning expansion, and we witnessed the birth of many companies independent of the big corporations, some of which became more powerful than the old traditional multinationals. By the end of the twentieth century, the most competitive were Chandos, Hyperion, ASV, Telarc, BIS, Naxos, Reference Recordings, and Koch; they reached an undeniably international level.

Some record labels that had begun as a mere family business in a garage became, within a few years, thanks to the boom of the CD—and its high price—rich and powerful companies distributed throughout the world. Multinationals like Sony (which had absorbed CBS Records, which itself had bought Columbia Records) or DGG/Decca, EMI, or BMG (which had acquired RCA) tried to compete or even to imitate the methods of operation of some small independent labels.

When the "small" brands began to record contemporary music and, to everyone's surprise, show a profit, the Decca company reissued its ARGO series, devoted mostly to new music—which it recorded and broadcast only if a substantial grant covered the costs. Sony went further, putting several composers under permanent contract. These CDs, which surprised no one, did not sell enough to meet the expectations of this large label. For an independent label, the sale of three thousand copies of a CD over four years could be considered a success, but for a major multinational label, anything below twenty thousand could be considered close to financial disaster. This pathetic result broke the heart of several prominent composers. Alas, this became the norm: a large phonographic company would record the symphony of a famous living composer, who thought that it had finally "happened"! But we would see the recording disappear from catalogs in less than six months. In other cases, the recordings were never marketed because people knew in advance that sales would prove so weak that it wasn't worth printing the discs. The consequence was that composers would begin to wonder if it might be preferable for their music to be distributed by certain small labels that, though less prestigious, would maintain their oeuvres in their catalogs, unlike those large firms, where exclusion was automatic, whatever the disc might be, if it did not sell sufficiently. The computer was ruthless: a method nothing less than brutal and expeditious.

It was in the last decade of the twentieth century that we witnessed the birth of dynamic and imaginative companies, such as Naxos, active around the world today. Naxos's director, Klaus Heymann, had great experience with marketing and distribution, having previously worked in several companies. His wife, Takako Nishizaki, is a brilliant and sensitive violinist. I met them when Takako was my soloist with the Melbourne Orchestra during my first Australian tour. We liked each other immediately. Takako invited me to dine with members of her family living in Melbourne. It was the first time that I had entered a typical Japanese home. I still remember that night. Klaus Heymann had long held the reins of a Hong Kong–based label, Marco Polo. What had made his own companies competitive in major markets was undoubtedly his great sense of marketing. He offered his CDs at a relatively low price at the precise time when the public and the press had begun to complain openly about exorbitant prices. By selling his CDs at a third of the current price, Heymann developed a new market that surpassed his expectations and hugely influenced the entire recording industry. Immediately, most other companies, whatever their size, created their own CD departments at reduced prices, but Naxos had already found its place in the sun and was not affected. After a modest start, Naxos could soon record the best and largest orchestras, with noteworthy artists, and frequently received the most laudatory reviews. In a short time, in addition to being the most economical label, Naxos became qualitatively the most innovative and efficient. The "majors" tried to imitate, often without success.

With the advent of the third millennium, some of the large record companies only had their own disintegration as their prospective future. BMG/RCA started out in denial and then grew to recognize the truth in the press allegations and rumors stating that its most important artists' contracts would not be extended, that it would stop reissuing most of its classic stock, including reissues of its heritage recordings—although it would only cost them the price of the reprint—the commercial value being too negligible. An example: the hundred CD boxes by Arthur Rubinstein, which were taking up considerable storage space, were soon covered with dust, unsold. A year after the release of this collection of historical recordings—"live" or studio—the computer showed that only two hundred sets had been sold. However, if officials at BMG Records had listened to the grievances of their employees, they would have learned that this important operation had been launched without the right kind of advertising and without appropriate marketing. The project had probably been too ambitious and costly for record collectors.

It was quickly understood that the classic CD market, as it was known, would soon cease to be and that many traditional or specialized shops would have to close their doors. We were seeing a new era with the advent of the Internet, with its phenomenal development and lower costs. At the time, the future seemed catastrophic, and even independent labels, worried, revised their policies and released fewer titles. The CD seemed doomed when the new cars and all new computers were built without CD players. Many music lovers have since kept their older cars to have access to the CD players.

As the world population increases, culture orients itself toward the large masses with simplified art. Of course we must not despair, because at the same time we can witness a gigantic flowering musical creation. The orchestras of today play much more contemporary music than they had during the twentieth century. Before that time, during earlier centuries, most of the music being performed was obviously "new." This can be explained because music composed at the end of the twentieth century was generally more accessible, and a new generation of conductors—Leonard Slatkin, David Zinman, Marin Alsop, Simon Rattle, JoAnn Falletta, and many others—delighted in discovering new music. Additionally, the Classical and Romantic repertoire had been rehashed to the extreme. And while it is indeed great to go back to Beethoven and Brahms, there is no need to interpret them in a routine-like way to appreciate them again.

One of the major problems encountered by the music industry was that a CD was virtually indestructible while a vinyl record had to be replaced after repeated hearings. It was clear that even the most ardent collector was reluctant to buy a new complete set of symphonies by Beethoven and Brahms when they already owned several versions. A tiny number would try new—or old but relatively unknown—composers, and a few would purchase high-quality CDs to test their expensive sound equipment.

Locked into technology, the record industry inevitably condemned itself to a slow form of suicide. But there was another reason that no one ever brought this to light in the media.

Before the era of CDs, the latest recordings by the greatest artists had been eagerly awaited. A new interpretation of a Classical or Romantic *chef d'oeuvre* was expected as an indicator of musical secrets. Excitement would be in the air, and the new version would be the subject of the most enthusiastic recommendations by salespeople in specialty shops—this before the birth of mass retailers, whose employees were incapable of spelling the names of either performers or composers.

Until the end of the twentieth century, when the hidden but actual cause of falling sales was revealed, interpretations had become standardized, sanitized, homogenized, reflections of one another in a mirror. The romantic *rubato*, the personal freedoms of interpretation, had disappeared. Many recordings began to sound almost identical. So why record and buy new versions? For the ears of our time, the beautiful and original interpretations by artists such as Pierre Monteux might seem extravagant. (One should listen to his version of Tchaikovsky's Fourth Symphony, considered in his time to be "historical.")

Whatever the case may be, the main problem of the phonographic industry was not solely a problem of sales; and neither was it caused by the vicissitudes of time. Rather, it was the inability of major record companies to anticipate the future, their lack of foresight about undiscovered potential markets, and the instability created by their lack of knowledge, musical and commercial.

If independent labels such as Hyperion, BIS, Chandos, Naxos, and RR were successful, it's because they were headed by lone entrepreneurs who accurately predicted the future and worked toward their goal with skill and perseverance.

WHAT WILL THE FUTURE BRING?

The Paris Conservatory, the Juilliard School, the Curtis Institute, Oberlin, the San Francisco Conservatory, and all the great music schools, such as Indiana University's, to name just a few major institutions, are as crowded as ever and buzzing with activity. Without pause, hundreds of young artists graduate—especially in wind and brass—and cannot find a post in the best ensembles. Pianists also have great difficulty developing a career. Even the first-prize winners of international competitions are not assured future solo careers. If they prove to be independent of mind, to think outside the box, or to not play routinely, showing an original personality, they could be excluded from the finals in most competitions.

The cause—and the CD shoulders its share of the responsibility—is that interpretations mostly sound alike. An "interpretation" is considered ideal if it conforms to the printed page, a carbon copy of any other!

I was asked once, in the United States, to serve on the jury of a piano competition sponsored the Xerox company. This competition was presented by Affiliate Artists, a powerful independent musical organization, in existence in New York at the time, and the winner of the competition would be named "the Xerox pianist." Composed of ten major pianists and me, the jury could not bring itself to choose a winner. The Xerox competition was never held again.

Even before the dawn of the third millennium, composers had many more opportunities to be performed at public concerts. For the first time since the days of Benjamin Britten and Aaron Copland, some composers have managed to survive thanks to an income from commissions and performances, in addition to teaching.

It is possible that there is a future for orchestral music, but probably with fewer orchestras, as they have become so much more expensive, due to their deserved need for full-time employment. To continue to exist, orchestras are having to add additional functions besides classical and pop concerts They are having to be even closer to communities, playing multiple roles. Structured in small or large groups according to need, they will give regular, short concerts in schools, hospitals, public parks—even in an impromptu fashion in malls. Of course, this is not a new concept, but it has become imperative to conform with contemporary times to justify essential public subsidies and private donations. Concert music needs to serve a broad range of society rather than just a tiny, dwindling minority.

The Internet, I sincerely hope, will help save the recording industry. We can already see interesting initiatives on the horizon, because there's no limit to human imagination. The musical arts should flourish as never before. The tiny percentage of people interested in classical music should explode in huge proportions. Music education in schools will regain the importance it once had long ago.

Letters from Leopold Stokowski

29 October 64

Maestro Jose Serebrier
Hotel Diplomat
108 West 43rd Street
New York, New York 10036

Dear Maestro

Thank you for your kind suggestion to help with the music for
the next program, but it looks as though everything is in order.
If not, I will telephone you quickly.

It is quite the contrary at Trivi where we need a strong man who
plays Soccer, and always brings a different girl.

I know that American Symphony Orchestra has made application to
one of the great Foundations for funds for extra rehearsals for
the Ives Symphony, but if that application fails, then of course
we would like to follow your kind suggestion about the Ditson Fund,
through your friend Mr. Beeson. I shall try to speed up this
question, otherwise it might be too late.

Always with friendly thoughts.

1067 Fifth Avenue
New York, New York 10028
ATwater 9-3689

LEOPOLD STOKOWSKI

11 December 64

Maestro Jose Serebrier
Hotel Diplomat
108 West 43rd Street
New York, New York

Dear Maestro

Thank you for your suggestion of Beethoven and Chausson for
the first half of the program. I am glad you will conduct on
December 5 and 6, '65.

                                 Sincerely

1067 Fifth Avenue
New York, New York 10028

LEOPOLD STOKOWSKI

23 December 64

Maestro Jose Serebrier
Hotel Diplomat
108 West 43rd Street
New York, New York

Dear Maestro

Thank you for your card and good wishes, and the mysterious package
which I shall open and enjoy at Christmas Time, and particularly
thank you for your friendship and all your skillful assistance in
the difficulty of making the American Symphony Orchestra reach up
to our ideals.

Wishing you Health and Well-Being in the New Year.

                                 Your friend

LEOPOLD STOKOWSKI

2 February 65

Maestro José Serebrier
Hotel Diplomat
108 West 43rd Street
New York, New York 10036

Dear Maestro

Thank you for your first draft of the program for December 5 and
6, '65. I am very glad you will conduct Chausson's beautiful
symphony. As we already have rather much music of Beethoven
on the programs, would you consider before Chausson, music of a
Spanish or Uruguayan or French composer to go with Chausson?
I am trying to make the programs for the whole season have great
variety, and include all kinds of music, and we are already very
strong on German music.

Sincerely

Leopold Stokowski

1067 Fifth Avenue
New York, New York 10028
ATwater 9-3689

LEOPOLD STOKOWSKI

13 May 65

Dear Maestro

Last night I listened to the music you have composed for the
Shakespearean scenes for Channel 5. I think you have done
splendidly in expressing the mood of the moment in each case, and
doing this with only a few instruments because then it is more trans-
parent, and more expressive musically. When there is a street scene
of confusion and agitation, what would you think of background
played by two pecussionists, each playing three instruments so
that six instruments would be heard, such as snare drum, cymbals,
bass drum, wood block, xylophone, chimes, and possibly one trumpet.

These are only suggestions. What you have already done showed
great talent on your part for such dramatic music.

Sincerely

Leopold Stokowski

LEOPOLD STOKOWSKI

17 February 69

Mr. Jose Serebrier
The Commodore
11311 Euclid Avenue at Ford Drive
Cleveland
Ohio 44106

Dear Maestro

At your convenience please send me the score of your composition for woodwinds, brass and percussion.

I shall not be able to go to San Salvador because all my time is already filled. At present we cannot plan an American Symphony Orchestra tour in Europe because of other commitments.

Greetings

1067 Fifth Avenue
New York, N.Y. 10028

Published Works

PUBLISHED BY PEERMUSIC

Adagio for string orchestra
Composed in 1964
Arranged by the composer from his *Vocalise* for mixed chorus
Premiered by St. Michael Strings, Finland
Recorded by St. Michael Strings (Alba ABCD 341, 2012) and RTÉ National Symphony Orchestra (BIS 2423, 2020)
Duration: 4:00

Aires de Tango for solo violin
Composed in 2009
Commissioned by Rachel Barton Pine
Recorded by Rachel Barton Pine (Cedille Records CDR90000124, 2011)
Duration: 6:00

Andante Cantabile for string orchestra
Composed in 1990
Orchestrated from Tchaikovsky's String Quartet no. 1 in D, op. 11
Multiple recordings on various record labels
Duration: 7:30

at dusk, in shadows . . . Fantasy for solo flute
Composed in 1988
Recorded by Martha Councell (Blue Griffin Recording BG 375, 2015)
Duration: 4:30

Canción del Destino (Song of Destiny) for mixed chorus (SATB a cappella)
Composed in 1955

Text by Francisco Villaespesa
English translation by José Serebrier
Duration: 4:00

Candombe for flute and chamber orchestra
Composed in 2019
Instrumentation: flute solo; piccolo, 1-2-1-1; 1-1-1-1; timpani-percussion; strings
Recorded by Nestor Torres and the Málaga Philharmonic Orchestra (2020) (Reference Recordings RR 2021)
Flute and piano reduction also published by Peermusic
Duration: 3:00

Casi un Tango (Almost a Tango) for English horn and string orchestra
Composed in 2002
Instrumentation: solo English horn (or flute, oboe, clarinet, horn, or trumpet); string orchestra
Recorded by Barcelona Symphony Orchestra (BIS 1175, 2005; BIS 2423, 2020) and the Bournemouth Symphony Orchestra (Naxos 8559648, 2010) (Reference Recordings RR 2021)
Duration: 4:00

Colores Mágicos, Variations for harp and chamber orchestra
Composed in 1971
Instrumentation: harp solo; 2 piccolos, 0-0-0-0; 2-2-1-1; timpani (optional)-2 percussion-piano-cello (optional); strings
(Reference Recordings RR 2021)
Duration: 12:00

Saxophone Quartet
Composed in 1955
Recorded by The Australian Saxophone Quartet (Phoenix USA 144, 2000)
Duration: 16:00

Dorothy and Carmine! for two flutes and string orchestra
Composed in 1989
Recorded by The Royal Philharmonic Orchestra (Phoenix USA 144, 2000); Orchestre de Chambre de Toulouse (Naxos 8559183, 2003) and Málaga Philharmonic Orchestra ((Reference Recordings RR 2021)
Duration: 7:00

Elegy for Strings for string orchestra
Composed in 1954
Recorded by Orchestre de Chambre de Toulouse (Naxos 8559183, 2003)
Duration: 8:00

Erotica for soprano (or trumpet) and woodwind quintet
Composed in 1968
Recorded by Carole Farley, soprano, and the Australian Wind Virtuosi (Phoenix USA 144, 2000)
Duration: 5:00

Fantasia for string quartet or string orchestra
Composed in 1960
Commissioned by the Harvard Musical Association
Duration: 12:00
Recorded by Orchestre de Chambre de Toulouse (Naxos 8559183, 2003) and the London Philharmonic Orchestra (Naxos 8559303, 2007; Naxos 8572087, 2008)
Duration: 12:00

Flute Concerto with Tango for flute and string orchestra
Composed in 2008
Recorded by Sharon Bezaly, flute and Australian Chamber Orchestra (BIS 1789, 2012; BIS 2423, 2020)
Duration: 22:00

Danza for flute and string orchestra
Revised in 2019
Finale of Flute Concerto with Tango
Recorded by Nestor Torres and Málaga Philharmonic Orchestra (Reference Recordings RR 2021)
Duration: 4:00

George and Muriel for solo double bass and double bass ensemble
Composed in 1986
Recorded by Lucas Drew (Phoenix USA 144, 2000) and Renaud Gruss (Naxos 8559183, 2003)
Duration: 7:00

If I Can Stop One Heart from Breaking for horn in F, violin, and narrator
Composed in 2017
Commissioned by Elmira Darvarova and Howard Wall
Premiered by Elmira Darvarova and Howard Wall, Carnegie Hall, New York, 2019
Recorded by Elmira Darvarova and Howard Wall (Affetto AF 2000 and 2021)
Duration: 4:00

Laments and Hallelujahs for orchestra (with optional choir)
Composed in 2016
Instrumentation: 2-2-2-2; 4-2-3-1; timpani-2 percussion-cello-piano; mixed choir (optional); strings

Commissioned by Saint Martha Concerts as a part of its Martha and Mary Medita-
tions, and sponsored by Olga and David Melin
Recorded by RTÉ National Symphony Orchestra (BIS 2423, 2020)
Duration: 10:00

Last Tango before Sunrise for string orchestra
Composed in 2018
Recorded by the Ukrainian Festival Orchestra (Toccata Classics TOCC 0370, 2019),
the RTÉ National Symphony Orchestra (BIS 2423, 2020), Málaga Philharmonic
of Spain (Reference Recordings RR 2021)
Duration: 3:00

Manitowabing for flute and oboe
Composed in 1966
Recorded by Claudia Anderson and William McMullen (Centaur Records 2775, 2006)
Duration: 8:00

Mexican Dance for symphonic band
Composed in 1971
Excerpt arranged for Symphonic Band from Revueltas's *Redes*
Recorded by "The President's Own" United States Marine Band (Naxos 8570727,
2008)
Duration: 5:00

Momento Psicológico for string orchestra (with backstage trumpet)
Composed in 1957
Recorded by Orchestre de Chambre de Toulouse (Naxos 8559183, 2003) and The
Royal Philharmonic Orchestra (Decca CDDCA785, 2011)
Duration: 4:00

Moto Perpetuo for voice (or woodwind instrument or French horn) and piano
Composed in 2013
Arranged by the composer from his *Vocalise* for mixed chorus
Duration: 2:30

Night Cry for four horns in F, two trumpets in C, three trombones, and tuba
Composed in 1994
Recorded by "The President's Own" United States Marine Band (Naxos 8570727, 2008)
Duration: 6:00

None but the Lonely Heart for cello ensemble
Arranged in 2018
Arranged from Tchaikovsky's *Six Romances*, op. 6, no. 6
Arranged by José Serebrier for eight cellos
Duration: 3:00

None but the Lonely Heart for string orchestra
Arranged in 2018 from Tchaikovsky's *Six Romances*, op. 6, no. 6
Recorded by the RTÉ National Symphony of Ireland (BIS SACD 2423)
Duration: 3:00

Nostalgia for solo viola
Composed in 2020
Recorded by Hiyoli Togawa (BIS SACD 2021)
Duration: 3:00

Nueve (Nine), Concerto for double bass and chamber ensemble
Composed in 1970
Instrumentation: double bass solo; narrator, choir; 0-0-2-0; 4-2-3-1; timpani-percussion-piano (cello, strings, no viola)
Recorded by Gary Karr, double bass and Bournemouth Symphony Orchestra (Naxos 8559648, 2010) and Gary Karr, double bass and Plainfield Symphony Orchestra (Urlicht UAV 5985, 2016)
Duration: 12:00

Orpheus Times Light, Ballet for harp and orchestra
Composed in 1976
Instrumentation: harp and soprano solo; 2(pic)-1-0-0; 2-2-1-1; timpani-percussion-harp-piano and strings
Premiered by Joffrey Ballet with choreography by Gerald Arpino, City Center, New York, 1976
Duration: 24:00

Passacaglia and Perpetuum Mobile for accordion and chamber orchestra
Composed in 1966
Instrumentation: accordion solo; 2 horns, trumpet, B trombone, percussion, strings
Recorded by Yi Yao, accordion and Orchestre de Chambre de Toulouse (Naxos 8559183, 2003)
Accordion and piano reduction also available
Duration: 7:00

Pequeña Música (Little Suite) for woodwind quintet
Composed in 1955
Recorded by The Australian Wind Virtuosi (Phoenix USA 144, 2000)
Duration: 10:00

Piano Sonata
Composed in 1957
Recorded by Nadia Shpachenko (Reference Recordings RR 2021)
Duration: 10:00

"Poema Elegíaco" for orchestra
Composed in 1958; revised in 1963
Instrumentation: piccolo, 2-2, English horn-2, B clarinet-2, contrabassoon-alto saxophone; 4-3-3-1; timpani-percussion-strings
Premiered by Leopold Stokowski, American Symphony Orchestra, Carnegie Hall, New York, 1963
Recorded by The Royal Philharmonic Orchestra (Decca CDDCA785, 2011) and Orchestre Symphonique de la RTBF Bruxelles (Urlicht UAV 5985, 2016)
Duration: 9:00

Preludio Fantástico y Danza Mágica for five percussionists
Composed in 1973
Commissioned by the National Autonomous University of Mexico, UNAM
Duration: 11:00

Samson and Buddha for two clarinets in B-flat
Composed in 2014
Duration: 4:00

Samson and Buddha for two solo flutes
Composed in 2014
Recorded in 2020 (Reference Recordings RR, 2021)
Duration: 4:00

Seis por Televisión (Six on Television) for woodwind quintet and percussion
Composed in 1965
Recorded by The Australian Wind Virtuosi (Phoenix USA 144, 2000)
Duration: 10:00

Sonata for viola solo
Composed in 1955
Duration: 9:00

Sonata for violin solo
Composed in 1954
Recorded by Gonzalo Acosta (Naxos 8559303, 2007)
Duration: 12:00

"Song without Name or Words No. 1" for high voice and piano
Composed in 1956
Duration: 2:30

"Song without Name or Words No. 2" for high voice and piano
Composed in 1958
Duration: 2:00

Suite Canina (Canine Suite) for woodwind trio
Composed in 1957
Recorded by The Australian Wind Virtuosi (Phoenix USA 144, 2000)
Duration: 16:00

Suite for solo cello
Composed in 2006
Commissioned by Carlos Prieto
Duration: 12:30

Symphonic B A C H Variations for piano and orchestra
Composed in 2017
Instrumentation: piano solo; 2 (piccolos)-2-2, bass clarinet-2; 4-2-3-1; timpani-
percussion; strings
Recorded by Alexandre Kantorow, piano / *Serebrier* / RTÉ National Symphony Or-
chestra (BIS 2423, 2020)
Duration: 20:00

Symphony for Percussion for five solo percussionists
Composed in 1964
Recorded on LP Direct-to-Disc by Sir John Eliot Gardiner
Recorded in Moscow by Gnessins Russian Academy of Music (Reference Recordings
RR, 2021)
Duration: 9:00

Symphony No. 1 for orchestra
Composed in 1956
Instrumentation: piccolo, 2-2, English horn-2, bass clarinets-2, contrabassoon; 4-3-
3-1; timpani-percussion-harp-cello-organ; strings
Premiered by Leopold Stokowski and the Houston Symphony Orchestra, Houston,
1957
Recorded by Leopold Stokowski / Houston Symphony Orchestra (Guild 2347,
released 2010) and Bournemouth Symphony Orchestra (Naxos 8559648, 2010)
Duration: 18:00

Symphony No. 2, *Partita*, for orchestra
Composed in 1958
Instrumentation: 3-3-3-3-alto saxophone; 4-3-3-1; timpani-percussion-piano; strings
Premiered by the National Symphony Orchestra, DAR Constitution Hall, Wash-
ington, DC, 1960
Recorded by the Louisville Orchestra (LP)
Recorded by the London Philharmonic Orchestra (Reference Recordings RR)
Recorded by the London Philharmonic Orchestra (Naxos 8559303, 2007)
Duration: 28:00

Symphony No. 3, *Symphonie Mystique*, for string orchestra (with soprano obbligato in final movement)
Composed in 2003
Recorded by Carole Farley, soprano, and Orchestre de Chambre de Toulouse (Naxos 8559183, 2003) and Carole Farley, soprano, and the National Youth Orchestra of Spain (Naxos DVD 2110230, 2008)
Duration: 25:00

Tango in Blue for clarinet and piano
Composed in 2001
Arranged by the composer from the orchestral original
Duration: 3:00

Tango in Blue for flute and piano
Composed in 2001
Arranged by the composer from the orchestra original
Duration: 3:00

Tango in Blue for flute and string orchestra
Composed in 2001
Arranged by the composer from the orchestral original
Duration: 3:00

Tango in Blue for orchestra
Composed in 2001
Instrumentation: 2 (piccolos)-2-2-2; 2-2-1-0; timpani-2 percussion-piano; strings
Recorded by Barcelona Symphony Orchestra (BIS 1175, 2005; BIS 2423, 2020) and by the Bournemouth Symphony Orchestra (Naxos 8559648, 2010) and by the Málaga Philharmonic (Reference Recordings RR 2021)
Arranged by the composer from the orchestral original, and published separately for clarinet and piano, flute and piano, flute and string orchestra, saxophone quartet, string orchestra, string quartet, violin and piano.
Duration: 3:00

Tango Perpétuel (Perpetual Tango) for orchestra
Arranged in 2003 for orchestra after Erik Satie's solo piano work, no. 17 of *Sports et Divertissements*
Instrumentation: 1 (piccolo)-1-1-1, alto sax, tenor sax; 0-2-2-0; percussion; strings
Duration: 3:00

They Rode into the Sunset: Music for an Imaginary Film for orchestra
Composed in 2009
Instrumentation: 2-2-2-2; 4-2-3-1; timpani-percussion-piano-cello; SATB choir (optional); strings
Recorded by the Bournemouth Symphony Orchestra (Naxos 8559648, 2010)
Duration: 13:30

Variations on a Theme from Childhood for trombone and string quartet (or string orchestra)
Composed in 1974
Recorded by Orchestre de Chambre de Toulouse (Naxos 8559183, 2003)
Duration: 8:00

Violin Concerto, *Winter*, for violin and orchestra
Composed in 1992
Instrumentation: violin solo; 2 (piccolo)-2 (English horn optional)-2 (bass clarinet)-2; 4-2-3-1; timpani-3 percussion; strings
Recorded by Michael Guttman, violin, / Royal Philharmonic Orchestra (ASV 855, 2004) and Philippe Quint, violin, / Bournemouth Symphony Orchestra (Naxos 8559648, 2010)
Duration: 16:00

Vocalise for mixed chorus (SATB a cappella)
Composed in 1964
Duration: 3:00

Windance for string orchestra
Composed in 2019
Recorded by Concerto Málaga (2021)
Duration: 5:00

Winterreise for orchestra
Composed in 1999
Arranged by the composer from his Violin Concerto, *Winter*
Instrumentation: 2 (piccolo)-2 (English horn)-2 (bass clarinet)-2; 4-2-3-1; timpani-3 percussion; strings
Recorded by the London Philharmonic Orchestra (Naxos 8559303, 2007)
Duration: 6:00

The Year 2020 for woodwind quintet
Composed in 2020
Duration: 9:00

Peermusic Classical New York

152 W. 57th St., 10th floor
New York, NY 10019
(212) 265-3917
peerclassical@peermusic.com
www.peermusicclassical.com

PEERMUSIC AGENTS AND DISTRIBUTORS

United States and Canada

Exclusive distributor for sales:

Hal Leonard Corporation
7777 W. Bluemound Rd.
PO Box 13819
Milwaukee, WI 53213
Tel: (800) 554-0626
Fax: (414) 774-3259
Retail Orders: halinfo@halleonard.com
Wholesale Orders: sales@halleonard.com
www.halleonard.com

Exclusive distributor for Peermusic rentals:

Subito Music Corp.
60 Depot Rd.
Verona, NJ 07044
Tel: (973) 857-3440
Fax: (973) 857-3442
rental@subitomusic.com
www.subitomusic.com
Rental reservation: https://www.subitomusic.com/rental/place-rental-order/
For perusal materials, contact Peermusic Classical.

Continental Europe

Sales and rentals:

Peermusic Classical GmbH
Sierichstraße 39
Germany
Tel: +49 (40) 278 379-28
Fax: +49 (40) 278 379-40
Sales: https://shop.peermusic-classical.de/en/
Rentals: https://www.peermusic-classical.de/en/catalogues/rental_material

Great Britain

Rentals, grand rights, and promotion:

Faber Music Ltd.
Bloomsbury House

74-77 Great Russell Street
London
WC1 3DA
United Kingdom
Tel: (44-207) 278 7436
Fax: (44-207) 833 7939
hire@fabermusic.com
www.fabermusic.com
Sales: Hal Leonard Corporation, USA

Latin America

Rentals and grand rights:

Boosey & Hawkes Rental Library
229 West 28th Street, 11th Floor
New York, NY 10001 USA
Tel: +1 (212) 358-5300, opt. 2
USRental@boosey.com
Sales: Hal Leonard Corporation, USA

Australia and New Zealand

Rentals, grand rights, and synchronizations:

Hal Leonard Australia
Music Hire and Licensing Department
4 Lentara Court
Cheltenham
Victoria, Australia
Tel: +61 3 9585 3300
Fax: +61 3 9585 8729
mstapleton@halleonard.com.au
Sales: Hal Leonard Corporation, USA

For all other territories, Peermusic Classical, New York

TRANSCRIPTIONS

Tchaikovsky/Serebrier   *Andante Cantabile* for string orchestra
Peermusic

Tchaikovsky/Serebrier   *None but the Lonely Heart* for string orchestra
Peermusic

Tchaikovsky/Serebrier Peermusic	*None but the Lonely Heart* for violoncello ensemble
Bizet/Serebrier Chester	*Carmen Symphony* for symphony orchestra
Bizet/Serebrier Hal Leonard	*Carmen Symphony* for band
Rachmaninoff/Serebrier Boosey & Hawkes	*Vocalise* for chamber orchestra
Grieg/Serebrier C. F. Peters Corp.	*Fourteen Songs* for soprano and small orchestra
Gershwin/Serebrier Warner Chappell	"Lullaby" for orchestra
Gershwin/Serebrier Warner Chappell	*Three Preludes* for orchestra
Janáček/Serebrier Universal Edition	*Makropulos Case*, Symphonic Synthesis for orchestra

Chester

Bizet/Serebrier   *Carmen Symphony*
Recorded by the Barcelona Symphony Orchestra on BIS
Latin GRAMMY, Best Recording of the Year

Peters Corporation / CF Peters

14 Grieg Songs, orchestrated by J. Serebrier
Recorded by Carole Farley and the London Philharmonic Orchestra on ASV

Boosey & Hawkes

Rachmaninoff/Serebrier   *Vocalise*
Recorded by the Russian National Orchestra on Warner Classics

Universal Edition

Janáček/Serebrier   *Makropulos Case*, Symphonic Synthesis
Recorded by the Brno Symphony Orchestra on Reference Recordings RR

Warner Chappell

Gershwin-Serebrier   *Three Preludes*; "Lullaby"
Recorded by the Royal Scottish National Orchestra on SOMM

Hal Leonard

Bizet/Serebrier   *Carmen Symphony* version for symphonic band
Recorded on Naxos by the United States Marine Band

Peermusic

Moto Perpetuo for accordion solo
Commissioned by the American Accordionists' Association

Discography, 1966–2021

Samuel ADLER (1928–)
Symphony No. 6
Concerto for cello and orchestra—Maxmillian Hornung, violoncello
Drifting on Winds and Currents
Royal Scottish National Orchestra—José Serebrier, conductor
Linn CKD 545 (world-premiere recordings)

Isaac ALBÉNIZ (1860–1909)
Iberia (orchestrated by Enrique Arbós)
SWF Symphony Orchestra, Baden-Baden—José Serebrier, conductor
Phoenix USA PH CD 147

Isaac ALBÉNIZ (1860–1909)
Tango, op. 165, no. 2
Mallorca, op. 202
Concerto Málaga—José Serebrier, conductor
SOMM CD 0171

Tomaso ALBINONI (1671–1751)
Adagio (orchestrated by Remo Giazotto)

Johann Sebastian BACH (1685–1750)
Air, from Suite No. 3, BWV 1068
Adelaide Symphony Orchestra—José Serebrier, conductor
Tioch CD 1004
Koch 321 850
Concerto Digital CD 3011 and Dante DNCD 012

Johann Sebastian BACH (1685–1750)
Toccata and Fugue in D minor (transcribed by Leopold Stokowski)

Bournemouth Symphony Orchestra—José Serebrier, conductor
Naxos 8.578305

Johann Sebastian BACH (1685–1750) (transcribed by Leopold Stokowski)
Air, from Suite No. 3, BWV 1068
"Sheep May Safely Graze," from Cantata No. 208
Fugue in G minor, BWV 578
Bournemouth Symphony Orchestra—José Serebrier, conductor
Naxos 8.578305 and Naxos 8.557883

"Komm, süsser Tod"
Chorale, from *Easter Cantata*
"Es ist Vollbracht!"
"Wir glauben all'an einen Gott"
Nun komm, der Heiden Heiland
Bournemouth Symphony Orchestra—José Serebrier, conductor
Naxos 8.557883

Johann Sebastian BACH (1685–1750) (transcribed by Leopold Stokowski)
Arioso
Wachet auf
Ich ruf zu dir
Adagio
"Mein Jesu"
"Jesu, Joy of Man's Desiring"
Prelude in B minor
Siciliano
Fugue in C minor
Bournemouth Symphony Orchestra—José Serebrier, conductor
Naxos 8.572050

Leonardo BALADA (1933–)
Concierto Mágico for guitar and orchestra—Eliot Fisk, guitar
Concerto No. 3 for piano and orchestra—Rosa Torres-Pardo, piano
Music for flute and orchestra—Magdalena Martínez, flute
Barcelona Symphony Orchestra—José Serebrier, conductor
World-premiere recordings
Naxos 8.555039

Samuel BARBER (1910–1981)
Souvenirs, Suite de Ballet, op. 28
London Symphony Orchestra—José Serebrier, conductor
ASV CD DCA 737
Desto (LP) DC 6433
Phoenix USA PHCD 111

Samuel BARBER (1910–1981)
Canzonetta for oboe and strings
World-premiere recording
Julia Girdwood, oboe—Scottish Chamber Orchestra—José Serebrier, conductor
ASV CD DCA 737
Desto (LP) DC 6433
Phoenix USA PHCD 111

Robert BEASER (1954–)
Guitar Concerto—Eliot Fisk, guitar solo
"Notes on a Southern Sky"
"Evening Prayer"
"Ground 0"
Royal Scottish National Orchestra—José Serebrier, conductor
World-premiere recordings
Linn CKD 528

Ludwig van BEETHOVEN (1770–1827)
Symphony No. 3, op. 55
Sydney Symphony Orchestra—José Serebrier, conductor
IMG Records CD 1615
RCA VRL 1 0532 (LP)
Trax Classique TRXCS 117

Symphony No. 8, op. 93

The Creatures of Prometheus, Overture, op. 43
Egmont, Overture, op. 84
Fidelio, Overture, op. 72
Sydney Symphony Orchestra—José Serebrier, conductor
Trax Classique TRXCS 117
IMG Records CD 1615
RCA VRL 1 053 (LP)

Elmer BERNSTEIN (1922–2004)
To Kill a Mockingbird: Suite
Royal Philharmonic Orchestra—José Serebrier, conductor
RPO 022 CD

The Magnificent Seven: Overture
Royal Philharmonic Orchestra—José Serebrier, conductor
RPO 017 CD

Luigi BOCCHERINI (1743–1805)
Minuet (transcribed by Leopold Stokowski)
Bournemouth Symphony Orchestra—José Serebrier, conductor
Naxos 8.572050

Georges BIZET (1838–1875)
Carmen Suites No. 1 and 2
Adelaide Symphony Orchestra—José Serebrier, conductor
Tioch Digital TC 1003, cassette and LP
KEM Disc KD 1003 CD
Koch 321870 DAT and K-Tel 1415 CD and cassette

Ernest BLOCH (1880–1959)
Concerto for violin and orchestra
Baal Shem for violin and orchestra
Michael Guttman, violin—Royal Philharmonic Orchestra—José Serebrier, conductor
ASV CD DCA 785

Ernest BLOCH (1880–1959)
Violin Concerto
Baal Shem
Suite Hebraique
Royal Scottish National Orchestra—Zina Schiff, violin—José Serebrier, conductor
Naxos 8.557757

Luigi BOCCHERINI (1743–1805)
Minuet, op. 11, no. 2
Adelaide Symphony Orchestra—José Serebrier, conductor
Tioch Digital TC 1003 cassette and LP
Koch 321 850 DAT
Concerto Digital CD 3011
Dante DNCD 012

Georges BIZET (1838–1875)—José SEREBRIER (1938–)
Carmen Symphony, in 12 Scenes
United States Marine Band—José Serebrier, conductor
Naxos 8.570727

Georges BIZET (1838–1875)
Carmen Symphony, in 12 Scenes by Bizet-Serebrier
L'Arlésienne, Suites No. 1 and 2
Barcelona Symphony Orchestra—José Serebrier, conductor
Latin GRAMMY for best recording of the year
BIS 1305-CD

Alexander BORODIN (1833–1887)
Symphonies 1, 2, 3 (original versions)
Rome RAI Symphony Orchestra—José Serebrier, conductor
ASV CD DCA 706

Alexander BORODIN (1833–1887)
Polovtsian Dances, from the opera *Prince Igor*
Sydney Symphony Orchestra—José Serebrier, conductor
RCA VRL 1 0529 (LP)
Trax Classique TRXCD 118 (CD and cassette)

Benjamin BRITTEN (1913–1976)
Young Apollo for piano and strings, op. 16 (world-premiere recording)
Peter Evans, piano—Scottish Chamber Orchestra—José Serebrier, conductor
ASV CD DCA 737
Phoenix USA PHCD 111

Les Illuminations (text by Arthur Rimbaud), op. 18
Carole Farley, soprano—Scottish Chamber Orchestra—José Serebrier, conductor
ASV CD DCA 737
Phoenix USA PHCD 111

Geoffrey BURGON (1941–2010)
Brideshead Variations Suite (world-premiere recording)
Adelaide Symphony Orchestra—José Serebrier, conductor
ABC Audiophile LP 1201

William BYRD (1543–1623)
Pavane and Gigue (transcribed by Leopold Stokowski)
Bournemouth Symphony Orchestra—José Serebrier, conductor
Naxos 8.572050

Elliott CARTER (1908–2012)
Elegy
St. Michael Strings—José Serebrier, conductor
ALBA ABCD 341

George CHADWICK (1854–1931)
Melpomene, Overture
Tam O'Shanter, Symphonic Poem
Brno Czech State Philharmonic—José Serebrier, conductor
Reference Recordings RR-64CD

George CHADWICK (1854–1931)
Aphrodite (world-premiere recording)
Elegy (world-premiere recording)
Symphonic Suite (world-premiere recording)
Brno Czech State Philharmonic—José Serebrier, conductor
Reference Recordings RR-74CD

Aphrodite
Symphonic Sketches
Melpomene, Overture
Tam O'Shanter
Elegy
Czech State Philharmonic—José Serebrier, conductor
Reference Recordings RR-2104CD

Ruperto CHAPÍ (1851–1909)
Nocturno, from the Zarzuela *El Rey que Rabió*
Concerto Málaga—José Serebrier, conductor
SOMM CD 0171

Ernest CHAUSSON (1855–1899)
Chanson Perpétuelle (text by Charles Cross), op. 37
Carole Farley, soprano—RTBF Symphony Orchestra of Belgium—José Serebrier,
    conductor
ASV CD DCA 605 CD and cassette

Poème de l'Amour et de la Mer (text by Maurice Bouchor), op. 19
Chanson Perpétuelle (text by Charles Cross), op. 37
Carole Farley, soprano—RTBF Symphony Orchestra of Belgium—José Serebrier,
    conductor
ASV CD DCA 643 CD and cassette

Symphony in B-flat major, op. 20
Soir de Fête, op. 32
La Tempête, op. 18
L'Orchestre Symphonique de la RTBF, Brussels—José Serebrier, conductor
CHANDOS CD 8369 and cassette ABT D 135 LP1135
MHS 512703K

Jeremiah CLARKE (1674–1707)
Trumpet Prelude (transcribed by Leopold Stokowski)
Bournemouth Symphony Orchestra—José Serebrier, conductor
Naxos 8.572050

Claude DEBUSSY (1862–1918)
"Le Balcon" (world-premiere recording)
"Le Jet d'Eau" (world-premiere recording)
Carole Farley, soprano—RTBF Symphony Orchestra of Belgium—José Serebrier,
    conductor
ASV CD DCA 643 CD and cassette

Léo DELIBES (1836–1891)
Coppélia, Ballet Suite

Adelaide Symphony Orchestra—José Serebrier, conductor
Tioch Digital TD 1002 MX (LP)
Arista DC 1002 MX
Kem-Disc KD 1003
Koch Digital 321870 DAT and CD
K-Tel 1415 CD and cassette

Frederick DELIUS (1862–1934)
Sept Chansons Danoises
Cinq Chansons Anglaises et Scandinaves (first recording)—Carole Farley, soprano
Irmelin, Orchestral Suite (first recording)—Rheinische Philharmonie—José Serebrier, conductor
Air and Dances Deux Acquarelles (orchestrated by Eric Fenby)—Philharmonia Orchestra—José Serebrier, conductor
Dinemec Classics DCCD 019

Vincent D'INDY (1851–1931)
Symphonie sur Chant Montagnard Français, op. 25
Valerie Traficante, piano—Royal Philharmonic Orchestra—José Serebrier, conductor
IMP Masters / Pickwick MCD 71

Henrí DUPARC (1848–1933)
Cinque Mélodies
Carole Farley, soprano—RTBF Symphony Orchestra of Belgium—José Serebrier, conductor
ASV CD DCA 605

Antonín DVOŘÁK (1841–1904)
Symphony No. 8, op. 88
Sydney Symphony Orchestra—José Serebrier, conductor
RCA Red Seal VRL1 0269 (LP) and RCA Red Seal ARL1 3550 (LP)
Trax Classique TRXCD127 (CD)
IMG Records CD 1614 (CD)

Symphony No. 9, op. 95, *From the New World*
Sydney Symphony Orchestra—José Serebrier, conductor
RCA Red Seal VRL1 0485 (LP)
Trax Classique TRXCD128 (CD)
IMG Records CD 1614 (CD)

Legends, op. 39
Scottish Chamber Orchestra—José Serebrier, conductor
ASV CD DCA 765

Carnival Overture, op. 92
Brno Czech State Philharmonic—José Serebrier, conductor
Not released

Violin Concerto, op. 53—Michael Guttman, violin
Romance for violin and orchestra, op. 11
Mazurek for violin and orchestra, op. 49
Legends, Nos. 1 and 3, op. 59
Scherzo Capriccioso, op. 66
Royal Philharmonic Orchestra—José Serebrier, conductor
IMP PCD 1110

Symphony No. 1 in C minor, op. 3, *The Bells of Zlonice*
Symphony No. 2 in B-flat major, op. 4
Symphony No. 3 in E-flat major, op. 10
Symphony No. 4 in G major, op. 88
Symphony No. 5 in E minor, op. 95
Symphony No. 6 in D minor, op. 60
Symphony No. 7 in D minor, op. 70
Symphony No. 8 in G major, op. 88
Symphony No. 9 in E minor, op. 95, *From the New World*
Slavonic Dances, op. 46, Nos. 1 and 6
Slavonic Dances, op. 72, Nos. 2, 3, 4, 6, 7, and 8
In Nature's Realm, op. 91
Scherzo Capriccioso, op. 66
Legends, op. 59
Czech Suite
Bournemouth Symphony Orchestra—José Serebrier, conductor
Warner Classics 0825646132010
Warner Classics 0825646287871
Warner Classics 2564 66656-2
Warner Classics 2564 66656-3
Warner Classics 2564 66656-6
Warner Classics 2564 69627.0

Symphony No. 9 in E minor, op. 95, *From the New World*
Czech State Philharmonic—José Serebrier, conductor
Conifer Classics 75605 51522 2

Czech Suite, op. 39
Legends, op. 59
Scottish Chamber Orchestra—José Serebrier, conductor
Musical Heritage Society 513437L

Manuel de FALLA (1876–1946)
Nights in the Gardens of Spain
Joaquín Soriano, piano—English Chamber Orchestra—José Serebrier, conductor
ASV CD DCA 775

"Ritual Fire Dance"
Interlude and Dance, from *La Vida Breve*

SWF Symphony Orchestra, Baden-Baden—José Serebrier, conductor
Phoenix USA PHCD 147

Gabriel FAURÉ (1845–1924)
Ballade for piano and orchestra
Valerie Traficante, piano—Royal Philharmonic Orchestra—José Serebrier, conductor
IMP Masters / Pickwick MCD 71

Orlando Jacinto GARCÍA (1954–)
Auschwitz (They Will Never Be Forgotten)
Varadero Memories
In Memoriam Earle Brown
Málaga Philharmonic Orchestra—Florida International University Concert Choir—
    José Serebrier, conductor
World-premiere recordings
Toccata Classics TOCC 0239

Ge GAN-RU (1954–)
Six Pentatonic Tunes
Chinese Rhapsody
Wu for piano and orchestra—Margaret Len Tan, piano
Royal Scottish National Orchestra—José Serebrier, conductor
World-premiere recordings
BIS-1509 SACD

George GERSHWIN (1898–1937)
An American in Paris
Three Preludes (orchestrated by José Serebrier)
"Lullaby" (orchestrated by José Serebrier)
Concerto in F for piano and orchestra—Leopold Godowsky III, piano
Royal Scottish National Orchestra—José Serebrier, conductor
Dinemec Classics DCCD 025
SOMM Ariadne 5003

George GERSHWIN (1898–1937)
Rhapsody in Blue—Shelly Berg, piano
An American in Paris
Three Preludes (orchestrated by José Serebrier)
"I Loves You, Porgy"—Monica Mancini, voice
"My Man's Gone Now"—Monica Mancini, voice
"I Got Rhythm"—Shelly Berg Trio
Royal Philharmonic Orchestra—José Serebrier, conductor
DECCA 28948 17407

Ricard Lamote de GRIGNON (1899–1962)
Lento Expresivo

Concerto Málaga—José Serebrier, conductor
SOMM CD 0171

Edvard GRIEG (1843–1907)
"Solveig's Cradle Song," from *Peer Gynt*
"Fiddlers," op. 25, no. 1
"A Swan," op. 25, no. 2
"Album Lines," op. 25, no. 3
"With a Water-Lily," op. 25, no. 4
"Departed," op. 25, no. 5
"A Bird-Song," op. 25, no. 6
The Mountain Thrall, op. 32
"A Vision," op. 33, no. 6
"Fra Monte Pincio," op. 39, no. 1
"Greeting," op. 39, no. 1
"One Day, O Heart of Mine," op. 48, no. 2
"The Way of the World," op. 48, no. 3
"The Nightingale's Secret," op. 48, no. 4
"The Time of Roses," op. 48, no. 5
"A Dream," op. 48, no. 6
"To the Motherland," op. 58, no. 2
The Princess, EG 135
"Little Kirsten," op. 60, no. 1
"The Mother's Lament," op. 60, no. 2
"On the Water," op. 60, no. 5
"A Bird Cried Out," op. 60, no. 4
"Eros," op. 70, no. 1
Carole Farley, soprano—José Serebrier, conductor—London Philharmonic
    Orchestra—Philharmonia
DINEMEC DCCD 022
SOMM Ariadne 5001

Alberto GINASTERA (1916–1983)
Estancia, Suite, op. 8a
United States Marine Band—José Serebrier, conductor
Naxos 8.570727

Alexander GLAZUNOV (1865–1936)
Symphony No. 1 in E major, op. 5
Symphony No. 2 in F-sharp minor, op. 16
Symphony No. 3 in D major, op. 33
Symphony No. 4 in E-flat major, op. 48
Symphony No. 5 in B-flat major, op. 55
Symphony No. 6 in C minor, op. 58
Symphony No. 7 in F major, op. 77, *Pastoral*

Symphony No. 8 in E-flat major, op. 83
Symphony No. 9 in D major, *Unfinished*
La Mer, op. 28
Introduction and Dance from *Salome*, op. 90
The Seasons, complete Ballet
Raymonda, Ballet Suite
Royal Scottish National Orchestra—José Serebrier, conductor
Violin Concerto, op. 82—Rachel Barton Pine, violin
Meditation for violin and orchestra, op. 32—Rachel Barton Pine, violin
Concerto Ballata for cello and orchestra, op. 108—Wen-Sinn Yang, violoncello
Chant du Ménestrel for cello and orchestra, op. 71—Wen-Sinn Yang, violoncello
Piano Concerto No. 1, op. 92—Alexander Romanovsky, piano
Piano Concerto No. 2, op. 100—Alexander Romanovsky, piano
Concerto for alto saxophone, op. 109—Marc Chisson, saxophone
Russian National Orchestra—José Serebrier, conductor
Warner Classics 2564 66467.4 DDD LC 04281
Warner Classics 0190295651435
Warner Classics 2564-61939-2
Warner Classics 2564-61434-2
Warner Classics 2564-69627-0
Warner Classics 2564-63236-2
Warner Classics 2564-65775-3
Warner Classics 2564-66656-2
Warner Classics 2564-64526-6
Warner Classics 2564-67946-5

Enrique GRANADOS (1867–1916)
Andaluza, from *Danzas Españolas*, op. 37 no. 5
Oriental, from *Danzas Españolas*, op. 37 no. 2
Pequeña Romanza, H. 107
El Himno de los Muertos, H. 67
Intermezzo, from *Goyescas* (transcribed by José Luis Turina)
Concerto Málaga—José Serebrier, conductor
SOMM CD 0171

Jay GREENBERG (1991–)
Symphony No. 5
London Symphony Orchestra—José Serebrier
World-premiere recording
SONY Classical CD 81804

Edvard GRIEG (1843–1907)
Carole Farley Sings Grieg
14 Lieder—orchestrated by José Serebrier—Carole Farley, soprano
London Philharmonic Orchestra—Philharmonia Orchestra—José Serebrier, conductor
Dinemec Classics DCCD 022

Charles GRIFFES (1884–1920)
Three Poems of Fiona MacLeod, op. 11
Carole Farley, soprano—Czech State Philharmonic Brno—José Serebrier, conductor
Not released

George Frideric HANDEL (1685–1759)
Air, from *Water Music*
Largo, from *Xerxes*
Adelaide Symphony Orchestra—José Serebrier, conductor
Tioch Digital CD 1004
Koch 321 850 DAT and CD
Concerto Digital CD 3011
Dante DNCD 012

George Frideric HANDEL (1685–1759)
"Pastoral" Symphony, from *Messiah* (transcribed by Leopold Stokowski)
Bournemouth Symphony Orchestra—José Serebrier, conductor
Naxos 8.557883

Franz Joseph HAYDN (1732–1809)
Andante Cantabile (transcribed by Leopold Stokowski)
Bournemouth Symphony Orchestra—José Serebrier, conductor
Naxos 8.572050

Ferdinand HÉROLD (1791–1833)
Le Pré aux Clercs, Opera in two acts
Soloists and Chorus of the Royal Scottish National Opera—BBC Scottish Symphony
   Orchestra
BBC Production, Broadcast on BBC Radio 3
Not released on CD

Bernard HERRMANN (1911–1975)
Psycho Suite: Prelude, "The Stairs," "The Murder," Finale
Taxi Driver: Main Theme
Royal Philharmonic Orchestra—José Serebrier, conductor
RPO 017 CD

Vertigo: Prelude, "The Nightmare," "Scene d'Amour"
North by Northwest: Overture
Citizen Kane: Prelude and Finale
Royal Philharmonic Orchestra—José Serebrier, conductor
RPO 022 CD

Paul HINDEMITH (1895–1963)
Concerto for orchestra, op. 38
Violin Concerto, op. 30, no. 3—Michael Guttman, violin

Kammermusik No. 4, op. 36, no. 3
Ragtime
Suite of French Dances (world-premiere recording) Philharmonia—José Serebrier,
   conductor
ASV DCA 945CD

Gustav HOLST (1874–1934)
The Planets, op. 32
Melbourne Symphony Orchestra—José Serebrier, conductor
RCA Red Seal VRL1 0412 LP
ASV CD/2L QS 6078
Trax Classique TRXCD 109
RCA Australia VRL1 0412 (LP)

Charles IVES (1874–1954)
Symphony No. 3
"Decoration Day"
The Unanswered Question
Adelaide Symphony Orchestra—José Serebrier, conductor
Not released

Symphony No. 4
World-premiere recording
American Symphony Orchestra—Leopold Stokowski—José Serebrier and David
   Katz, associate conductors—Schola Cantorum of New York, Hugh Ross, director
CBS ML/MS 6775 (LP USA)
72403 Europe LP
Sony CD MPK 46726

Symphony No. 4
London Philharmonic Orchestra—José Serebrier, conductor
RCA Red Seal ARL1 0589 (LP)
Q8 ART1 0589
Chandos CD 839
RCA CD HP 09026 63316-2
GRAMMY nomination for best classical recording of the year

Leoš JANÁČEK (1854–1928)
Sinfonietta
Taras Bulba
Lachian Dances
Brno Czech State Philharmonic—José Serebrier, conductor
Reference Recordings RR 65 CD

The Makropulos Affair, Orchestral Suite by José Serebrier (world-premiere recording)
The Cunning Little Vixen, Suite
Jenufa: "Jalousie," Prelude

The House of the Dead: Prelude
Brno Czech State Philharmonic—José Serebrier, conductor
Reference Recordings RR 75 CD

Jerome KERN (1885–1945)
Showboat, Symphonic Scene (orchestrated by Robert Russell Bennett)
WDR Symphony Orchestra, Köln—José Serebrier, conductor
Not released

Zoltán KODÁLY (1882–1967)
Háry János, Concert Suite
SWF Symphony Orchestra, Baden-Baden—José Serebrier, conductor
Bodensee International Festival 6MBH CD (live concert recording)

Zoltán KODÁLY (1882–1967)
Háry János, Concert Suite
Dances of Galánta
Le Paon, Orchestral Variations
Marosszék Dances
SWF Symphony Orchestra, Baden-Baden—José Serebrier, conductor
BIS CD 875

Erich Wolfgang KORNGOLD (1897–1957)
The Sea Hawk: Main Theme
Royal Philharmonic Orchestra—José Serebrier, conductor
RPO 017 CD

Erich Wolfgang KORNGOLD (1897–1957)
The Adventures of Robin Hood: "The Fight," "Victory," Epilogue
Royal Philharmonic Orchestra—José Serebrier, conductor
RPO 022 CD

William F. LEE (1929–2011)
Veri (World-premiere recording)
Adelaide Symphony Orchestra—José Serebrier, conductor
Finnadar Atlantique 90937 (LP)
UAV 5995 (CD)

Aubert LEMELAND (1932–2010)
Time Landscapes
Memorial
Symphony No. 6
World-premiere recordings
Carole Farley, soprano—Rheinische Philharmonie—José Serebrier, conductor
Skarbo DSK3104 / UPC 3375250310405

Franz LISZT (1811–1886)
Mephisto Waltzes (orchestrated by Matthias Weigmann)—Jitka Cechova, piano
The Preludes
SWF Symphony Orchestra, Baden-Baden—José Serebrier, conductor
Bodensee International Festival 6MBH CD (live concert recording)

Otto LUENING (1900–1996)
Lyric Scene for flute and strings
Legend for oboe and strings
Per Øien, flute—Erik Larsen, oboe—Oslo Philharmonic—José Serebrier, conductor
World-premiere recordings
ASV CD DCA 741
Desto DC 6466 (LP)
Phoenix USA PHCD 101

Concerted Piece for Tape Recorder and Orchestra
Oslo Philharmonic—José Serebrier, conductor
World-premiere recording
Composers Recordings Inc CRI LP 227 (LP)

Frederick LOEWE (1901–1988)
My Fair Lady, Orchestral Suite (orchestrated by Robert Russell Bennett)
WDR Symphony, Köln—José Serebrier, conductor
Not released

Leevi MADETOJA (1887–1947)
Elegy
St. Michael Strings—José Serebrier, conductor
ALBA ABCD 341

Joaquim MALATS (1872–1912)
"Serenata Española," from *Impresiones de España*
Concerto Málaga—José Serebrier, conductor
SOMM CD 0171

Alessandro MARCELLO (1673–1747)
Oboe Concerto—Jean-Marie Quenon, oboe
RTBF Symphony Orchestra—José Serebrier, conductor
Concerto Digital 3011 CD/LP/cassette
Koch Digital DA 321 850
Dante DN CD 012

Tomás MARCO (1942–)
Árbol de Arcángeles
SWF Symphony Orchestra, Baden-Baden—José Serebrier, conductor

World-premiere recording
Phoenix USA PHCD 147

Carlo MARTELLI (1935–)
Serenade for strings
World-premiere recording
Philharmonia—José Serebrier, conductor
Not released

Symphony No. 2
World-premiere recording
Royal Scottish National Orchestra—José Serebrier, conductor
Not released

Jules MASSENET (1842–1912)
Prelude: *La Vierge (Légende Sacrée)*
Adelaide Symphony Orchestra—José Serebrier, conductor
Tioch Digital TD 1003 (LP)
Kem Disc CD 1003
K-Tel NEV1415 C

Johann MATTHESON (1681–1764)
Air (transcribed by Leopold Stokowski)
Bournemouth Symphony Orchestra—José Serebrier, conductor
Naxos 8.572050

Clark MCALISTER (1946–)
Aguae Sulis
St. Michael Strings—José Serebrier, conductor
World-premiere recording
ALBA ABCD 341

Felix MENDELSSOHN (1809–1847)
Symphony No. 3, *Scottish*, op. 56
Symphony No. 4, *Italian*, op. 90
Scherzo, op. 20, original version (world-premiere recording)
Scottish Chamber Orchestra—José Serebrier, conductor
ASV CD 700 UK Music Retailers Association Award for best orchestral recording

The Hebrides, Overture, op. 26
Scottish Chamber Orchestra—José Serebrier, conductor
Not released

Peter MENNIN (1923–1983)
Symphony No. 9
Adelaide Symphony Orchestra—José Serebrier, conductor

World-premiere recording
Finnadar Atlantic 90937-1 (LP) and cassette

Gian Carlo MENOTTI (1911–2007)
Sebastian
World-premiere recording of the complete ballet
London Symphony Orchestra—José Serebrier, conductor
Desto 6432 (LP) ASV CD DCA 741
Phoenix USA PHCD 101

Darius MILHAUD (1892–1974)
Concertino de Printemps, op. 136
Michael Guttman, violin—Royal Philharmonic Orchestra—José Serebrier, conductor
ASV CD DCA 855

Jesús de MONASTERIO (1836–1903)
Andante Religioso
Andante Expresivo
Concerto Málaga—José Serebrier, conductor
SOMM CD 0171

Xavier MONTSALVATGE (1912–2002)
Cinco Canciones Negras
Carole Farley, soprano—SWF Symphony Orchestra, Baden-Baden—José Serebrier,
    conductor
Phoenix USA PHCD 147

Enric MORERA (1865–1942)
Desolació
St. Michael Strings—José Serebrier, conductor
SOMM CD 0171

Jerome MOROSS (1913–1983)
The Big Country: Main Theme
Royal Philharmonic Orchestra—José Serebrier, conductor
RPO 017 CD

Modest MUSSORGSKY (1839–1881) (transcribed by Leopold Stokowski)
Entr'acte (Act IV) from *Khovanshchina*
Russian National Orchestra—José Serebrier, conductor
Warner Classics 2564 68025-5

Modest MUSSORGSKY (1839–1881)
Pictures at an Exhibition (orchestrated by Leopold Stokowski)
Boris Godunov: A Symphonic Synthesis (orchestrated by Leopold Stokowski)

Night on Bald Mountain (orchestrated by Leopold Stokowski)
Bournemouth Symphony Orchestra—José Serebrier, conductor
Blu-ray Audio

Pictures at an Exhibition
Boris Godunov: A Symphonic Synthesis
Night on Bald Mountain
Bournemouth Symphony Orchestra—José Serebrier, conductor
Blu-ray Audio

Night on Bald Mountain (transcribed by Leopold Stokowski)
Boris Godunov: A Symphonic Synthesis
Pictures at an Exhibition
Bournemouth Symphony Orchestra—José Serebrier, conductor
Acoustic Reality Experience CD

Jacques OFFENBACH (1819–1880)
Can-Can, from *Orpheus in the Underworld*
Entr'acte and Barcarolle from *The Tales of Hoffmann*
Adelaide Symphony Orchestra—José Serebrier, conductor
Tioch Digital TD 1003 (LP)
Kem-Disc 1003 CD

Johann PACHELBEL (1653–1706)
Canon
Adelaide Symphony Orchestra—José Serebrier, conductor
Tioch Digital TD 1004 (LP)
Koch 321 850 (DAT and CD)
Concerto Digital CD 3011
Dante DNCD 012

Giovanni Pierluigi da PALESTRINA (1525–1594)
Adoramus Te (transcribed by Leopold Stokowski)
Bournemouth Symphony Orchestra—José Serebrier, conductor
Naxos 8.572050

Carter PANN (1972–)
Miami Concerto for piano and orchestra
Dance Partita
Two Portraits of Barcelona
Deux Séjours
Barry Snyder, piano—Czech State Philharmonic Brno—José Serebrier, conductor
World-premiere recordings
Naxos 8.559043

Manuel PONCE (1882–1948)
Concierto del Sur
Sharon Isbin, guitar—New York Philharmonic—José Serebrier, conductor
Warner Classics 2564,60296-2

Francis POULENC (1899–1963)
La Voix Humaine, Opera in one act
Carole Farley, soprano—Adelaide Symphony Orchestra—José Serebrier, conductor
RCA RL 70114 (LP)
Andante / Varese Sarabande AD 72405 (LP)
Chandos CD 8331
Phoenix USA CD PHCD 131

John POWELL (1963–)
A Prussian Requiem
Philharmonia Orchestra—José Serebrier
Javier Camarena—Steven Pence—The Philharmonia
5 Cat Studios FCS 001 (world-premiere recording)

Film Suites, volume 1
1. "Building the Crate" from *Chicken Run*
2. "Assassin's Tango" from *Mr. & Mrs. Smith*
3. Suite from *How to Train Your Dragon*
4. Love Theme from *Two Weeks Notice*
5. Main Title from *The Bourne Identity*
6. Suite from *Ice Age: The Meltdown*
7. Suite from *X-Men: The Last Stand*
8. "The Great Tree" from *Endurance*
9. Suite from *How to Train Your Dragon 2*
Philharmonia Orchestra—José Serebrier, conductor
5 Cat Studios FCD010 (digital only)

Rio 2 (original motion picture score)
Hollywood Symphony Orchestra—José Serebrier, conductor
88843 04845 2 Atlantic Records

Sergey PROKOFIEV (1891–1953)
Sketch d'Automne, op. 8
"The Ugly Duckling," op. 18
Symphony No. 1, *Classical*, op. 25
Jour d'Été, op. 65a
Feu de Joie en Hiver, op. 122
Carole Farley, soprano—Pisley Abbey Choir
Scottish Chamber Orchestra—José Serebrier, conductor
ASV CD DCA 760

Giacomo PUCCINI (1858–1924)
Crisantemi
St. Micahel Strings—José Serebrier, conductor
ALBA ABCD 341

Henry PURCELL (1659–1695)
"Dido's Lament," from *Dido and Aeneas* (transcribed by Leopold Stokowski)
Timothy Walden, cello solo—Bournemouth Symphony Orchestra—José Serebrier,
    conductor
Naxos 8.578305

Sergey RACHMANINOFF (1873–1943)
The Bells, op. 35
Lyubov Petrova, soprano—Andrei Popov, tenor—Sergei Leiferkus, baritone
The Moscow State Chamber Choir, Vladimir Minin, director
Russian National Orchestra—José Serebrier, conductor
Warner Classics 2564 68025-5 (recorded live in Moscow, Rostropovich Festival)

Vocalise (orchestrated by José Serebrier)
Russian National Orchestra—José Serebrier, conductor
Warner Classics 2564 68025-5

Einojuhani RAUTAVAARA (1928–2016)
Divertimento
St. Michael Strings—José Serebrier, conductor
ALBA ABCD 341

Angels and Visitations
Helsinki Radio Philharmonic—José Serebrier, conductor
Not released (broadcast recording by Finnish Radio)

Maurice RAVEL (1875–1937)
Boléro
Melbourne Symphony Orchestra—José Serebrier, conductor
Tioch Digital TD 1001
Trax Clasique TRXCD 118
ASV CD ZCQS 6078

Boléro
SWF Symphony Orchestra, Baden-Baden—José Serebrier, conductor
Phoenix USA PHCD 147

Ottorino RESPIGHI (1879–1936)
Concerto Gregoriano
Ruggiero Ricci, violin—Adelaide Symphony Orchestra—José Serebrier, conductor
Not released

Silvestre REVUELTAS (1899–1940), José SEREBRIER (1938–)
Mexican Dance
United States Marine Band
Naxos 8.570727

Nicolay RIMSKY-KORSAKOV (1844–1908)
Scheherazade, Symphonic Suite, op. 35
Russian Easter Overture, op. 36
London Philharmonic Orchestra—José Serebrier, conductor
Reference Recordings CD RR 89

Richard RODGERS (1902–1979)
The King and I
Oklahoma!
Juliet and Me (orchestral suites by Robert Russell Bennett)
WDR Symphony Orchestra Köln—José Serebrier, conductor
Not released (recorded for broadcast on WDR Radio)

Joaquín RODRIGO (1901–1999)
Concierto de Estío
Michael Guttman, violin—Royal Philharmonic Orchestra—José Serebrier, conductor
ASV CD DCA 855

Concierto de Aranjuez
Sharon Isbin, guitar—New York Philharmonic—José Serebrier, conductor
Warner Classics 2564 60296-2

Ned ROREM (1923–)
Piano Concerto No. 2—Simon Mulligan, piano
Cello Concerto—Wen-Sinn Yang, cello
Royal Scottish National Orchestra—José Serebrier, conductor
Naxos 8.559315

Symphonies 1, 2, and 3
Bournemouth Symphony Orchestra—José Serebrier, conductor
Naxos 8.559149

Flute Concerto—Jeffrey Khaner, flute
Violin Concerto—Philippe Quint, violin
Royal Liverpool Philharmonic Orchestra—José Serebrier, conductor
Naxos 8.559278

Nino ROTA (1911–1979)
The Godfather: Sicilian Pastorale, "Michael and Kay," Love Theme
Royal Philharmonic Orchestra—José Serebrier, conductor
RPO 022 CD

Miklós RÓZSA (1907–1995)
The Private Life of Sherlock Holmes: Violin Concerto
Royal Philharmonic Orchestra—José Serebrier, conductor
RPO 022 CD

Spellbound Concerto
Ben-Hur: Love Theme and "Parade of the Charioteers"
Royal Philharmonic Orchestra—José Serebrier, conductor
RPO 017 CD

Anton RUBINSTEIN (1829–1894)
Piano Concerto no. 3, op. 45
Caprisse Russe, op. 102
Valerie Traficante, piano—Royal Philharmonic Orchestra—José Serebrier, conductor
Vox 7533

Charles-Camille SAINT-SAËNS (1835–1921)
"Dance of the Priestesses," from *Samson and Delilah*
Adelaide Symphony Orchestra—José Serebrier, conductor
Tioch Digital TD 1003 (LP)
Kem Disc CD 1003

Reinhard SCHWARZ-SCHILLING (1904–1985)
Violin Concerto—Kirill Troussov
Partita
Polonaise
Staatskapelle Weimar—José Serebrier, conductor
Naxos 8.572801

Sinfonia Diatonica
Symphony in C
Introduction and Fugue
Staatskapelle Weimar—José Serebrier, conductor
Naxos 8. 570435

William SCHUMAN (1910–1992)
Violin Concerto—Philippe Quint, violin
New England Triptych
Bournemouth Symphony Orchestra—José Serebrier, conductor
Naxos 8.559083

José SEREBRIER (1938–)
Symphony No. 1
Houston Symphony Orchestra—Leopold Stokowski, conductor
Guild GHCD 2347

Symphony no. 1
Bournemouth Symphony Orchestra—José Serebrier, conductor
Naxos 8.559648

Symphony for Percussion—Moscow's Gnessin Percussion Ensemble—Ilia Melikhov, director
Piano Sonata—Nadia Shpachenko, piano
Colores Mágicos, Harp Concerto—Sara Cutler, harp—Solène Le Van, soprano
Tango in Blue
Candombe—Néstor Torres, flute
Samson and Buddah— Néstor Torres and Gabriel Goñi, flutes
Málaga Philharmonic Orchestra—José Serebrier, conductor
Reference Recordings RR-743

Symphony No. 2, *Partita* (1958)
Fantasia (1960)
Sonata for violin solo (1947)—Gonzalo Acosta, violin
London Philharmonic Orchestra—José Serebrier, conductor
RR 90CD
Naxos 8.572087

Symphony No. 3, *Symphonie Mystique*—Carole Farley, soprano
Passacaglia and Perpetum Mobile, for accordion and orchestra
George and Muriel, for double bass, choir and bass ensemble
Elegy for Strings
Variations on a Theme from Childhood
Momento Psicológico
Dorothy and Carmine!
Toulouse National Chamber Orchestra—José Serebrier
Naxos 8.559183

Manitowabing for woodwind duo—Claudia Anderson, flute—William McMullen, oboe
Centaur CRC 2775

Symphonic B A C H Variations for piano and orchestra
Alexandre Kantorow, piano
RTÉ National Symphony Orchestra of Ireland—José Serebrier, conductor
BIS-2423 SACD

Violin Concerto, *Winter*
Philippe Quint, violin—Bournemouth Symphony and Chorus—José Serebrier, conductor
Naxos 8.559648

Violin Concerto, *Winter*
Michael Guttman, violin—Royal Philharmonic Orchestra—José Serebrier, conductor
ASV CD DCA 855

Laments and Hallelujahs
RTÉ National Symphony Orchestra of Ireland—José Serebrier, conductor
BIS-2423 SACD

Last Tango before Sunrise
RTÉ National Symphony Orchestra of Ireland—José Serebrier, conductor
BIS-2423 SACD

Last Tango before Sunrise
Ukrainian Festival Orchestra—Paul Mann, conductor
Toccata Classics TOCC 0370

Adagio
RTÉ National Symphony Orchestra of Ireland—José Serebrier, conductor
BIS-2423 SACD
St. Michael Strings—Jose Serebrier, conductor
Alba ABCD 341

Flute Concerto with Tango
Sharon Bezaly, flute—Australian Chamber Orchestra—Richard Tognetti, director
BIS-2423 SACD
BIS-CD-1789

Casi un Tango
Tango in Blue
Molly Judson, English horn—Barcelona Symphony Orchestra—José Serebrier, conductor
BIS-2423 SACD
BIS 1175

Nueve, Concerto for double bass and chamber orchestra with narrator
Gary Karr, double bass and narrator
Plainfield Symphony Orchestra—José Serebrier, conductor
UAV 5995

Nueve, Concerto for double bass and chamber orchestra with narrator
Simon Callow, narrator—Gary Karr, double bass
Bournemouth Symphony and Chorus—José Serebrier, conductor
Naxos 8.559648

"Poema Elegíaco" (subtitled "Funeral March," second movement of *Partita*, Symphony No. 2)
Adelaide Symphony Orchestra—José Serebrier, conductor
UAV-5995

"Poema Elegíaco" (subtitled "Funeral March," second movement of *Partita*, Symphony No. 2)
London Philharmonic Orchestra
RR 90CD

Aires de Tango—Rachel Barton Pine, violin
Cedille CDR 9000 124

Dmitry SHOSTAKOVICH (1906–1975)
Festive Overture, op. 96
Russian National Orchestra—José Serebrier, conductor
Warner Classics 2564 68025-5

Music from the film *Hamlet*
Suite, op. 116
Belgian Radio Symphony Orchestra (RTBF)—José Serebrier, conductor
RCA 74321 2412 2
RCA 82876 55-183-2

Music from the films *Pirogov, The Gadfly, Hamlet, King Lear, Five Days-Five Nights,*
   Michurin, The Fall of Berlin, Golden Mountains
Belgian Radio Symphony Orchestra (RTBF)—José Serebrier, conductor
Warner Classics 2564 69070-2

Jean SIBELIUS (1865–1957)
Symphony No. 1 in E minor, op. 39
Melbourne Symphony Orchestra—José Serebrier, conductor
RCA Red Seal VRL1 0334 (LP)
RCA Gold Seal A6L1 4093 cassette
ASV CD DCA 612
ASV CD QS 604
Chandos

Bedřich SMETANA (1824–1884)
"Vltava" (from *Má Vlast*)
The Bartered Bride, Overture
Czech State Philharmonic—José Serebrier, conductor
Conifer Classics 75605 51522 2

John Philip SOUSA (1854–1932)
"The Stars and Stripes Forever"
United States Marine Band—José Serebrier, conductor
Naxos 8.570727

Max STEINER (1888–1971)
Gone with the Wind: "Tara"
Casablanca: Suite
Royal Philharmonic Orchestra—José Serebrier, conductor
RPO 017 CD

The Caine Mutiny: "March"
Royal Philharmonic Orchestra—José Serebrier, conductor
RPO 022 CD

Leopold STOKOWSKI (1882–1977)
Two Ancient Liturgical Melodies
Bournemouth Symphony Orchestra—José Serebrier, conductor
Naxos 8.557883

Cristina SPINEI (1984–)
Synched
St. Michael Strings—José Serebrier, conductor
ALBA ABCD 341

Richard STRAUSS (1864–1949)
Capriccio, final scene
Daphne, final scene
Carole Farley, soprano
RTBF Symphony Orchestra of Belgium—José Serebrier, conductor
Chandos CD 8364

Four Last Songs
Carole Farley, soprano—Czech State Philharmonic Brno—José Serebrier, conductor
MG 7605-70022

Guntram: Prelude
Intermezzo, Symphonic Interludes
Czech State Philharmonic Brno—José Serebrier, conductor
MG 7605-70022

Francisco TÁRREGA (1852–1909)
Recuerdos de la Alhambra
Gran Valse (Grande Valse)
Concerto Málaga—José Serebrier, conductor
SOMM CD 0171

Pyotr Ilich TCHAIKOVSKY (1840–1893)
Romeo and Juliet, Fantasy Overture
Sydney Symphony Orchestra—José Serebrier, conductor
Tioch Digital TD 1001 (LP)
Trax Classique TRXCD 128
ASV CDQ 6040
K-Tel CD 1513

Romeo and Juliet, Fantasy Overture
Royal Philharmonic Orchestra—José Serebrier, conductor
IMG Records CD 1601

Romeo and Juliet, Fantasy Overture
Francesca da Rimini, op. 32
Capriccio Italien, op. 45
Bamberger Symphoniker—José Serebrier, conductor
BIS 2001

1812 Overture, op. 49
Francesca da Rimini, op. 32
Royal Philharmonic Orchestra—José Serebrier, conductor
IMG Records CD 1601

Francesca da Rimini, op. 32
Royal Philharmonic Orchestra—José Serebrier, conductor
IMG Records CD 1601

Symphony No. 4, op. 36
The Tempest, op. 18
Fatum
Bamberger Symphoniker—José Serebrier, conductor
BIS 2001

Serenade for strings, op. 48
Elegy
Andante Cantabile, op. 11 (orchestrated by José Serebrier)
Sleeping Beauty, op. 66 (orchestrated by Igor Stravinsky—world-premiere recording)
Scottish Chamber Orchestra—José Serebrier, conductor
ASV CD DCA 719

Andante Cantabile, op. 11 (orchestrated by José Serebrier)
Elegy
Czech State Philharmonic Brno—José Serebrier, conductor
IMG CD2001

Andante Cantabile, op. 11 (orchestrated by José Serebrier)
Elegy
Bamberger Symphoniker—José Serebrier, conductor
BIS 2001

Waltzes, Marches, and Melodies
Royal Philharmonic Orchestra—Czech State Philharmonic—José Serebrier, conductor
IMG Records CD 1617

Opera arias from *Pique Dame, Eugene Onegin, The Maid of Orleans*
Carole Farley, soprano—Melbourne Symphony Orchestra—José Serebrier, conductor
RCA Red Seal VRL1 0380 (LP)
Chandos CD 1128

Opera arias from *Mazeppa, Iolanta, Oprichnik*, and other works
Carole Farley, soprano

Melbourne Symphony Orchestra—Orchestra Sinfonica Siciliana—José Serebrier, conductor
IMP Masters MCD 64

The Nutcracker Suite, op. 71 A
Adelaide Symphony Orchestra—José Serebrier, conductor
Trax Classique TRXCD 118
Tioch LP and cassette

Solitude, op. 73, no. 6 (transcribed by Leopold Stokowski)
Bournemouth Symphony Orchestra—José Serebrier, conductor
Naxos 8.578305

Concert Fantasy in G major, op. 56
İdil Biret, piano—Bilkent Symphony Orchestra—José Serebrier, conductor
Naxos 8.571280

"None but the Lonely Heart" (transcribed by Jose Serebrier)
RTÉ National Symphony Orchestra of Ireland—José Serebrier, conductor
BIS 2423 SACD

Dimitri TIOMKIN (1894–1979)
Dial M for Murder: Theme
Royal Philharmonic Orchestra—José Serebrier, conductor
RPO 022 CD

The Guns of Navarone: Main Theme
Royal Philharmonic Orchestra—José Serebrier, conductor
RPO 017 CD

Eduard TOLDRÀ (1895–1962)
Nocturno, from *Vistas al Mar*
Concerto Málaga—José Serebrier, conductor
SOMM CD 0171

Joaquín TURINA (1882–1949)
La Oración del Torero, op. 34
Symphonic Rhapsody for piano and orchestra, op. 66
Joaquín Soriano, piano—English Chamber Orchestra—José Serebrier, conductor
ASV CD DCA 775

La Oración del Torero
St. Michael Strings—José Serebrier, conductor
ALBA ABCD 341

Giuseppe VERDI (1813–1901)
Complete Ballet Music from the Operas
Otello, Act III, Scene 1

Macbeth, Act III, Scene 1
Jérusalem, Act III, Scene 1
Don Carlo, Act III, Scene 2
Aida, Act I, Scene 2
Aida, Act II, Scenes 1 and 2
Il Trovatore, Act III, Scenes 1 and 2
I Vespri Siciliani, Act III, Scene 2, *The Four Seasons* Ballet
Bournemouth Symphony Orchestra—José Serebrier, conductor
Naxos 8.572818-19

Heitor VILLA-LOBOS (1887–1959)
Guitar Concerto
Sharon Isbin, guitar—New York Philharmonic—José Serebrier, conductor
Warner Classics 2564,60296-2

Concerto Grosso for wind quintet and wind orchestra
United States Marine Band, José Serebrier, conductor
Naxos 8.570727

Antonio VIVALDI (1678–1741)
The Four Seasons
Michael Guttman, violin—Scottish Chamber Orchestra—José Serebrier, conductor
IMG Records CD 1602

Richard WAGNER (1813–1883)
Tristan und Isolde, Prelude and "Liebestod"
The Mastersingers of Nuremberg, Prelude
Lohengrin, Prelude to Act III
Die Walküre, Act III
Sydney Symphony Orchestra—José Serebrier, conductor
RCA VRL1 0486 (LP)
ASV CDA 644
IMG Records 1613

Richard WAGNER (1813–1883) (transcribed by Leopold Stokowski)
"Entrance of the Gods into Valhalla," from *Das Rheingold*
"Ride of the Valkyries," from *Die Walküre*
Bournemouth Symphony Orchestra—José Serebrier, conductor
Naxos 8.578305

Franz WAXMAN (1906–1967)
Sunset Boulevard: Suite
A Place in the Sun: Suite
Royal Philharmonic Orchestra—José Serebrier, conductor
RPO 022 CD

Kurt WEILL (1900–1950)
Violin Concerto, op. 12
Der Neue Orpheus for soprano, violin, and chamber orchestra, op. 16
Der Silbersee: 2 arias
Street Scene: Selections
Michael Guttman, violin—Carole Farley, soprano
Staatsorchester Rheinische Philharmonie—José Serebrier, conductor
ASV CD DCA 987

Ermanno WOLF-FERRARI (1876–1948)
L'Amore Medico: Overture
Il Campiello: Intermezzo
La Doma Boba: Overture
I Gioielli della Madonna: "Festa Popolare," Intermezzo, Serenata, and Danza Napoli-
    tana
I Quatro Rusteghi: Overture and Intermezzo
Il Segreto di Susanna: Overture
Royal Philharmonic Orchestra—José Serebrier, conductor
ASV CD DCA 861

Xiaogang YE (1955–)
Symphony No. 3—Hila Plittmann, soprano
The Last Paradise—Cho-Liang Lin, violin
Royal Philharmonic Orchestra—José Serebrier, conductor
BIS—2083

December Chrysanthemum, for Flute and Orchestra, Sharon Bezaly, flute
Winter
Starry Sky, Noriko Ogawa, piano
Royal Scottish National Orchestra—José Serebrier
BIS—2113

DVD AND VHS

Georges BIZET, *L'Arlésienne*, Suite no. 2 : *Farandole*
José Serebrier, *Symphony No. 3*, Carole Farley, soprano
Pictures at an Exhibition by Mussorgsky, transcribed by Stokowski

Wagner, *Mastersinger Prelude*
National Youth Orchestra of Spain / Joven Orquesta Nacional de España,
(JONDE) —José Serebrier
Naxos DVD 2.110230

Francis POULENC (1899–1963)
La Voix Humaine, Opera in one act
Carole Farley, soprano—Scottish Chamber Orchestra—José Serebrier, conductor

Gian Carlo MENOTTI (1911–2007)
The Telephone, Opera in one act
Carole Farley, soprano—Russell Smythe, baritone
Scottish Chamber Orchestra—José Serebrier
VAI Video Arts International 4374
DECCA VHS 071 243-3

Sergey PROKOFIEV (1891–1953)
Alexander Nevsky: Cantata
Sydney Symphony Orchestra—Philharmonia Choir
Ruth Gurner, mezzo-soprano—José Serebrier

Ludwig van BEETHOVEN (1770–1827)
Symphony No. 3, *Eroica*
Pyotr Ilich TCHAIKOVSKY (1840–1893)
Symphony No. 1
Melbourne Symphony Orchestra—José Serebrier
KULTUR VHS 1110

José Serebrier: Live in Beijing
Alexander GLAZUNOV, *The Seasons*, op. 67
Giuseppe VERDI, *The Four Seasons*, Ballet from the opera *I Vespri Siciliani*
Xiaogang YE, *Winter*
Johann Sebastian BACH, Air, from Suite no. 3 in D Major, BWV 1068
Manuel de FALLA, "Ritual Fire Dance"
Georges BIZET, Farandole, from L'Arlesienne, Suite no. 2
RTE National Symphony Orchestra of Ireland—José Serebrier
Video Arts International VAI 4504

Index

About the Authors

Michel Faure is music and movie critic for a large daily newspaper in the south of France. He has worked for the French Federation of Film Societies, 20th Century Fox, and for many international festivals. Faure founded and hosted various radio and television programs in France dedicated to American cinema and classical music.

Paul Conway is a musicologist and writer specializing in contemporary music. He has reviewed frequently for *The Independent* newspaper, *Tempo Journal*, and *Musical Opinion* magazine; has provided program notes for BBC Proms and for the Edinburgh, Brighton, and Three Choirs festivals; and has contributed chapters to books on the composers John McCabe, Robert Simpson, and José Serebrier.

Bernard Jacobson served for eight seasons as the Philadelphia Orchestra's program annotator and as musicological adviser to Riccardo Muti and later as artistic director of the Residentie Orkest in The Hague. He has written *A Polish Renaissance*, a study of the music of Andrzej Panufnik and his compatriots, a memoir titled *Star Turns and Cameo Appearances*, various books on conducting, and one on Brahms.

ACKNOWLEDGMENTS

Thomas Corfield, indexing
Cristina Spinei, technical support
Françoise Marcus, translator
Marie Presswell, translator

CPSIA information can be obtained
at www.ICGtesting.com
Printed in the USA
BVHW052352070821
613667BV00002B/3